T0321961

Applications of Encryption and Watermarking for Information Security

Boussif Mohamed
University of Tunis El Manar, Tunisia

A volume in the Advances in
Information Security, Privacy, and
Ethics (AISPE) Book Series

Published in the United States of America by
    IGI Global
    Information Science Reference (an imprint of IGI Global)
    701 E. Chocolate Avenue
    Hershey PA, USA 17033
    Tel: 717-533-8845
    Fax: 717-533-8661
    E-mail: cust@igi-global.com
    Web site: http://www.igi-global.com

Library of Congress Cataloging-in-Publication Data

Names: Mohamed, Boussif, 1989- editor.
Title: Applications of encryption and watermarking for information security
  / Boussif Mohamed.
Description: Hershey, PA : Information Science Reference, 2022. | Includes
  bibliographical references and index. | Summary: "This book will aim to
  provide relevant theoretical frameworks and the latest empirical
  research findings in the domain of security and privacy. It will be
  written for professionals who want to improve their understanding of the
  strategic role of trust at different levels of the information security,
  that is, trust at the level of cryptography and watermarking, finally,
  trust at the level of securing multimedia data"-- Provided by publisher.

Identifiers: LCCN 2022041680 (print) | LCCN 2022041681 (ebook) | ISBN
  9781668449455 (h/c) | ISBN 9781668449462 (s/c) | ISBN 9781668449479
  (eISBN)
Subjects: LCSH: Data encryption (Computer science) | Digital watermarking.
  | Electronic information resources--Access control.
Classification: LCC QA76.9.D335 A67 2022 (print) | LCC QA76.9.D335
  (ebook) | DDC 005.8/24--dc23/eng/20221115
LC record available at https://lccn.loc.gov/2022041680
LC ebook record available at https://lccn.loc.gov/2022041681

This book is published in the IGI Global book series Advances in Information Security, Privacy, and Ethics (AISPE) (ISSN: 1948-9730; eISSN: 1948-9749)

British Cataloguing in Publication Data
A Cataloguing in Publication record for this book is available from the British Library.

For electronic access to this publication, please contact: eresources@igi-global.com.

Advances in Information Security, Privacy, and Ethics (AISPE) Book Series

Manish Gupta
State University of New York, USA

ISSN:1948-9730
EISSN:1948-9749

MISSION

As digital technologies become more pervasive in everyday life and the Internet is utilized in ever increasing ways by both private and public entities, concern over digital threats becomes more prevalent.

The **Advances in Information Security, Privacy, & Ethics (AISPE) Book Series** provides cutting-edge research on the protection and misuse of information and technology across various industries and settings. Comprised of scholarly research on topics such as identity management, cryptography, system security, authentication, and data protection, this book series is ideal for reference by IT professionals, academicians, and upper-level students.

COVERAGE

- Network Security Services
- Access Control
- Information Security Standards
- Risk Management
- Tracking Cookies
- Security Information Management
- Cookies
- Data Storage of Minors
- Global Privacy Concerns
- Electronic Mail Security

IGI Global is currently accepting manuscripts for publication within this series. To submit a proposal for a volume in this series, please contact our Acquisition Editors at Acquisitions@igi-global.com or visit: http://www.igi-global.com/publish/.

Titles in this Series

For a list of additional titles in this series, please visit: *http://www.igi-global.com/book-series/*

Emerging Perspectives in Systems Security Engineering, Data Science, and Artificial Intelligence
Maurice Dawson (Illinois Institute of Technology, USA)
Information Science Reference • © 2023 • 315pp • H/C (ISBN: 9781668463253) • US $250.00

Protecting User Privacy in Web Search Utilization
Rafi Ullah Khan (ICS&IT, The University of Agriculture Peshawar, Pakistan)
Information Science Reference • © 2023 • 325pp • H/C (ISBN: 9781668469149) • US $240.00

Fraud Prevention, Confidentiality, and Data Security for Modern Businesses
Arshi Naim (King Kalid University, Saudi Arabia) Praveen Kumar Malik (Lovely Professional University, India) and Firasat Ali Zaidi (Tawuniya Insurance, Saudi Arabia)
Business Science Reference • © 2023 • 347pp • H/C (ISBN: 9781668465813) • US $250.00

Handbook of Research on Cybersecurity Issues and Challenges for Business and FinTech Applications
Saqib Saeed (Department of Computer Information Systems, College of Computer Science and Information Technology, Imam Abdulrahman Bin Faisal University, Dammam, Saudi Arabia) Abdullah M. Almuhaideb (Department of Networks and Communications, College of Computer Science and Information Technology, Imam Abdulrahman Bin Faisal University, Dammam, Saudi Arabia) Neeraj Kumar (Thapar Institute of Engineering and Technology, India) Noor Zaman (Taylor's University, Malaysia) and Yousaf Bin Zikria (Yeungnam University, South Korea)
Business Science Reference • © 2023 • 552pp • H/C (ISBN: 9781668452844) • US $315.00

Cybersecurity Issues, Challenges, and Solutions in the Business World
Suhasini Verma (Manipal University Jaipur, India) Vidhisha Vyas (IILM University, Gurugram, India) and Keshav Kaushik (University of Petroleum and Energy Studies, India)
Information Science Reference • © 2023 • 288pp • H/C (ISBN: 9781668458273) • US $265.00

701 East Chocolate Avenue, Hershey, PA 17033, USA
Tel: 717-533-8845 x100 • Fax: 717-533-8661
E-Mail: cust@igi-global.com • www.igi-global.com

Table of Contents

Detailed Table of Contents

    Boussif Mohamed, University of Tunis El Manar, Tunisia
    Aymen Mnassri, University of Tunis El Manar, Tunisia

Data encryption is one of the security solutions used to protect secret data. The use of image encryption techniques in DICOM (digital imaging and communications in medicine) data to secure it in unprotected networks or storage is the focus of this chapter. Therefore, based on the improvement of a 3D (three dimension) s-box proposed previously, the authors provide a novel efficient images encryption method for medical imaging. The technique also encrypts the DICOM tags and Jpeg compressed DICOM imaging because 512-bit-based blocks of data are processed. A function named encrypt_block() is used for the diffusion and confusion. This function processes a block with subblocks each of 8-bit. For each subblock it uses the s-box for data transformation. The cryptanalysis of the proposed encryption system shows its strength and security. The runtime and the speed of the algorithm demonstrate its low time complexity, which makes it suitable for much electronics hardware, especially embedded systems.

    Milan Gupta, Auckland University of Technology, New Zealand
    Wei Qi Yan, Auckland University of Technology, New Zealand

A digital watermark, which is embedded in an image sequence or video frames as the form of a binary string or visual logo, is a small size of visible data. Thus, the quality of embedded videos is often slashed due to the watermarking. Comparative video watermarking is a highly innovative method that was designed to unravel this issue. In this chapter, the authors make use of singular value decomposition (SVD) and discrete wavelet transform (DWT) for video watermarking; the authors employed inverse transform (IDWT) to extract the video watermark. The digital signature is also utilised to increase the authenticity of watermarks and verify any changes. The authors combine this approach with digital fingerprinting as well as to get the improved results. Throughout the designed attacks, the merits of the new watermarking paradigm such as robustness, convergence, and stability are attained with security and authenticity by calculating the metrics such as MSE, PSNR, entropy, SSIM, etc.

Chapter 3

Duo Tong, Auckland University of Technology, New Zealand
Wei Qi Yan, Auckland University of Technology, New Zealand

Banknote identification plays an increasingly important role in financial fields due to the diffusion of automatic bank systems in terms of vending machines. Nowadays, YOLOv5 has become the state-of-the-art detector of visual objects because of its relatively outperformed accuracy with a high speed of computing. In this chapter, the squeeze-excitation (SE) attention module is mingled with the terminal of the backbone in YOLOv5 to further improve visual watermark recognition of paper banknotes. The main contribution of this chapter is that the excellent precision reaches 99.99% by utilizing the novel model YOLOv5+SE.

Chapter 4

Boussif Mohamed, University of Tunis El Manar, Tunisia
Mnassri Aymen, University of Tunis El Manar, Tunisia

Digitalization of media has exploded in recent years. It has resulted in the rise of private data hacking, which has been increased by the growth of the data exchange system, i.e., the Internet, as well as the simple access to storage media. New approaches, such as watermarking in (C. Iwendi et al., 2020; D. Datta et al, 2021; Randhir Kumar et al,2021), are being used to combat these hackers. The application of image watermarking technologies to medical images, as proposed in (Nazari, M., et al, 2021; Thanki, R, 2021; Manoj K., 2020), is the focus of this research. In this chapter, we propose a new robust blind crypto-watermarking solution for medical imaging or DICOM file (Digital Imaging and Communications in Medicine) security based on masking (or hide) electronic patient information (patient name, patient ID, patient age...) in its medical imaging, then, erases them from the tag of the DICOM.

Before being included into medical imaging, DICOM patient information, or EPR, is encrypted using a modified AES (Advanced Encryption Standard) encryption technique. The image is broken into 8x8 pixel chunks. In each block, we use the 2D-LWT (Lifting wavelet transform), 2D-DCT (discrete cosine transforms), and SVD (singular value decomposition) to insert one bit of the encrypted watermark into the hybrid transform domain. Various attacks, such as noise, filtering, scaling, and compression, are used to test the method. According to the obtained results the watermark (EPR) is imperceptible in the imaging, and the suggested technique has passed the attacks test with success.

Chapter 5

>   *Donia Ammous, Laboratory of Electronics and Information*
>   *Technologies, National Engineering School of Sfax, Tunisia*
>   *Amina Kessentini, Laboratory of Electronics and Information*
>   *Technologies, National Engineering School of Sfax, Tunisia*
>   *Naziha Khlif, Laboratory of Electronics and Information Technologies,*
>   *National Engineering School of Sfax, Tunisia*
>   *Fahmi Kammoun, Laboratory of Electronics and Information*
>   *Technologies, National Engineering School of Sfax, Tunisia*
>   *Nouri Masmoudi, Laboratory of Electronics and Information*
>   *Technologies, National Engineering School of Sfax, Tunisia*

Several lossless video compression methods have been developed and published in the literature. The authors focused on the hierarchical lossless video compression methods that consist of two layers: The EL layer is used to code the error's information realized by both the transformation and the quantization. The BL layer contains the common chain of the H264/AVC standard's lossy coding. They integrated some features into two-layer lossless video compression in order to enhance their performance. The simulation results demonstrated that, in comparison to earlier work, the approach reduces the total bit of the coded sequence.

Chapter 6

>   *Mnasri Aymen, University of Tunis El Manar, Tunisia*
>   *Oussama Boufares, University of Tunis El Manar, Tunisia*

Creating a system that can hear and respond accurately like a human is one of the most critical issues in human-computer interaction. This inspired the creation of the automatic speech recognition system, which uses efficient feature extraction and selection techniques to distinguish between different classes of speech signals.

In order to improve the ASR (automatic speech recognition), the authors present a new feature extraction method in this study which is based on modified MFCC (mel frequency cepstral coefficients) using lifting wavelet transform LWT (lifting wavelet transform). The effectiveness of the proposed approach is verified using the datasets of the ATSSEE Research Unit "Analysis and Processing of Electrical and Energy Signals and Systems." The experimental investigations have been carried out to demonstrate the practical viability of the proposed approach. Numerical and experimental studies concluded that the proposed approach is capable of detecting and localizing multiple under varying environmental conditions with noise-contaminated measurements.

Identification of system is one of the most important steps in industrial process automation studies. The modeling of a process aims to establish a representation linking the variables of the process, either from an approach of understanding the phenomena involved or from a mathematical processing of the data collected on the process. The object of identification is to estimate the parameters of the models thus obtained. In this chapter, the convergence of a prediction error method applied for the identification of multivariable delayed systems is proven. Indeed, a multivariable system with multiple time delays is used. Then a convergence study is given. A numerical example based on a thermostatic mixing valves process is finally introduced to prove the robustness of the proposed scheme.

Chapter 8

Moving object detection is a fundamental task on smart CCTV systems, as it provides a focal point for further investigation. In this study, an algorithm for moving object detection in video, which is thresholded using a stationary wavelet transform (SWT), is developed. In the detection steps, the authors perform a background subtraction algorithm; the obtained results are decomposed using discrete stationary wavelet transform 2D, and the coefficients are thresholded using Birge-Massart strategy. This leads to an efficient calculation method and system compared to existing traffic estimation methods.

Chapter 9
Speech Recognition System Implementation of a Method Based on Wave
Atom Transform and Frequency-Mel Cepstral Coefficients Using SVM..........176

Walid Mohamed, University of Orleans, Orleans, France
Yosssra Ben Fadhel, University of Tunis El Manar, Tunisia

In the field of human-machine interaction, automatic speech recognition (ASR) has been a prominent research area since the 1950s. Single-word speech recognition is widely used in voice command systems, which can be implemented in various applications such as access control systems, robots, and voice-enabled devices. This study describes the implementation of a single-word speech recognition system using wave atoms transform (WAT) and frequency-mel cepstral coefficients (MFCC) on a Raspberry Pi 3 (RPi 3) board. The WAT-MFCC approach is combined with a support vector machine (SVM). The experiment was conducted on an Arabic word database, and the results showed that the proposed WAT-MFCC-SVM method is highly reliable, achieving a detection rate of 100% and a real-time factor (RTF) of 1.50.

Preface

With the rapid development of multimedia and communication technologies, as Internet, the sharing and remote access to data has become very easy. Therefore, the demand for data security is increasing. Information security is one of the most important topics in the research, especially with the great and rapid technological development that our world is witnessing today, as individuals, companies, and large facilities in particular today they are looking for ways and technologies that enable them to protect their information from any threat. Therefore, information security is one of the topics that attract the most attention of individuals and companies who seek to ensure the safety of their information from any risks that may lead to its demise or destruction. It is one of the basics that every company or individual seeks to secure, with the aim of maintaining the confidentiality of information and avoiding theft and deliberate sabotage. Because of the high competition between companies, some of them seek to harm their competitors by carrying out systematic attacks in order to disrupt, sabotage or steal their information in order to imitate it and know its secrets. The importance of protecting information is reflected in a number of points, the most important of which are:

- Determine who is authorized to access information.
- Avoid random hacks by amateurs or professionals.
- Ensure the continuity of the production process and prevent it from being obstructed by sabotaging information.
- Ensuring the excellence of companies and establishments by protecting the confidentiality of information and preventing its leakage.
- Reduce costs and avoid losses, by protecting information there is less need to reproduce it from scratch.

The most known techniques on information security are cryptography and watermarking. Encryption, or cryptography, is used for data security and privacy purposes. Long before the arrival of computers and networks, encryption already existed, in other forms. Encryption consists of making the data incomprehensible or readable. For example, "Hello" becomes "a68f5469a1" when encrypted. This action is carried out by algorithms which are few in number and known to all. But then, if these algorithms are available to everyone, how to ensure that the encryption is secure? Cryptanalysis is the technique of deducing plaintext from ciphertext without possessing the encryption key. The process by which one attempts to understand a particular message is called an attack.

Watermarking is appeared in the late 1990s, applicable on multimedia data as videos, images or audios. This research theme, designated in publications by the term watermarking. One of the primary motivations was the protection of the copyright. This technique is effective for several applications, but, as in cryptography, the watermark can be attacked. There are two types of attacks that affect the robustness of the watermarking algorithm: benevolent attacks and malicious attacks.

The malicious attacks are manipulations intended to remove, prevent detection of the mark or render the mark unusable. All attackers can consciously use all malicious attacks to achieve their goals.

Benevolent attacks include manipulations on the watermarked data whose purpose is to allow better exploitation of the image, and which are not intended to destroy the mark or prevent its detection as compression in Chapter 5 or the manipulation of MFCC used for denoising audio before the reconnaissance in Chapter 6.

In Chapter 1, the authors applied image encryption techniques in DICOM (Digital Imaging and Communications in Medicine) data to secure it in unprotected networks or storages. Therefore, based on the improvement of a 3D (three dimension) S-Box proposed previously (Boussif et al., 2021), the authors provide a novel efficient images encryption method for medical imaging. The technique also encrypts the DICOM tags and Jpeg compressed DICOM imaging because 512-bit based block of data are processed. A function named encrypt_block() is used for the diffusion and confusion. This function processes a block with subblocks each of 8-bit. For each subblock it uses the s-box for data transformation. The cryptanalysis of the proposed encryption system shows it strength security. The runtime and the speed of the algorithm demonstrates it low time complexity which makes it suitable for many electronics hardware especially embedded systems. In Chapter 2, the authors concentrated on a digital watermark, which is embedded in an image sequence or video frames as the form of a binary string or visual logo, is a small size of visible data. Thus, the quality of embedded videos is often slashed due to watermarking. Comparative video watermarking is a highly innovative method that was designed to unravel this issue. In this chapter, singular value decomposition (SVD) and discrete wavelet transform (DWT) are employed for video watermarking, inverse transform (IDWT) is adopted to extract the video watermark. The digital signature is also utilized to increase the authenticity of watermarks and verify any changes. This approach is combined with digital fingerprinting as well to get the improved results.

Throughout the designed attacks, the merits of the new watermarking paradigm such as robustness, convergence, and stability are attained with security and authenticity by calculating the metrics such as MSE, PSNR, entropy, SSIM, etc. The focus of Chapter 3 is on banknote identification which plays an increasingly important role in financial fields due to the diffusion of automatic bank systems in terms of vending machines. Nowadays, YOLOv5 has become the state-of-the-art detector of visual objects because of its relatively outperformed accuracy with a high speed of computing. In this book chapter, the squeeze-excitation (SE) attention module is mingled with the terminal of the backbone in YOLOv5 to further improve visual watermark recognition of paper banknotes. The main contribution of this chapter is that the output precision reaches 99.99% by utilizing the novel model YOLOv5+SE. The application of image watermarking technologies to medical images, as proposed in Nazari (2021), Thanki (2021), and Manoj (2020), is the focus of Chapter 4. In this chapter, the authors propose a new robust blind crypto-watermarking solution for medical imaging or DICOM file (Digital Imaging and Communications in Medicine) security based on masking (or hide) electronic patient information (patient name, patient ID, patient age) in its medical imaging, then, erases them from the tag of the DICOM. Before being included into medical imaging, DICOM patient information, or EPR, is encrypted using a modified AES (Advanced Encryption Standard) encryption technique. The image is broken into 8x8 pixel chunks. In each block, the method uses the 2D-LWT (Lifting wavelet transform), 2D-DCT (discrete cosine transforms), and SVD (singular value decomposition) to insert one bit of the encrypted watermark into the hybrid transform domain. Various attacks, such as noise, filtering, scaling, and compression, are used to test the method. According to the obtained results the watermark (EPR) is imperceptible in the imaging, and the suggested technique has passed the attacks test with success. Several lossless video compression methods have been currently developed and published in the literature as in Chapter 5 where the authors focused on the hierarchical lossless video compression methods that consist of two layers: The EL layer is used to code the error's information realized by both the transformation and the quantization. The BL layer contains the common chain of the H264/AVC standard's lossy coding. We integrated some features into two-layer lossless video compression in order to enhance their performance. The simulation results demonstrated that, in comparison to earlier work, our approach reduces the total bit of the coded sequence. Creating a system that can hear and respond accurately like a human is one of the most critical issues in human-computer interaction. This inspired the creation of the automatic speech recognition system, which uses efficient feature extraction and selection techniques to distinguish between different classes of speech signals. In order to improve the ASR (Automatic Speech Recognition), in Chapter 6, the authors present a new feature extraction method in this study which is based on modified MFCC (Mel Frequency Cepstral Coefficients) using lifting wavelet transform LWT (Lifting Wavelet Transform). The effectiveness of this proposed approach is verified using the datasets of the ATSSEE Research Unit "Analysis and Processing of Electrical and Energy Signals and Systems." The experimental investigations have been carried out to demonstrate the practical viability of the proposed approach. Numerical and experimental studies concluded that the proposed approach could detect and localizing multiple under varying environmental conditions with noise-contaminated measurements. In Chapter 7, the convergence of a prediction error method applied for the identification of multivariable delayed systems is proven. Indeed, a multivariable system with multiple time delays is used. Then a convergence study is given. A numerical example based on a thermostatic mixing valves process is finally introduced to prove the robustness of the proposed scheme. Chapter 8 presents an algorithm for moving object detection in video which is thresholded using a stationary wavelet transform (SWT). In the detection steps the authors perform a background subtraction algorithm, the obtained results are decomposed using discrete stationary wavelet transform 2D and the coefficients are thresholded using Birge-Massart strategy. This leads to an efficient calculation method and system compared to existing traffic estimation methods. Chapter 9 describes the implementation of a single-word speech recognition system using Wave Atoms Transform (WAT) and Frequency-Mel Cepstral Coefficients (MFCC) on a Raspberry Pi 3 (RPi 3) board. The WAT-MFCC approach is combined with a Support Vector Machine (SVM). The experiment was conducted on an Arabic word database, and the results showed that the proposed WAT-MFCC-SVM method is highly reliable, achieving a detection rate of 100% and a real-time factor (RTF) of 1.50.

In this book our objective was to provide novel algorithms of encryption and watermarking for information security. Chapter 1 presents an encryption method for DICOM. In Chapters 2, 3, 4 novel watermarking methods was presented. Finally, Chapters 5, 6, 7, 8, and 9 present novel methods for multimedia data manipulation using transformations. These methods are examples of watermarking attacks.

Boussif Mohamed
University of Tunis El Manar, Tunisia

REFERENCES

Boussif, M., Bouferas, O., Aloui, N., & Cherif, A. (2021), A Novel Robust Blind AES/LWT+DCT+SVD-Based Crypto-Watermarking schema for DICOM Images Security. *IEEE International Conference on Design & Test of Integrated Micro & Nano-Systems (DTS)*. 10.1109/DTS52014.2021.9497916

Nazari, M., & Mehrabian, M. (2021). A novel chaotic IWT-LSB blind watermarking approach with flexible capacity for secure transmission of authenticated medical images. *Multimedia Tools and Applications*, *80*(7), 10615–10655. doi:10.100711042-020-10032-2

Singh, M. K., Kumar, S., Ali, M., & Saini, D. (2020). Application of a novel image moment computation in X-ray and MRI image watermarking. *IET Image Processing*. Advance online publication. doi:10.1049/ipr2.12052

Thanki, R., & Kothari, A. (2021). A. Multi-level security of medical images based on encryption and watermarking for telemedicine applications. *Multimedia Tools and Applications*, *80*(3), 4307–4325. doi:10.100711042-020-09941-z

Acknowledgment

The editor would like to thank everyone who helped in the creation of this publication.

He would like to publicly thank the authors of the chapters in the present book for their enthusiastic involvement in the project.

Also deserving of praise are the anonymous reviewers, whose helpful suggestions and insightful comments helped authors improving the quality of chapters during the review process.

We are appreciative to the Publisher IGI global for giving us the chance to edit a book on the application of watermarking and encryption on the security.

Boussif Mohamed
University of Tunis El Manar, Tunisia

Chapter 1
Novel Fast Improved 3D S-Box-Based Cryptography Algorithm for Protecting DICOM Images

Boussif Mohamed

https://orcid.org/0000-0003-3198-7605
University of Tunis El Manar, Tunisia

Aymen Mnassri
University of Tunis El Manar, Tunisia

ABSTRACT

Data encryption is one of the security solutions used to protect secret data. The use of image encryption techniques in DICOM (digital imaging and communications in medicine) data to secure it in unprotected networks or storage is the focus of this chapter. Therefore, based on the improvement of a 3D (three dimension) s-box proposed previously, the authors provide a novel efficient images encryption method for medical imaging. The technique also encrypts the DICOM tags and Jpeg compressed DICOM imaging because 512-bit-based blocks of data are processed. A function named encrypt_block() is used for the diffusion and confusion. This function processes a block with subblocks each of 8-bit. For each subblock it uses the s-box for data transformation. The cryptanalysis of the proposed encryption system shows its strength and security. The runtime and the speed of the algorithm demonstrate its low time complexity, which makes it suitable for much electronics hardware, especially embedded systems.

DOI: 10.4018/978-1-6684-4945-5.ch001

INTRODUCTION

The development of new telecommunications technology and especially the internet network, has increased the complexity of data security problems such as hacking, unauthorized access to data, spyware in network. The need to be able to send data securely is probably as old as communications itself. In our modern world, where various methods of communication are used for transferring any data, the need for confidentiality is more present than ever on a multitude of levels. For example, it is normal for a firm to want to protect its new software against piracy, for banking institutions to want to ensure that transactions are secure, and that all individuals want their personal data to be protected. Furthermore, the need for secure communications has given rise to a discipline known as cryptology. Etymologically, cryptology appears to be the science of secrecy. However, it has only recently been considered a science since it combines the art of secrecy with that of piracy. Indeed, cryptology consists of two complementary parts: cryptography and cryptanalysis. The first part consists of studying and designing information encryption methods while the second aims at analyzing cipher texts by extracting the hidden information. This information may be in the form of textual data, audio, or in the form of digital images and other multimedia. There are many contexts where encryption is used to protect data like industrially, military, and especially medical where patient data are secret and only patient's doctors have authorized to access their data. DICOM, a secret data in medical profession, is a series of fields named Tag contain information of patient, information of the image, and the pixels of the medical imaging. For protecting this DICOM against unauthorized viewed, recently, we proposed many recherché paper for securing these DICOM data (Boussif et al., 2017, 2018, 2019, 2020, 2021), in this chapter, we propose a novel improved 3D S-Box-based encryption system for encrypt imaging, and text data or tags (all DICOM data) because the images encryption system scalable with text data. It is manipulating the data in blocks of 512 bit. A function named encrypt_block() is used for the confusion and diffusion in the image encryption.

The rest of this paper is organized as follow: In Section 2, we discus some related works (images and DICOM encryption algorithms). Then, the proposed method is detailed in Section 3. Section 4 dedicated to the result of cryptanalysis and its comparison with the state-of-the-art. Limitations of the work is presented in Section 5. The paper is end by a conclusion and our future works (Section 6).

RELATED WORKS

Images encryption is a known research axis in a common field between data security and images processing. In the last years researcher have proposed several images encryption methods. Wang X. et al. (Wang et al., 2021) used the DNA encoding and the PWLCM (linear chaotic mapping system) for encrypting any number of still images with different sizes. The method is robust august differential attack, brute force attack, statical attack, entropic attack, lossless data in network. So, the security of the system is good, however the paper doesn't discuss the runtime and the complexity of the method. Iqbal N. et al (Iqbal et al, 2021) proposed a grayscale image encryption method using the variable length row-column swapping operations. The method is robust august differential attack, brute force attack, statical attack, entropic attack, lossless data in network and its encryption speed and complexity are acceptable, however, the method doesn't resolve the problem of encryption key exchange. Also, it cannot resist to chosen-plaintext attacks, cipher text only attacks, chosen cipher text attacks, and known-plaintext attacks. Priya et al. (2019) employed the watermarking for the secure transmission and authentication of DICOM images. Riaz et al. (2012) improved the advanced encryption standard for images encryption. It encrypts only a selected part of the images. Even though the AES is modified to minimize the runtime, the system remain slow comparing with the novel proposed encryption algorithm. In Sneha (2020) the authors have proposed a cryptography method for image data by combining the Walsh–Hadamard transform and the Arnold maps. A method based on genetic algorithm and 4-D chaotic maps has been proposed by Gupta et al. (2020). Shaheen et al. (2019) used a combined signal processing transformation for an image encryption algorithm. As still images, medical imaging has the same problematic due to its strength correlation of adjacent pixels where El-Shafai et al. (2021) used DNA code for a chaos system used to medical images encryption. In our previous work (Boussif et al., 2017) we used the matrix product for medical images encryption. A selective encryption method-based edge has been proposed by Khashan et al. (2020). Kumar et al. (2022) proposed a method for encrypting medical images using the complex entropy.

ENCRYPTION METHOD

As shown in Figure 1, the encryption system is used in unsafe network channel or storage, the DICOM file that contain information of a patient and its imaging is secretly exchanged to the patient's doctor. The encryption system encrypts the imaging and the related patient information. The correspondent doctor, who has the key, decrypts the DICOM for restore the original data. Detail explanations of the proposed encryption and decryption processes are given in the bellow subsection where we present:

1. The improved 3D S-box: where we present the original schema and the improved algorithm with samples from an S-box generated with the new S-box generation algorithm.
2. The encryption method: where we present the processes of encryption and decryption of the imaging.
3. DICOM Tag encryption: where we present how we encrypt text data especially DICOM tag using the proposed algorithm.

Table 1. Samples from a 3D generated S-box: S-box-E(:,1,1)

The first sub sbox obtained in direction I (or S-box-E(:,1,1))
Columns 1 through 19
123 154 10 134 234 127 101 139 221 234 214 145 233 115 148 21 129 239 159
Columns 20 through 38
22 93 66 142 117 158 52 24 43 164 217 21 77 228 138 239 215 106 10
Columns 39 through 57
177 34 94 65 96 44 189 62 106 252 185 149 212 51 105 26 143 154 246
Columns 58 through 76
194 126 150 166 180 143 181 9 189 221 58 160 50 100 111 129 49 201 221
Columns 77 through 95
154 219 161 14 164 180 32 76 46 68 137 52 154 44 122 80 137 236 8
Columns 96 through 114
256 120 240 88 108 231 8 77 243 102 59 20 25 135 182 118 90 72 70
Columns 115 through 133
229 52 56 18 210 2 116 216 152 191 32 105 135 124 199 57 50 223 57
Columns 134 through 152
104 145 134 189 104 61 147 199 10 73 162 31 236 88 117 30 210 121 209
Columns 153 through 171
78 145 108 236 122 59 123 95 194 142 72 71 189 50 85 12 145 67 21
Columns 172 through 190
61 27 217 89 81 239 212 224 143 160 43 145 154 38 244 213 182 59 130
Columns 191 through 209
251 118 9 139 28 34 129 245 61 97 40 201 72 138 84 162 132 116 94
Columns 210 through 228
239 107 240 162 75 232 162 169 159 32 151 52 245 127 101 227 225 237 122
Columns 229 through 247
12 118 164 59 157 27 129 183 39 85 110 128 12 54 214 164 51 53 129
Columns 248 through 256
207 101 129 243 62 147 93 178 60

Figure 1. The proposed protection system for DICOM data

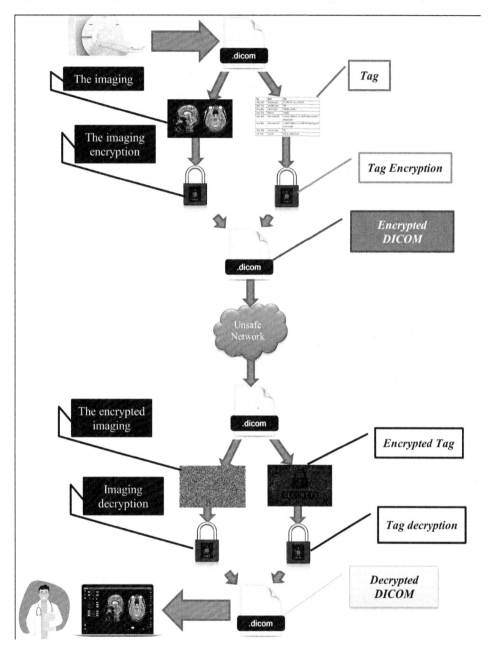

Improved 3D S-Box Generation

Here, we start by presented the original schema, the S-box is three-dimensionally (as shown in Figure 2). Each dimension is of size 256, therefore, the size of the S-box is 256x256x256, or it is constituted of 256 under (or sub) S-box. Each under S-box is a matrix of 256 line and 256 columns. For the encryption S-box, In the first, each line is initialized to 1:2N, i.e., the ith value of each line is set to i.

$$SboxE(i,j,k)=j \qquad (1)$$

Where S-boxE denotes the encryption S-box, then we applied a random permutation for each line.

$$SboxE(I,:,k)=randpermute(S\text{-}boxE(i,:,k)) \qquad (2)$$

Table 2. Samples from a 3D generated S-box: S-box-E(1,:,1)

The first sub s-box obtained in direction J (or S-box-E(1,:,1))
Columns 1 through 19
123 99 174 244 32 40 22 175 34 152 92 170 91 146 119 190 112 127 241
Columns 20 through 38
165 35 6 121 228 160 236 55 148 3 96 166 136 68 16 140 135 69 115
Columns 39 through 57
11 101 54 105 176 218 30 133 186 149 224 45 184 216 77 211 235 60 217
Columns 58 through 76
219 113 214 254 171 249 147 150 163 74 78 72 62 70 229 129 232 242 107
Columns 77 through 95
134 51 33 7 86 182 237 212 196 221 103 38 238 100 157 58 76 205 143
Columns 96 through 114
81 172 187 159 202 89 42 162 28 128 145 164 230 151 17 239 223 131 220
Columns 115 through 133
194 41 227 120 47 195 111 180 250 98 213 80 14 193 247 255 156 46 155
Columns 134 through 152
56 63 240 197 198 144 253 104 93 204 117 252 8 181 67 84 139 208 90
Columns 153 through 171
97 169 248 138 83 59 210 231 106 233 79 142 209 256 188 5 201 48 179
Columns 172 through 190
177 108 53 29 21 25 52 185 109 37 64 31 49 234 246 178 27 183 110
Columns 191 through 209
61 88 50 87 26 43 124 192 94 189 161 19 102 200 44 130 15 243 203
Columns 210 through 228
73 1 125 199 173 36 116 82 71 215 23 141 126 137 207 65 158 153 225
Columns 229 through 247
2 132 114 4 18 85 222 245 75 191 24 95 206 167 154 39 168 13 9
Columns 248 through 256
66 20 57 122 251 10 12 226 118

Where randpermute is the function that randomly permutes a vector. The improved algorithm is presented in algorithm 1. As see in this algorithm we generate only one s-box named S-Box-E where we try, using the permutation, that each value is unique in the direction I and k (we note that each value is unique in the direction J). this improvement makes the s-box more suitable to the encryption in term of security and runtime. Tables 1, 2, and 3 present the subs-boxes from a generated S-box in the three dimensions, respectively.

The function in(**a,b**) used in algorithm 1 allows to determine if the pixel **a** exist in a vector of pixels **b**. Therefore, if the algorithm of generation finds the pixel, it permutes until find a unique value. We note that this procedure is applied from 2 to 255 for reasons of time complexity.

Table 3. Samples from a 3D generated S-box: S-box-E(1,1,:)

The first sub s-box obtained in direction k (or S-box-E(1,1,:))
Columns 1 through 19
123 196 97 104 79 237 46 182 144 65 200 58 58 251 189 19 117 10 251
Columns 20 through 38
64 29 111 65 41 141 3 181 176 5 204 62 201 247 218 54 119 104 9
Columns 39 through 57
184 24 256 122 29 73 67 19 42 101 157 149 85 142 173 173 56 221 107
Columns 58 through 76
193 245 92 197 203 83 3 119 207 74 184 37 244 97 174 190 202 148 63
Columns 77 through 95
252 43 178 196 192 148 72 221 109 74 229 129 145 69 98 69 173 57 87
Columns 96 through 114
11 231 28 241 29 238 222 146 78 231 66 73 99 184 248 213 168 182 26
Columns 115 through 133
6 180 3 250 159 236 36 125 208 3 126 169 239 108 252 53 31 112 115
Columns 134 through 152
116 252 44 119 90 224 221 212 213 108 246 33 120 47 155 200 215 78 204
Columns 153 through 171
228 41 140 7 240 191 164 67 200 153 207 208 105 202 172 166 251 118 17
Columns 172 through 190
121 148 214 216 222 10 244 147 215 236 35 167 96 115 161 184 124 189 256
Columns 191 through 209
62 144 143 184 100 152 154 170 60 166 167 80 68 185 245 13 48 21 54
Columns 210 through 228
130 248 185 49 141 240 130 120 37 27 235 182 159 11 80 5 184 129 159
Columns 229 through 247
105 79 54 169 143 222 14 154 10 172 251 30 169 7 114 129 110 198 20
Columns 248 through 256
202 247 12 6 83 120 52 32 26

Figure 2. schema of the three dimensionally S-box

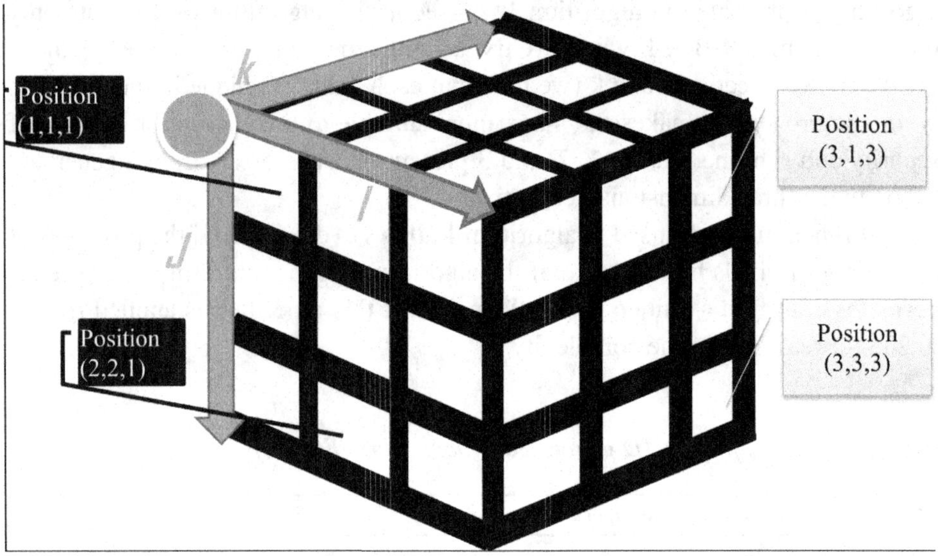

Encryption Process

The encryption process is presented in algorithm 2. It uses a function named encryt_block (presented in algorithm 3) for the diffusion and confusion criteria. This function uses a 3D s-box generated by algorithm 1, the data to be encrypted or decrypted, the key, and a variable named d which is initialized by the function Fn_XOR (see algorithm 6) and after each block is incremented to give more randomness to the system.

Algorithm 1: The encryption algorithm

```
1)        Input: sbox_E, img, e
2)        L←size(img)
3)        key←reshape(e,[1,64])
4)        imgb←reshape img to line of 64
5)        d←Fn_XOR(key,sbox_E)+1
6)        etemp←encrypt_block(key,key,d,sbox_E)
7)        for i from 1 to the number of blocks do
      temp←imgb(:,i)
      t←temp ⊕ etemp
    etemp←encrypt_block(t,key,d,sbox_E)
    increment d/* d must be in [1..256]*/
```

```
ctimgb(:,i)←t;
            endfor
```
8)   `encimg←reshape ctimgb to original size`
9)   `output: encimg`

For the decryption, practically the same algorithm used with s-box, encrypted imaging, key are the inputs, however, for the function encrypt_block we must respect domain (the input must be the encrypted domain). The output of the algorithm wile be the restored data. The function encrypt_block is presented in algorithm 2, it encrypts a block of 512-bit using the s-box.

Algorithm 2: The function encrypt_block() used in encryption algorithm

1)   `Input:`
```
            data: block of 512-bit
            key: encryption key of 512 bit
            d: parameter d in [1..256]
             s: the s-box
```
2)   `initialize enc to 64 zeros of 8-bit`
3)   `for i from 1 to 64 do`
```
         enc(i) ←s(key(i)+1, data(i)+1, d)-1;
         increment d /* d must be in 1..256 */
     end for
```
4)   `Output:`
```
            Enc: Encrypted block
```

The function Fn_XOR used in the encryption algorithm is define as:

$$Fn_{XOR(m,s,i)} = s\left(m_i + 1, m_{L-i+1}, Fn_{XOR(m,s,i-1)}\right) \oplus Fn_{XOR(m,s,i-1)}$$

$$Fn_{XOR(m,s,1)=m(1)}$$

$$i = 1 \dots L \tag{3}$$

Where m and s are a vector of 64 pixel each of 8-bit, the S-box. L is the length of m. this function used initially before starting the blocks encryption. It is determine a variable d from 1...256 used for the first encrypt_block(). The images are presented in

DICOM Tag Encryption

DICOM Tag must be regrouped in one block of 512 bit, then, we crypt them using the previous presented algorithm as one block (previous section). Finally, we replace original Tag by 4 encrypted each of 128-bit since in DICOM the max tag length is 128-bit. If DICOM tags are more than 512-bit, in this case, we must regroup them in two blocks.

SECURITY ANALYSIS AND COMPARISON

Simulation Strategy and Used Tool and Hardware

Results and presented values are obtained under Matlab 2021a running on laptop using Windows 11 and ADM processor 1.20 GHz base frequency with 4 Gb RAM. We have taken 20 images of different type. Then, obtained values is the average value of these 20 images. In each encryption test we use a new encryption key. Figure 3 present 6 samples from our dataset: A grayscale Lena image of 512x512 pixels and 8-bit (named Lena), a grayscale zeros image of 512x512 pixels and 8-bit (named Black). a grayscale medical imaging of 460x460 pixel and 12-bit (named MR), a grayscale medical imaging of 2022x1736 pixels and 14-bit (named DX). Color image of 512x512x3 (named Python). Color image of 460x460x3 pixels (named I). The images are presented in Figure 3.

Encryption Test

In this section, we present some encrypted version of our dataset. As shown in Figure 4, all encrypted images are noise. Therefore, the proposed system encrypts all king of images. Foremother, we test the system with nonrandom key (key equal to zeros) and we find similar results. For measure the effect of encryption we use the PSNR (peak signal to noise ratio) between original image and its encrypted version. As shown in Table 4, the PSNR is around 7 db. So, the proposed system has good visual difference between original and encrypted images. The formula of the PSNR is:

$$PSNR\left(I, I_w\right) = 10 Log_{10}\left(\frac{\left[2^{dep} - 1\right]^2}{MSE\left(I, I_w\right)}\right)$$

$$MSE\left(I, I_w\right) = \frac{1}{L} \sum_{k=1}^{L} \left[I\left(k\right) - I_w\left(k\right)\right]^2 \tag{4}$$

Where L corresponds to the number of imaging pixels, and *dep* denotes imaging depth. MSE is the mean squared error.

Table 4. PSNR between original images and encrypted images

Images	PSNR (db)
Lena	9.2565
black	4.2455
MR	7.3598
DX	7.2154
Python	7.1558
I	7.9544
Image1	9.2514
Image2	8.9564
Image3	7.2564
Image4	9.2548
Image5	9.5648
Image6	9.4265
Image7	7.8546
Image8	8.8546
Image9	9.6548
Average	9.0545

Key Sensitivity

The sensitivity of the key is evaluated by making a slight modification in one of the elements constituting the key in the decryption phase. The objective is to show that only the encryption key can restore the original image. As shown in Table 5, the NPCR (number of pixels change rate) of decrypted images is near to 100%, therefore, only the correct key, or the encryption key, can decrypt an encrypted image (see Figure 5). The formula of NPCR is given in equation (9).

Figure 3. Six samples from our dataset: Lena, black, MR, DX, python, and I images, respectively

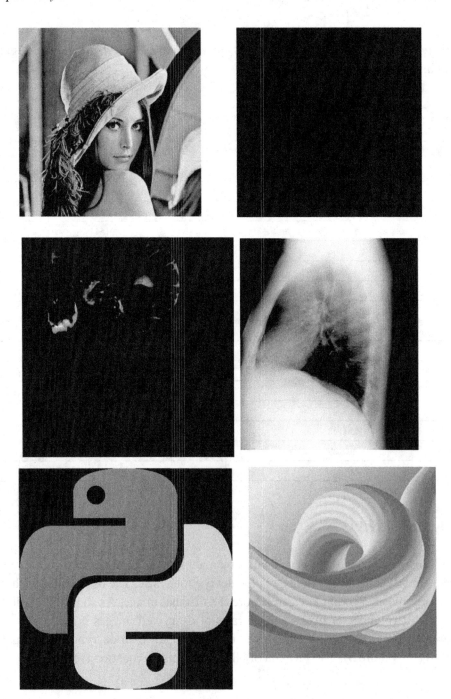

Figure 4. Encrypted images of Figure 3, respectively

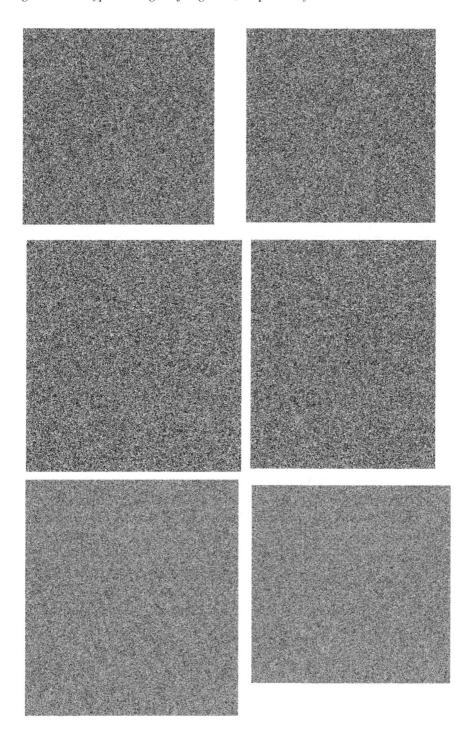

Table 5. NPCR Values with minimally incorrect key

Number of Incorrect Bits in Decryption Key	NPCR
1	0.9935
2	0.9955
3	0.9987
4	0.9954
5	0.9992
6	0.9976
7	0.9999
8	0.9981
9	0.9955
10	0.9971
11	0.9988
12	0.9944
13	0.9994
14	0.9944
15	0.9995
16	0.9954
30	0.9984
40	0.9994

Key Space

The key space of an encryption or decryption algorithm is the total of the different keys that can be used in the encryption or decryption process. An image encryption method is said to be secure if it has the largest possible encryption key space, it must resist brute force attacks where the attacker tries to find the correct key by manipulating all possible combinations. If we assume that the size of this key is n, finding the correct key will take 2^n operations to successfully find it. On our algorithm, the key is of 512-bit, so, it has a space of 2^{512}. Therefore, the system can resist force brute attacks. The comparison of key space with state-of-the-art is presented in Table 6 where our algorithm has the biggest space.

Figure 5. Two decrypted images with minimally wrong key, respectively

Table 6. Comparison of key space

Methods	Key Space
Our encryption system	2^{512}
(Khashan, O.A et al, 2020)	2^{100}
(Kumar, V. et al, 2022)	2^{180}

Statical Test

Histograms

Histogram is a commonly used metric as a qualitative check of the distribution of data, in order to assess the robustness of the cryptosystem against statistical attacks. For a well-designed cryptosystem, such a metric should obscure any notable information about the single image or the relationship between it and the encryption image. An image histogram is a graphical representation showing the distribution of pixel values, plotting the number of pixels in each grayscale value. The graphical representation of the histogram of the encrypted image is important, but not sufficient to ensure the uniformity of the distribution of the encrypted pixels for this reason, the Chi-square test is performed to indicate the uniformity characteristic of the given cipher image histogram. This statistical test Chi-square (X^2) is calculated by the following formula:

$$X^2_{exp} = \sum_{i=1}^{Nv} \frac{\left(oi - ei\right)^2}{ei} \tag{5}$$

Where Nv denotes the total number of levels (in the case of a grayscale image, Nv = 256), oi are the frequencies of occurrence of each gray level (0-255) and ei represents the frequency of expected occurrence of the uniform distribution, calculated as follows: ei = MxNxP / 256 (M is the number of rows, N number of columns and P the number of planes, for the grayscale image P = 1). Figure 6, Figure 7, and Table 7 illustrate the histogram plot and a few chi-square values, respectively. The results of the 2 tests may be used to determine if the pixels in cipher pictures are evenly distributed, and the histogram can be used to visually distinguish between plain and cipher images. Figures 6 and 7 show that the plain pictures have a distinct interval of pixel aggregation while the cipher images have a uniform distribution of pixels. Table 7 shows that the "Python" and "I" histograms of the cipher pictures' cardinality measurements are all smaller than the chi-square value of 255, which equals 310. Figures 6 and 7 as well as Table 7 can demonstrate that the suggested encryption method produces a uniform distribution of encrypted images.

Table 7. Some obtained Chi-square values from the dataset

Images	Chi-Square of Original Image Histogram	Chi-Square of Encrypted Image Histogram
Python	613319	266
I	582244	264

Correlation

It is well known that there is high redundancy and a strong correlation between adjacent pixels of a natural or still images, and such an encryption algorithm will always try to defuse the existing resemblance between these adjacent pixels to defense statical attacks. Here, we make two known analyses: 1) The correlation test between adjacent pixels involves randomly selecting a number of pairs of adjacent pixels from the original image and another numbers of pairs from the encrypted image and then analyzing the correlations in the horizontal, vertical and diagonal directions of the two original and encrypted images. The correlation diagrams between the pixels adjacent to the horizontal, vertical, and diagonal directions of the original Lena image and its encrypted image are shown in Figure 8 and 9, respectively. As shown in Table 8, the correlation coefficients of the original image in the three directions approximate 1, while those of its encrypted image approach 0. In this case, we say that the encryption considerably attenuated the correlation between pixels of the encrypted image, we also notice in Figure 8 that the distribution of the intensities of the pixels of the original image is focused on the diagonal, the pixels are then strongly correlated, while those of the encrypted image are uncorrelated and have a uniform distribution (Figure 9). The expression of the coefficient of correlation (CC) between I1 and I2 is given below:

$$CC\left(I1, I2\right) = \frac{Cov\left(I1, I2\right)}{\sigma_w \sigma_{ex}} \tag{6}$$

where $Cov(x,y)$, and σ_x are the covariance of x and y, and the standard deviation of x, respectively.

Figure 6. Histograms of original and encrypted image, respectively. The original image is sample from the dataset.

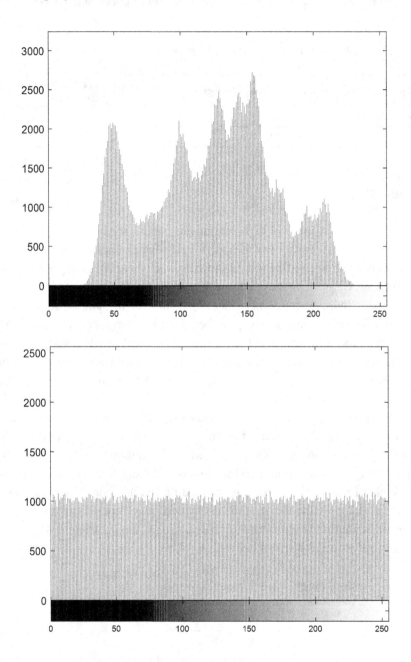

Figure 7. histograms of original and encrypted image, respectively. We use "BLACK" image sample.

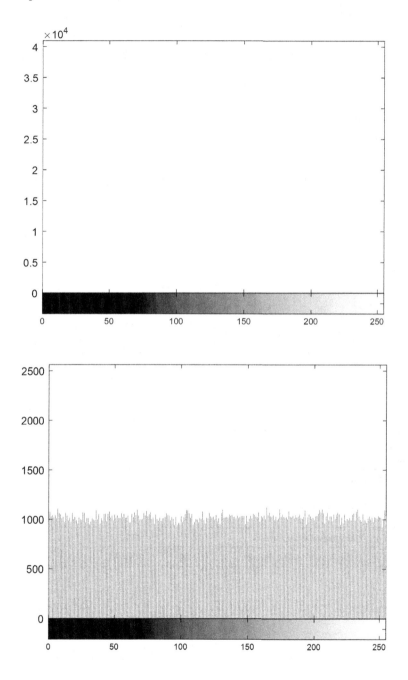

$$Cov(x, y) = \frac{1}{N} \sum_{i=1}^{N} (x_i - \bar{x})(y_i - \bar{y})$$

$$\sigma_x = \sqrt{E[x^2] - E[x]^2}$$

$$E[x] = \sum_{i=1}^{n} x_i p_i \qquad (7)$$

We denote by $\bar{x}$ and p_i the average value of x and the probability of x_i, respectively.

Table 8. Correlation coefficient of adjacent pixels

Images	Direction		
	Vertical	**Horizontal**	**Diagonal**
Original Lena	0.9554	0.9206	0.8914
Encrypted Lena	0.0088	-0.0102	0.0054
Original black	1.0000	1.0000	1.0000
Encrypted black	0.0055	0.0110	0.0019
Original MR	0.9954	0.9921	0.9952
Encrypted MR	0.0014	0.0077	0.0088
Original DX	0.9911	0.9851	0.9821
Encrypted DX	0.0069	-0.0051	0.0089
Original python	0.9985	0.9921	0.9852
Encrypted Python	0.0076	-0.0099	-0.0089
Original I	0.9751	0.9542	0.9684
Encrypted I	0.0055	0.0059	0.0065
Average of original images of the dataset	0.9910	0.9955	0.9955
Average of encrypted images of the dataset	0.0056	0.0042	0.0033

Figure 8. Adjacent pixels plotting of original Lena image in the three directions: V, D, and H, respectively

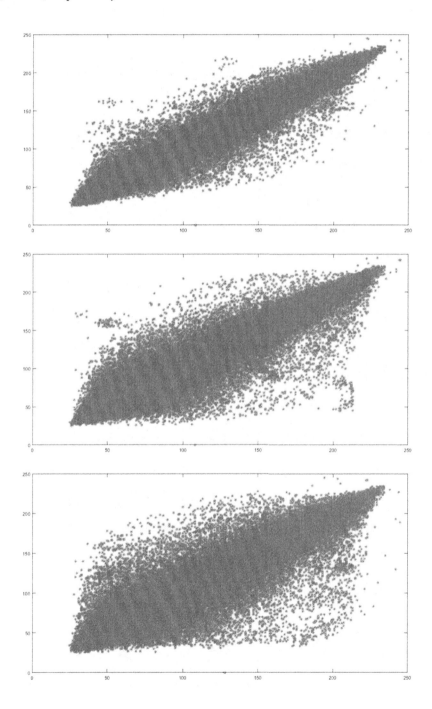

Figure 9. Adjacent pixels plotting of encrypted Lena image in the three directions: V, D, and H, respectively

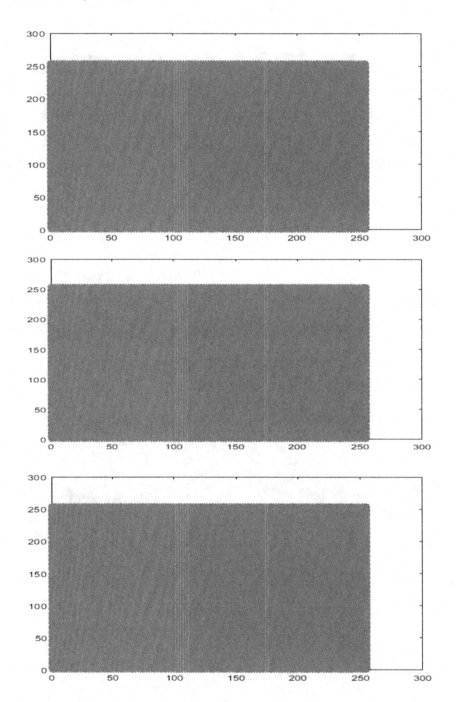

NIST Statistic Test

NIST (National Institute of Standards and Technology) tests are a statistical C/C++ package of tests that are designed to detect the randomness of binary sequences at the output of random or pseudo-random number generators used in applications requiring cryptography. The output of pseudo-random number generators should be unpredictable by ignoring the input. NIST tests focus on different types of non-random aspects that can be found in a sequence and compare them with a random sequence. Some tests can be broken down into a set of subtests. The order of application of the tests is arbitrary. However, the frequency test should be applied first, since it provides the most obvious proof of the non-random aspect, which is non-uniformity. If the test does not pass, the probability of subsequent tests failing is high. The result of each test is given by a P-Value which represents the probability that a perfect random number generator produces a less random sequence than the sequence already tested. This variable has a uniform distribution over the interval [0 1].

P-Value = 1: perfect random aspect.
P-Value = 0: non-random aspect.

Table 9. NIST Test of three encrypted Lena image with different key

NIST Test	Result (Pass/Fail) Test 1	Result (Pass/Fail) Test 2	Result (Pass/Fail) Test 3
Linear Complexity Test	*PASS*	*PASS*	*PASS*
Serial Test	*PASS*	*PASS*	*PASS*
Random Excursions Variant test	*PASS*	*PASS*	*PASS*
Random Excursions test	*PASS*	*PASS*	*PASS*
Approximate Entropy Test	*PASS*	*PASS*	*PASS*
Universal Test	*PASS*	*PASS*	*PASS*
Overlapping Template test	*PASS*	*PASS*	*PASS*
Non-Overlapping Template test	*PASS*	*PASS*	*PASS*
FFT Test	*PASS*	*PASS*	*PASS*
Rank Test	*PASS*	*PASS*	*PASS*
Longest Run Test	*PASS*	*PASS*	*PASS*
Runs Test	*PASS*	*PASS*	*PASS*
Cumulative Sums Test	*PASS*	*PASS*	*PASS*
Block Frequency Test	*PASS*	*PASS*	*PASS*
Frequency Test	*PASS*	*PASS*	*PASS*

A constant α is fixed in the interval [0.001-0.02]. It is called "level of significance". If the P-Values are greater than or equal to α, then the sequence passes the test otherwise it fails. The 15 NIST tests are on the Lena encrypted images are presented in Table 9. From the table we can confirm that the proposed system has a good randomness.

Entropy Test

We must examine the information entropy in order to test the suggested algorithm's resistance to entropic attacks. The amount of information contained in a sequence is expressed mathematically as the Shannon entropy. This series might be made up of text, a pixel, or any other binary file (byte collection). Let I stand for the information sequence, and the following formula displays Shannon's entropy H.

$$H\left(I\right) = \sum_{i=0}^{2^L-1} P_i log_2\left(\frac{1}{P_i}\right) \tag{8}$$

where L is the total number of potential grey level values and Pi is the likelihood that the ith grey value of i will occur. According to this formula, an ideal random source with 256 levels has an entropy of 8. (Case of an image). The information entropy test results are shown in Table 10. According to this table, the entropy of the encrypted data for the test dataset varied between 7.9992 and 7.9993, which is close to 8 and shows that the cipher images are nearly as random.

Table 10. Entropy of encrypted images

Image	Min Entropy	Max Entropy	Average Entropy
Lena	7.9992	7.9993	7.9993
black	7.9992	7.9993	7.9993
MR	7.9992	7.9993	7.9992
DX	7.9992	7.9994	7.9993
Python	7.9992	7.9993	7.9993
I	7.9992	7.9994	7.9992
Average	7.9992	7.9993	7.9993

Differential Attack Test

For the sake of secret key recovery, an attacker could attempt to distinguish any notable information between the normal image and its encryption version, by observing the influence of a one pixel change on the entire system output. encryption. A well-designed cryptosystem is a system in which a minor change in its simple image results in a major transformation of its encrypted image and, therefore, such type of attacks is nullified. To perform the experiment, the following procedure must be adopted: 1. The clear image P1 is encrypted to have an encryption image I1. 2. The simple image P2 here is obtained by applying a minor change to a randomly selected pixel in the first block, the corrupted ordinary image P2 is encrypted using the same secret key to produce the corresponding cipher image I2. Influence is measured quantitatively using two commonly used metrics:

- Number of pixel change rate (NPCR): it calculates the number of pixel differences between two images below I1 and I2, using the following formulas:

$$NPCR = 100 \frac{\sum D_{i,j}}{W \times H} \tag{9}$$

W and H correspond to the width and the height of the ciphered image, respectively; D(i,j) equal to 1 if I1(i,j) deferent to I2(i,j), 0 otherwise.

- Unified mean intensity of change (UACI): it calculates the average intensity of the differences between two numbered images I1 and I2, using the following formula:

$$UACI = 100 \sum \frac{\left| I_{1(i,j)} - I_{2(i,j)} \right|}{W \times H \times \left(2^d - 1 \right)} \tag{10}$$

As shown in Table 11, the mean values of NPCR and UACI for our dataset are estimated as 99.80% and 33.38% respectively, so, the observational values of NPCR and UACI are very close to the 100% and 33.33%, which proves the capability of the proposed algorithm to withstand differential attacks. The comparison of the NPCR and UACI are presented in Table 12. From this table, we can see that the proposed has a good robustness compared with Qobbi et al. (2022), Khashan et al. (2020), and Kumar et al. (2022). The difference between two images different in one pixel and encrypted with the same key are shown in Figure 10 where the plotted pixels confirm the robustness of the proposed algorithm.

Table 11. NPCR and UACI values

Images	NPCR	UACI
Lena	99.60	33.43
black	99.58	33.49
MR	99.88	33.34
DX	99.89	33.35
Python	99.81	33.38
I	99.71	33.34
Average	99.80	33.38

Figure 10. Difference between two images different in one pixel and encrypted with the same key

Table 12. NPCR and UACI comparison

Methods	NPCR	UACI
Our	99.80	33.38
(Qobbi Y. et al, 2022)	99.61	33.46
(Khashan O.A et al,2020)	99.40	33.45
(Kumar V. et al,2022)	99.64	33.42

Chosen/Know Attacks Analysis

In these types of attacks, we suppose that the cracker has applied a strength side channel attack (presented in the next subsection), Therefore, he accesses encrypted data, in this case he has a sample of encrypted data, or he can evaluate an encryption test, in this case he has the original and encrypted images, respectively. Using these data, he must compute the secret key. However, in the proposed system, we have an S-Box combined of 256 under S-boxes which make the determination of both s-box and key impossible. As shown in Table 13, where we test similarity of three S-box generated by the proposed s-box generation method, each s-box is different to another (NPCR equal to 100%) due to the random generation of the system.

Table 13. NPCR between three generated s-boxes

Images	Sbox1	Sbox2	Sbox3
Sbox1	-	100%	100%
Sbox2	100%	-	100%
Sbox3	100%	100%	-

Side-Channel Attack

In the field of computer security, an attack by side channel (SCA) refers to a computer attack which, without calling into question the theoretical robustness of security methods and procedures, searches for and exploits flaws in their implementation, software or hardware. Indeed, "mathematical" security does not necessarily guarantee security during "practical" use. Auxiliary channel attacks are many and varied and involve different parameters. There are two main categories:

- Invasive attacks that require interaction with hardware (potentially destructive):
- Survey attack: This attack consists in placing a probe directly in the circuit to be studied, in order to observe its behavior (generally used in the case of encrypted buses).
- Fault injection attack: This attack consists of deliberately introducing errors into the system to cause certain revealing behaviors (such as a laser or electromagnetic pulse, etc.).
- Non-invasive attacks that simply perform an external observation of the system (passive):
- Attack by fault: This attack consists of using the system outside of its nominal operating range, which causes it to fault, faults then analyzed to extract relevant information.
- Analysis of electromagnetic emanations: This attack is similar to acoustic cryptanalysis but using electromagnetic radiation (emission of waves, analysis of a thermal image, light emitted by a screen, etc.).
- Consumption analysis: Increased consumption indicates a large calculation and can give information about the key.
- Traffic analysis attack: Intercepting elements on the communication between its targets makes it possible to deduce clues about their activity.
- Branch prediction attack: The study of the branch prediction units of the new architectures of the processors can give interesting information.
- Temporal attack: This attack consists of studying the time taken to perform certain operations.
- Acoustic cryptanalysis: This attack consists of the study of the noise generated by a computer or a machine that encrypts. Indeed, the processor emits noise which varies in intensity and nature according to its consumption and the operations carried out (typically capacitors which charge, or discharge emit an easily measurable snap).

Table 14. PSNR between Lena decrypted without attack Lena decrypted with applied Noise and cropping for the encrypted image

Extracted Data	PSNR
SPN(0.001)	22.35
SPN(0.01)	21.20
Cropping 100x100 pixels	24.00

Figure 11. Noise and cropping attacks test. We note that the attacks are applied on the encrypted domain.

These attacks can be combined to obtain secret information like the encryption key. Their implementation is closely related to the attacked hardware or software.

Noise and Cropping Attack

The proposed encryption method should be able to tolerate some noise contamination as the image may become contaminated by noise during transmission. Figure 11 displays the results of testing the encryption algorithm's resilience against salt and pepper noise (SPN) attack and cropping attack. PSNR is used to gauge the effectiveness of image decryption, as illustrated in Table 14. Therefore, we can conclude that even under a mild noise attacks, the suggested encryption method can still decode most of the image data.

Table 15. Runtime results

Images	Encryption Time(s)	Decryption Time(s)	S-Box Gen(s)
Lena	0.0951	0.0944	
Black	0.0851	0.0855	320.3843
MR	0.0965	0.0992	

Runtime and Complexity

The execution time of an encryption algorithm is a crucial factor in cryptography because in the design of such algorithms. Care must always be taken to achieve the robustness-speed compromise, because the faster the encryption process, the more difficult its discovery in cryptanalysis, and as the proposed system finds its application in embedded system field, which is characterized by its speed in processing, the pre-encryption schemes proposed with a view to improving the sensitivity must meet this speed criterion. To evaluate the proposed pre-encryption from an execution time point of view, the tests are carried out on three standard test images of Lena, Black and MR, under MATLAB R2021a environment using a personal laptop running Windows 11, with a processor: ADM Atom with CPU1.20GHZ and 4G RAM, the test results are summarized in Table 15. The results summarized in this table confirm the speed of the proposed method. These results also confirm the need to always achieve the robustness-speed compromise according to the importance and the degree of security required in the specifications of the application to be secured.

LIMITATIONS AND FUTURE WORK

In this work. The exchange of S-box and encryption key is manually. In the future, we will propose a protocol for exchanging this secret data using Network by combining the RSA with large size keys and ECC for padding bit protocol in RSA. Also, the size of s-box is around 16 MB, for minimize this size two solutions: the first is to split a pixel of 8-bit to two-part L and H, then the s-box will be of 4x4x4. The second solution is the use of neural network to the optimization.

CONCLUSION

In this chapter, we have proposed a DICOM encryption system for protecting this file in unsafe storage or network. The novel method is based on an improved three dimensionally S-box which is used in diffusion using the function and confusion using the function. It encrypts the imaging in block of 512-bit which make it suitable for encrypting text part or DICOM tag. Results are demonstrated the performance of the proposed algorithm in term of security and runtime. compared avec the state-of-the-art the proposed schema has the best performance which make it suitable for used as standard for DICOM encryption.

REFERENCES

Boussif, M., Aloui, N., & Cherif, A. (2017). New Watermarking/Encryption Method for Medical Images Full Protection in mHealth. *Iranian Journal of Electrical and Computer Engineering*, 7(6), 3385–3394.

Boussif, M., Aloui, N., & Cherif, A. (2018). Secured cloud computing for medical data based on watermarking and encryption. *IET Networks*, 7(5), 294–298. doi:10.1049/iet-net.2017.0180

Boussif, M., Aloui, N., & Cherif, A. (2019). Images encryption algorithm based on the quaternion multiplication and the XOR operation. *Multimedia Tools and Applications*, 78(24), 35493–35510. doi:10.100711042-019-08108-9

Boussif, M., Aloui, N., & Cherif, A. (2020). Securing DICOM images by a new encryption algorithm using Arnold transform and Vigenère cipher. *IET Image Processing*, 14(6), 1209–1216. doi:10.1049/iet-ipr.2019.0042

Boussif, M., Bouferas, O., Aloui, N., & Cherif, A. (2021). A Novel Robust Blind AES/LWT+DCT+SVD-Based Crypto-Watermarking schema for DICOM Images Security. *IEEE International Conference on Design & Test of Integrated Micro & Nano-Systems (DTS)*, 1-6. 10.1109/DTS52014.2021.9497916

El-Shafai, W., Khallaf, F., El-Rabaie, E. S. M., & El-Samie, F. E. A. (2021). Robust medical image encryption based on DNA-chaos cryptosystem for secure telemedicine and healthcare applications. *Journal of Ambient Intelligence and Humanized Computing*, *12*(10), 9007–9035. doi:10.100712652-020-02597-5

Gao, X., Mou, J., Xiong, L., Sha, Y., Yan, H., & Cao, Y. (2022). A fast and efficient multiple images encryption based on single-channel encryption and chaotic system. *Nonlinear Dynamics*, *108*(1), 613–636. doi:10.100711071-021-07192-7

Gupta, A., Singh, D., & Kaur, M. (2020). An efficient image encryption using non-dominated sorting genetic algorithm-III based 4-D chaotic maps. *Journal of Ambient Intelligence and Humanized Computing*, *11*(3), 1309–1324. doi:10.100712652-019-01493-x

Iqbal, N., & Hanif, M. (2021). An efficient grayscale image encryption scheme based on variable length row-column swapping operations. *Multimed Tools Appl*, *80*, 36305–36339,

Khashan, O. A., & AlShaikh, M. (2020). Edge-based lightweight selective encryption scheme for digital medical images. *Multimed Tools Appl.*, *79*, 26369–26388.

Kumar, V., Pathak, V., & Badal, N. (2022). *Complex entropy based encryption and decryption technique for securing medical images*. Multimed Tools Appl. doi:10.100711042-022-13546-z

Mohamed, B., & Aymen, M. (2022). Secure Images Transmission Using a Three-Dimensional S-Box-Based Encryption Algorithm. In *5th International Conference on Advanced Systems and Emergent Technologies (IC_ASET)* (pp. 17-22). IEEE

Munir, N., Khan, M., & Al Karim Haj Ismail, A. (2022). Cryptanalysis and Improvement of Novel Image Encryption Technique Using Hybrid Method of Discrete Dynamical Chaotic Maps and Brownian Motion. *Multimed Tools Appl.*, *81*, 6571–6584.

Priya, S., & Santhi, B. (2019). A Novel Visual Medical Image Encryption for Secure Transmission of Authenticated Watermarked Medical Images. *Mobile Networks and Applications*, *26*(6), 2501–2508. doi:10.100711036-019-01213-x

Qobbi, Y., Jarjar, A., Essaid, M., & Benazzi, A. (2022). Image encryption algorithm based on genetic operations and chaotic DNA encoding. *Soft Computing*, *26*(12), 5823–5832. doi:10.100700500-021-06567-7

Riaz, F., Hameed, S., Shafi, I., Kausar, R., & Ahmed, A. (2012). Enhanced Image Encryption Techniques Using Modified Advanced Encryption Standard. *Emerging Trends and Applications in Information Communication Technologies*, *281*, 385–396.

Shaheen, A. M., Sheltami, T. R., Al-Kharoubi, T. M., & Shakshuki, E. (2019). Digital image encryption techniques for wireless sensor networks using image transformation methods: DCT and DWT. *Journal of Ambient Intelligence and Humanized Computing*, *10*(12), 4733–4750. doi:10.100712652-018-0850-z

Sneha, P. S., Sankar, S., & Kumar, A. S. (2020). A chaotic colour image encryption scheme combining Walsh–Hadamard transform and Arnold–Tent maps. *Journal of Ambient Intelligence and Humanized Computing*, *11*(3), 1289–1308. doi:10.100712652-019-01385-0

Song, W., Fu, C., & Zheng, Y. (2022). Protection of image ROI using chaos-based encryption and DCNN-based object detection. *Neural Comput & Applic.*, *34*, 5743–5756.

Wang, X., Li, B., & Wang, Y. (2021). An efficient batch images encryption method based on DNA encoding and PWLCM. *Multimed Tools Appl*, *80*, 943–971.

APPENDIX 1: MATLAB 2021A CODE OF S-BOX GENERATION

```
clear all
sbox_E=zeros(256,256,256);
sbox_D=zeros(256,256,256);
for i=1:256
    for j=1:256
            sbox_E(i,:,j)=randperm(256);
            for c1=1:255
                p=c1+1;
              if j>2
              while ((in(sbox_E(i,c1,j),sbox_E(1:(i-
1),c1,j))) &&(in(sbox_E(i,c1,j),sbox_E(i,c1,1:(j-1))))))
                    if p>=255
                        break
                    end
                    aux=sbox_E(i,c1,j);
                    sbox_E(i,c1,j)=sbox_E(i,p,j);
                    sbox_E(i,p,j)=aux;
                    p=p+1;

                end
              end
            end

    end
end
clear i j k l
save sbox
```

APPENDIX 2: MATLAB 2021A CODE OF ENCRYPTION AND DECRYPTION PROCESSES

Main

```
clear all;
tic;
load sbox
oupnet=toc;
 %I='sim/c.dcm';
%img=dicomread(I);
 %imginf=dicominfo(I);
%img= imread('sim/bg.bmp');
img=uint8(zeros(512));
%a=open('sim/lena512.mat');
%img=uint8(a.lena512);
l=size(img);
%N=double(imginf.BitDepth);
N=8;
e=key_ben();
key=reshape(e,[1,64]);
imgb=reshape(img,[64,4096]);
tic;
d=double(Fn_XOR(key,sbox_E))+1;
etemp=encrypt_block(key,key,d,sbox_E);
for i=1:fix(l(1)*l(2)/64)
    temp(:)=imgb(:,i);
    t=bitxor(uint8(temp),uint8(etemp));
    etemp=encrypt_block(t,key,d,sbox_E);
    d=mod(d+1,256)+1;
    ctimgb(:,i)=t;
end
encimg=reshape(ctimgb,[512,512]);
temps=toc;
%encimg(1:256-50,1:256)=0;
%h = fspecial('average', 1);
%encimg = imfilter(encimg, h);
%encimg= imnoise(encimg,'salt & pepper',0.01);
imgb=reshape(encimg,[64,4096]);
 d=double(Fn_XOR(key,sbox_E))+1;
```

```
etemp=encrypt_block(key,key,d,sbox_E);
for i=1:fix(l(1)*l(2)/64)
    temp(:)=imgb(:,i);
    t=bitxor(uint8(temp),uint8(etemp));
    etemp=encrypt_block(temp,key,d,sbox_E);
    d=mod(d+1,256)+1;
    ctimgb(:,i)=t;
end
rest=reshape(ctimgb,[512,512]);
```

encrypt_block Function

```
function out = encrypt_block(temp,key,d,s)
out(64)=0;
for i=1:64
out(i)=s(key(i)+1,temp(i)+1,d)-1;
d=mod(out(i)+1,256)+1;
end
end
```

Fn_XOR Function

```
function  output = Fn_XOR(m,s)
me=uint8(m(1));
for i= 2:length(m)

        me=bitxor(me,uint8(s(m(i)+1,m((length(m)-
i+1))+1,double(me)+1)-1));
end
    output=me;
end
```

Chapter 2
Video Watermarking With Digital Signature and Fingerprinting

Milan Gupta
Auckland University of Technology, New Zealand

Wei Qi Yan
Auckland University of Technology, New Zealand

ABSTRACT

A digital watermark, which is embedded in an image sequence or video frames as the form of a binary string or visual logo, is a small size of visible data. Thus, the quality of embedded videos is often slashed due to the watermarking. Comparative video watermarking is a highly innovative method that was designed to unravel this issue. In this chapter, the authors make use of singular value decomposition (SVD) and discrete wavelet transform (DWT) for video watermarking; the authors employed inverse transform (IDWT) to extract the video watermark. The digital signature is also utilised to increase the authenticity of watermarks and verify any changes. The authors combine this approach with digital fingerprinting as well as to get the improved results. Throughout the designed attacks, the merits of the new watermarking paradigm such as robustness, convergence, and stability are attained with security and authenticity by calculating the metrics such as MSE, PSNR, entropy, SSIM, etc.

DOI: 10.4018/978-1-6684-4945-5.ch002

INTRODUCTION

Digital watermarking is a way of embedding secure information into digital media for transcoding. A machine-detectable pattern that could be put on several documents for anti-counterfeiting purposes was identified in 1979. A number of years later, a method for embedding an identification code into an audio signal was identified by researchers. Researchers firstly employed the term digital watermark in 1988. The notion of digital watermarking gained widespread acceptance in the early 1990s. The first information hiding workshop (IHW), which included digital watermarking as one of its key topics, was held in 1996 (Gupta, 2021).

A watermark is visible where it is easily seen by the owner and observer or invisible where decoding algorithms can be identified by the originator (Gupta, 2021). The watermark needs to be durable for this application so that it cannot be broken by digital media alteration. The algorithm needs to be blind, another prerequisite for watermarking for copyright protection. The host media is not needed to remove the watermarking information for blind operations. Security is an important issue that requires only the owner to change the watermark. The number of special sessions held at recent conferences and the efforts made on related European projects such as Certimark and Encrypt are a good indication of the increasing interest in this topic, whereas watermarking robustness has usually been associated with the possibility of decoding error or resistance to removal of watermarks, the definition of watermarking protection is still fuzzy.

Recent work has been accepted that security attacks have wider applications than robustness attacks, as the former is concerned not only with the simple impairment of communication mechanism but also with the achievement of rights given by the system's hidden parameters. Watermarking helps to recognize the actual possessor of digital information. It is one of the potential strategies for securing digital information.

Digital watermarking is an effective approach for protecting intellectual property and copyrights by shielding multimedia data such as photographs, videos, or audio files from information such as signatures, logos, or manuscripts. However, a high risk of piracy is also seen by copyright owners, especially large Hollywood studios and music labels. Using analogue devices leads to a lower risk in the past than using digital media; copying an analogue file contributes to consistency degradation. However, songs and movies can be generated without any quality degradation using digital media recording, because the data is a stream of 0's and 1's.

Cryptography provides a small security measure; once the decrypted material enters the consumer, there will be no further security. Therefore, further content protection is required, even after it is decrypted. The watermarking is a popular approach that is used to comply with the creator's copyright rights. The knowledge is hidden inside the content in digital watermarking. Digital watermarking can withstand various types of attacks, including compression, conversion from digital to analogue, and changes in file format. In order to fulfil all these processes, a watermark can be created.

For copy prevention and copyright protection, watermarking has been well-thought-out. The watermark may be used in copyright protection applications to recognize the copyright holder and ensure sufficient payment of the royalties. Although copyright security and copy prevention have been major drivers of watermarking field research, there are a range of earlier applications for which watermarking has been used. It includes broadening, monitoring, monitoring activities, and confirmation. Medical photographs, satellite images, and photos taken by mobile phone cameras include other applications.

Usually, one hidden key is used in the watermarking process. The essential element of information that the material is legitimate or not by identifying the watermark is the hidden key. Insertion or embedding is called positioning in watermarking process. The process that the watermark is extracted is called watermark extraction. The use of a watermark is also a solution for copyright security and authentication of ownership; the digital data becomes much stable and is safe from infringement. There are various types of methods available for watermarking including watermark extraction. Each of them offers various characteristics and functions that can be used for multiple purposes.

Digital watermarking has been utilized for multiple functions, such as copyright protection, broadcast tracking like watermarked videos from an international news agency, hidden or subchannel communications, etc. If visible information is embedded in the media as a watermark, the watermark is termed as visible digital watermark. This may be a logo or a text that marks a digital medium (Po-Chyi et al., 2017; Langelaar et al., 2000).

In this chapter, we take advantage of digital videos as the host media for watermarking which is referred to as video watermarking. This is often applied to verify the believability of digital media or to acknowledge the identity of the owner of the media. So, the purpose of this research work is to come up with an approach that overcomes the limitations of the existing watermarking process by providing more secure and robust ways of video watermarking.

In this chapter, a watermarking method is proffered for copyright protection of digital videos. The watermarking is implemented based on two mathematical transforms. The first one is the discrete wavelet transformation (DWT), while the second is singular value decomposition (SVD). These two models are from frequency domain and spectrum domain respectively, thus are completely distinct and generate different outcomes, however, the levels of security against an attack are distinguished. A watermark is embedded in the video that carries the hidden data regarding sender and receivers to verify whether the watermark has been tampered or not (Natarajan & Govindarajan, 2015). The digital fingerprinting is combined with watermarking to achieve the improvised results. Video fingerprinting takes use of d a digital rights management (DRM) which is use of technological tools to identify, extract, and represent the attributes belonging to a video file. This is to identify the video by its unique "fingerprint".

In this book chapter, the selected literature will be surveyed, later the methodologies are delineated, the experimental results will be expounded as the follow, and the conclusion will be drawn finally.

RELATED WORK

In this book chapter, the work related to digital watermarking is explicated. Firstly, the digital watermarking approaches based on the frequency domain of digital videos are surveyed. We see that frequency domain is suitable for watermarking (Deepak & Prachi, 2018). In order to accomplish the watermark embedding, in this chapter, two singular value matrices are generated and have been employed to host watermarks. All video frames are taken as the watermarking objects by using the proffered algorithms. DWT is applied to watermark video frames. With high stability, SVD is conducted based on the obtained HL2 subbands, and watermark embedding is implemented (Muthumanickam & Arun, 2018).

A distinct method of video watermarking has been developed by paying zero cost, digital files are very easy to be copied. Users mostly download and share multimedia data such as images, audio clips, and video footages. Hence, there is a great possibility of digital information being duplicated. Therefore, it necessitates prohibiting the copyright of digital media (Anjali & Parul, 2018).

In order to support SVD and MR-SVD in fast motion frames, one of the algorithms based on wavelets, SVD, and transform split the frames of the cover video into red, green, and blue (RGB) bands. While most of the prevailing watermarking schemes have placed the watermark in each video frame, which spends enormous time and also has a noticeable impact on the quality of the video, the projected methodology selects only the fast motion frames in each shot to host the watermark (Imen, 2018).

Another approach took use of Haar wavelet transform and LSB in digital watermarking for the purpose of video authentication (Pallavi, 2018; Wahid et al., 2018; Harahap & Khairina, 2020). This aids to remove random noises by embedding a visual watermark so as to prevent attacks in the least significant part of the cover image. The results show that the planned method provided excellent hidden invisibility, reasonable security, and well-hidden attacks (Tasheva et al., 2017; Saqer & Barhoom, 2016).

Finally, Hash algorithms were introduced to apply cryptography on a watermarked image for achieving the purposes of authentication and security in watermarking. MD5 was accommodated with LSB substitution (Nurul et al., 2018; Pradhan et al., 2018; Khairina et al., 2018), similar approaches were proposed where Hash algorithm was applied to specifically the selected pixels (Mohd et al., 2018).

A watermarking approach mingling with the digital signature was taken advantage of Hash algorithm and asymmetric key cryptography together to achieve a high level of security and authenticity. Thus, the sender's private key was generated with a digital signature, the receiver's public key was employed to encrypt the media data and signatures (Antony & Uma, 2014; Li´skiewicz et al., 2017). Individual signature was computed from the selected pixels which are hidden in the designated pixels of the same image. This method preserved the size of the image and does not create any significant distortions which are visible to human eyes (Sahib et al., 2018). The digital watermarking was combined with fingerprinting techniques to identify the copyrights for colour images (Hsieh et al., 2014). It involved the fingerprint and watermarked image generation and the authentication of logo detection phase.

In this paper, we propose SVD in the frequency domain associated with DWT for video watermarking. The watermarked video is segmented into single frames. The LSB method has been applied to visual watermarking.

METHODS

The proposed algorithm encapsulates two branches: Watermark embedding and watermark extraction. The flowchart of the proposed watermarking scheme follows the steps shown as Figure 1.

The Steps for Watermark Embedding

- Decompose the watermark image into m different watermark images.

$$W = W_1, W_2, W_3, ..., W_m \tag{1}$$

- Apply singular value decomposition (SVD) for each of the watermark images.

$$[Uw(j). Sw(j) . Vw(j)] = SVD(W(j)) \tag{2}$$

where $j = 1,2,3,...,m$.

Figure 1. The proposed watermarking scheme

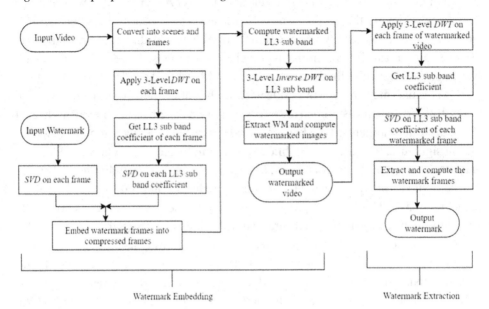

- Split the host video into scenes and frames.
- Apply DWT on each frame of the scene to retrieve the *LL3(j)* subband coefficients.
- Apply SVD for each compressed frame of the jth scene.

$$[U_i(j) . S_i(j) . V_i(j)] = svd(LL_{3i}(j)) \tag{3}$$

where *i* is the number of video frame in the seq *j*.

- Add watermark information into each compressed frame of the jth scene.

$$D_i(j) = S_i(j) + K \times S_w(j) \tag{4}$$

where *K* is watermarking strength.

- Compute watermarked *LL3'* subband coefficients and apply 3-level inverse DWT to get WM components.

$$LL3_i'(j) = U_i(j) \cdot Di(j) \cdot V_i(j) \tag{5}$$

- Reconstruct all watermarked frames and retrieve the watermarked video.

The Steps for Watermark Extraction

- Apply 3-level DWT to each frame of the jth sequence of watermarked video to retrieve $LL_3'(j)$ sub-band coefficients.
- Apply SVD to each compressed frame of the jth sequence of the watermarked video.

$$[U_i'(j) \cdot S_i'(j) \cdot V_i'(j)] = SVD\ (LL_{3i}'(j)) \tag{6}$$

where i is frame sequence in j-th scene, SVD($\cdot$) is the singular value decomposition function.

- Extract the watermark image $w'(j)$ for the jth sequence

$$W'(j) = U_w'(j) \cdot S_w'(j) \cdot V_w'(j) \tag{7}$$

where $S_w'(j) = (S_i'(j) - S_i(j))/K$

- Finally, a single watermark is reconstructed from the extracted watermark images.

$$W = W_1 + W_2 + W_3 + \cdots + W_m \tag{8}$$

A digital signature is a kind of cryptographical methods. The process of a digital signature is quite akin to the handwritten signature having a digital certificate that is applied to verify the identity. The signature affirms that the verifying information is originated from the party having the respective signature on it.

Cryptography, as well known, means keeping communication security and providing a better mechanism of information security by using encryption and decryption. Cryptography is implemented at present by using any of the following three ways: symmetric key (SKC), asymmetric key (AKC) – using public-private keys, hash functions (one-way cryptography).

The Hash function is to generate a unique value for the data on which it is being applied. Hashing is employed to provide authentication in a much better way than that of encryption, which is a way of generating a hash value according to the visual contents of the applied image. There are a wealth of Hash algorithms with different techniques like message Digest (MD5), secure hash algorithm (SHA), etc. MD5 is the most famous one in the family of Hash algorithms.

In digital signature, Hash is generated from the original message, the digital signature is produced with the sender's private key, this data is encrypted with the receiver's public key. On the receiver's side, the data is decrypted with the receiver's private key as it was encrypted by using the receiver's public key. The digital signatures will be verified with the sender's public key at the receiver side, which confirms that it has been sent by the intended sender without an intruder involved. Later, Hashing is calculated based on received data at the receiver's side and compared against what was sent with the message. If both match, then all good; Otherwise, it indicates there is a data breach or compromise of security in the data transfer.

Figure 2. The proposed scheme of digital signature

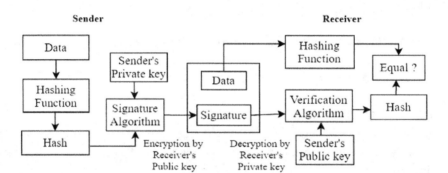

The proposed algorithm of video watermarking is extended further to uplift the privacy, security, and authentication in the field of video watermarking. As we know, digital signature guarantees that the contents of the transit message will not be altered, the message is originated via the intended sender only. Through considering the high degree of privacy, security, and authenticity provided by a digital signature, we fully make use of digital signature along with Hash algorithms to generate the watermarks. Now, this watermark is able to be used for video watermarking to verify the authenticity and ownership of any video footage. The proposed algorithm is combined with Hash algorithm and digital signature during the watermarking time. The steps of video watermarking with digital signature are:

- Segment the host video into frames.
- Apply the hash function (MD-5) to the cover image (or frame) to generate the message digest (Di).
- Apply encryption scheme (RSA) to this digest to generate the digital signature (Si).
- This digital signature itself is used as a watermark which will be embedded video frames, from where it is generated.

44

- Use the watermarking embedding steps for each video.
- Finally, the embedded watermark is reconstructed along with the digital signatures, the same is used as a watermark for corresponding frames/images.

The steps of watermark extraction with digital signature:

- Follow the watermarking extraction steps for each frame/image. It will provide the extracted watermark (Wi, i.e., the digital signature embedded as a watermark) and actual digital signature (Si) sent with each frame/image.
- Apply a decryption scheme (RSA) to this digital signature (Si) and retrieve the message digest (Di).
- Retrieve the message digest (Di') by applying the decryption scheme (RSA) on the extracted watermark (Wi).
- The two message digests (i.e., Di' and Di) are compared to verify the authenticity, integrity, and ownership of the respective image/frame or video.

The proposed approach in this chapter is combined with the digital fingerprinting method to have better efficiency and robustness. It takes use of image secret sharing (ISS) that generates a share image from two images. After generating the feature image from the base image, another identifiable (or logo) image is added to generate the secret shared image. This method has two phases:

(1) Initially, feature extraction is applied to extract the features of the base image and then scrambling is employed to disarrange the authentication logo to a scrambled logo image. After this, the fingerprint is generated by using extracted features and the scrambled logo, this is called fingerprint generating. Finally, the fingerprint is employed as a watermark and is embedded in the base image, to generate the watermarked image. We have stored the fingerprint in a database to use in the next phase.

(2) This phase detects the watermark first and procced with fingerprint detection. After watermark retrieval, the watermark features of the suspect image are extracted by using feature extractor. Now, logo restoration is conducted by using the extracted watermark and the extracted features to recover and rearrange the scrambled logo. Finally, logo comparison is accomplished and the detection is completed if the accuracy rate of the restored logo is high enough; Otherwise, the next available fingerprint is retrieved from the database, then it returns to logo restoration step, which takes as input the retrieved fingerprint instead of the extracted watermark. The process continues to loop until no fingerprint is available or authentication logo is discovered.

For various continuous frames of a video, we have a watermarking scheme from frame-by-frame perspective. In this scheme, we embed a different pseudo-random watermark in each video frame as shown in eq.(9).

$$F'_t = F_t + \alpha \cdot W_t(K) \tag{9}$$

where F'_t represents the luminance of the t-th video frame, F_t is the luminance of the t-th watermarked frame, α is the embedding strength and K is a secret key. Each inserted watermark $W_t(K)$ has a normal distribution with unit variance and zero mean which is different at every instant t. Regarding the pseudo-random generator, $K+t$ is employed as a seed to retrieve this property. The perceptual shaping is introduced to improve the invisibility of the watermark even if a global embedding strength has been used in practice.

Figure 3. Fingerprint and watermarked image generating and logo detection

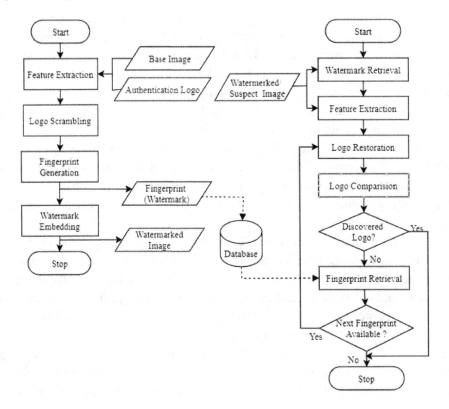

RESULTS

The proposed approach is applied to evaluate the performance. The videos are segmented into a sequence of frames to leverage and enrich the sample datasets. A rich assortment of images/frames are employed in the watermarking process with the proposed watermarking approach. Figure 4 shows the images from the datasets.

The proposed watermarking approach is employed to multiple images and video frames, so as to generate the watermarked images. SSIM is applied to measure the effectiveness of the watermarked image and extracted watermark, i.e., to evaluate the performance of the proposed watermarking approach with these samples.

Structural Similarity Index Measure (SSIM) is an alternative visual quality metric that is used to measure the similarity between two videos. It is a full reference metric. The weakness of PSNR and MSE metrics is that sometimes they do not represent the several distortions perceived by the human visual system. SSIM is more effective at estimating the perceptual quality of images than the PSNR and MSE as it considers image degradation as a perceived change in structural information. Structural information is the idea that the pixels have strong interdependencies especially when they are spatially close. These dependencies carry important information about the structure of the objects in the visual scene. The similarity measure using SSIM is already proven very robust and versatile in various environments. SSIM output varies from -1.0 to 1.0, where -1.0 represents very noticeable distortion and 1.0 stands for perfect quality. The SSIM is given as eq. (10).

$$SSIM\left(x,y\right)=\frac{\left(2\mu_x\mu_y+c1\right)\left(2\sigma_{xy}+c2\right)}{\left(\mu_x^2+\mu_y^2+c1\right)\left(\sigma_x^2+\sigma_y^2+c2\right)} \tag{10}$$

where μ_x is the average of x, μ_y is the average of y, σ_x^2 is the variance of x, σ_y^2 is the variance of y, σ_{xy} is the covariance of x and y, and c1,c2 are constant variables to stabilize the division. SSIM takes advantage of luminance, contrast, and structure comparison functions to estimate the perceived quality of an image. The luminance comparison is carried between the original image and the degraded image by using the eq. (11).

$$LC=\frac{2\mu_x\mu_y}{\mu_x^2+\mu_y^2} \tag{11}$$

where

$$\mu_x = \bar{x} = \frac{1}{N}\sum_{i=1}^{N} x_i, \quad \mu_y = \bar{y} = \frac{1}{N}\sum_{i=1}^{N} y_i.$$

The contrast comparison between the original image and the degraded image is calculated by using the eq. (12).

$$CC = \frac{2\sigma_x \sigma_y}{\sigma_x^2 + \sigma_y^2} \tag{12}$$

where

$$\sigma_x^2 = \frac{1}{N-1}\sum_{i=1}^{N}(x-\bar{x})^2, \quad \sigma_y^2 = \frac{1}{N-1}\sum_{i=1}^{N}(y-\bar{y})^2.$$

The structural comparison for the original and the degraded image is done by using eq. (13).

$$SC = \frac{\sigma_{xy}}{\sigma_x \sigma_y} \tag{13}$$

where

$$\sigma_x = \sqrt{\frac{1}{N}\sum_{i=1}^{N}(x_i - \mu_x)^2}, \quad \sigma_y = \sqrt{\frac{1}{N}\sum_{i=1}^{N}(y_i - \mu_y)^2},$$

$$\sigma_{xy} = \frac{1}{N-1}\sum_{i=1}^{N}(x-\bar{x})(y-\bar{y}),$$

N as the size of the image(s), x_i and y_i as the intensity of the original and the degraded image, and $\bar{x}$ and $\bar{y}$ as the mean intensity of respective images, all these three comparisons are combined to calculate SSIM as,

$$SSIM(x,y) = LC \cdot CC \cdot SC \tag{14}$$

$$SSIM(x,y) = \frac{2\mu_x \mu_y}{\mu_x^2 + \mu_y^2} \cdot \frac{2\sigma_x \sigma_y}{\sigma_x^2 + \sigma_y^2} \cdot \frac{\sigma_{xy}}{\sigma_x \sigma_y} \qquad (15)$$

This is as same as what we have seen earlier with c_1 and c_2 are 0.

$$SSIM(x,y) = \frac{(2\mu_x \mu_y + c1)(2\sigma_{xy} + c2)}{(\mu_x^2 + \mu_y^2 + c1)(\sigma_x^2 + \sigma_y^2 + c2)} \qquad (16)$$

Mean square error (MSE) for various images is quite low while the respective Peak Signal to Noise Ratio (PSNR) is quite high. This indicates that the effectiveness and performance of the proposed approach image watermarking from the given dataset are good. The other metric like similarity structure index measure (SSIM) is quite high and approaches 1.00, which reveals that the similarity of the images before and after watermarking remains intact by using the proposed. Similarly, mean, variance, and entropy in Table 1 signify the effectiveness and robustness of the proposed solution with a given dataset.

There are several types of tampering methods that is able to be implemented in a watermarked image before extracting the watermarks. The proposed approach is evaluated by applying several attacks on the watermarked images. The watermark is extracted post-attack(s) and the parameters are calculated to measure the performance of the applied process/approach as it is calculated in earlier cases.

Various signal processing operations to conduct the noise modifications/attacks (non-geometrical attacks) are implemented based on the watermarked image of Lena. The attacks of salt & pepper noises (with variance 0.05 and 0.01) are applied to evaluate the results of the proposed approach, it shows the respective PSNR and Normalized Correlation (NC) values for the attacked watermarked images and the extracted watermarks in Figure 5. The image dataset is shown as Figure 4.

Gaussian noisy attacks with variance 0.05 and 0.01 are also applied to show the attacked watermarked and extracted watermark along with the respective PSNR and NC values. Similarly, speckle attack is applied on watermarked images with variance equals 0.05 and 0.01. Figure 6 shows the respective PSNR and NC values along with attacked watermarked and extracted watermark.

The rotation attack is a geometric attack applied by moving/rotating the image clockwise/anti-clockwise to introduce modifications. The watermarked image of Lena is attacked with different angles and evaluated in each case. The extracted watermarks with respective PSNR and NC values are shown in Table 1 and Figure 7. The resizing and cropping attacks are also geometric attacks. The resizing attack is implemented by changing the size of the watermarked image and restoring it to the same level. These attacks were implemented based on the watermarked image of Lena like other attacks. The respectively extracted watermarks along with PSNR and NC values are shown in Figure 7.

Now, different datasets having multiple video frames are tackled with various approaches. These datasets are verified/tested against already existing watermarking attacks (i.e., SVD, 2-DWT). The same datasets were applied to our proposed approach and the combination of our approach with the digital signature as shown in Figure 4.

The average PSNR values for different datasets were calculated for watermarked images / videos against each of these three approaches. Table 2 represents the result classification of PSNR values for watermarked images/videos with different approaches.

The existing approach has adopted a 2-level DWT transform for the watermarking process while the proposed approach has employed a slightly different way with 3-level DWT for various videos and its frames to commence the video watermarking. Table 2 shows that the results of the proposed approach are much better than the existing approaches with respect to the PSNR values based on different datasets. The overall average result of all the datasets with the proposed approach is higher than the existing approach.

Figure 4. Sample images or video frames from datasets

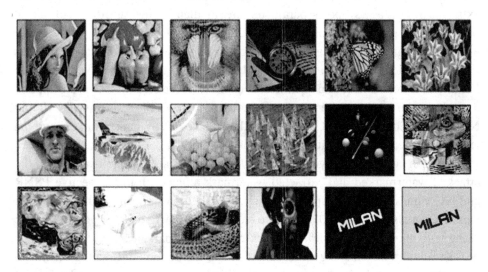

Figure 5. Watermarking images: (a) cover images, (b) watermark images, (c) watermarked images, (d) extracted watermarks, (e) SSIM for cover images/ watermarked images, (f) SSIM for extracted watermark

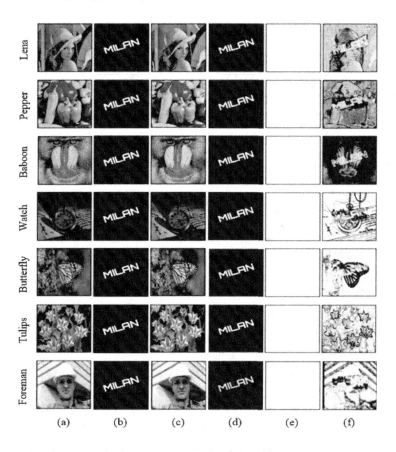

(a) (b) (c) (d) (e) (f)

Our approach is combined with the digital signature, we have calculated the average PSNR values for each dataset which has the mixed result as compared to the previous approach. Our proposed scheme outperforms the existing approach. We have applied digital signatures to achieve much security, privacy, and authenticity which may lead to little compromise based on PSNR values for a few datasets depending on the nature of videos and images.

Overall, we have witnessed that the proposed approach has performed better for video watermarking, if it is combined with digital signature which ensures more privacy, security, and authenticity as compared to the existing approaches.

Table 1. Results with watermarked images and extracted watermarks

Image	Parameters	MSE	PSNR	SSIM	Mean	Variance	Entropy
Lena	WM Image	2.65	54.71	0.99	131.56	3.86E+03	7.81
	Extracted WM	3.39	53.64	0.67	14.37	2.86E+03	2.84
Pepper	WM Image	1.74	56.54	0.99	114.08	4.84E+03	7.72
	Extracted WM	4.26	52.65	0.53	15.12	2.81E+03	3.23
Baboon	WM Image	2.43	55.09	0.99	129.77	3.55E+03	7.82
	Extracted WM	3.85	53.09	0.22	18.29	2.83E+03	3.79
Watch	WM Image	1.95	60.81	0.99	75.36	2.08E+03	7.30
	Extracted WM	3.83	57.89	0.78	13.90	2.85E+03	2.36
Butterfly	WM Image	1.76	58.25	0.99	107.17	3.20E+03	7.64
	Extracted WM	2.70	56.39	0.80	14.05	2.91E+03	2.42
Tulips	WM Image	1.36	59.37	0.99	104.83	5.48E+03	7.79
	Extracted WM	2.35	56.99	0.72	14.30	2.91E+03	2.70
Foreman	WM Image	2.20	49.49	0.99	158.72	3.99E+03	7.56
	Extracted WM	10.82	39.09	0.75	12.95	2.95E+03	2.79

Figure 6. PSNR and NC results for salt and pepper, Gaussian, and speckle attack

Attack	Salt & Pepper (var = 0.05)	Salt & Pepper (var = 0.01)	Gaussian (var =0.05)	Gaussian (var =0.01)	Speckle (var =0.05)	Speckle (var =0.01)
Attacked Frame	(PSNR = 50.90)	(PSNR = 52.23)	(PSNR = 52.11)	(PSNR = 53.217)	(PSNR= 48.15)	(PSNR = 51.14)
Extracted Watermark	(PSNR = 48.90) (NC = 0.73)	(PSNR = 49.44) (NC = 0.85)	(PSNR = 48.92) (NC = 0.66)	(PSNR = 52.68) (NC = 0.7)	(PSNR = 48.70) (NC = 0.85)	(PSNR = 50.44) (NC = 0.91)

CONCLUSION

In this book chapter, we have investigated and applied a little different way of watermarking process for videos by using SVD and DWT methods. As we know, most of the previously existing approaches and ways of the watermarking process are based on images only and not using digital signatures as a watermark, we have shown how the digital signatures are employed as a watermark along with the 3-level wavelet and SVD techniques. In particular, the use of Hash algorithm and digital signature as a watermark resolved the issue of achieving a high level of security, privacy, and authenticity.

For watermarking, we embed an image watermark to implement video watermarking. After tampered with various attacks, the performance of this new enhanced algorithm is evaluated through MSE, PSNR, Entropy, SSIM, etc. The proposed approaches are verified with different datasets and several attacks are implemented based on the watermarked videos/images.

Figure 7. PSNR and NC results for rotation, resizing, and cropping attack

Attacks	Rotate (10 degrees)	Rotate (5 degrees)	Rotate (2 degrees)	Resize (512 to 256 to 512)	Cropping
Attacked Frame	 (PSNR = 49.34)	 (PSNR = 52.23)	 (PSNR = 53.45)	 (PSNR = 48.34)	 (PSNR = 45.33)
Extracted Watermark	 (PSNR = 48.11) (NC = 0.68)	 (PSNR = 48.50) (NC = 0.71)	 (PSNR = 48.72) (NC = 0.76)	 (PSNR = 51.83) (NC = 0.88)	(PSNR = 15.58) (NC = 0.43)

Table 2. Comparisons with PSNR (watermarked images/videos)

Classes	SVD (2-DWT)	Our Approaches	Our Approach With Digital Signatures
Beach	52.1	54.15	52.83
Foreman	37.12	39.06	38.19
Multiple Scene Type	53.12	55.12	53.26
Different Times of Day	45.54	48.23	43.89
Plants and Butterfly	56.54	58.45	57.16
General Traffic	48.15	51.64	46.37
Average	48.76	51.10	48.61

The algorithmic solution of this book chapter is based on a cascading of two efficient mathematical transforms: SVD in spectrum domain and DWT in frequency domain (Ding et al., 2000, 2001, 2002; Yan & Qi, 2001; Ian et al., 2008, Thompson et al., 2008). The two transforms show a high degree of complementary, thus different levels of robustness are achieved by using combinations against the attacks. The use of Hash algorithm and digital signatures as a watermark took it further to attain the security and authenticity of the watermark (Bansal et al., 2003; Gupta, 2021; Liu & Yan, 2014; Weir & Yan, 2011, Yan, 2019).

The approaches implemented in this book chapter can be extended further to achieve more robustness, speed, and to cover different types of images and videos in future. The use of binary images like QR codes doesn't go well with the provided approach. The binary images do not use the concept of RGB so the given approach can be taken as a base and modified or improvised further to incorporate watermarking for binary images as well.

The evaluation or benchmarking of the watermarking process was conducted based on various parameters like PSNR, MSE, SSIM, Variance, Entropy, etc. in the given solution. The same can be extended to cover the evaluation on distributions which can give more accurate/close results and provide coverage over a wide range of parameters.

REFERENCES

Anjali, S., & Parul, B. (2018). Different video watermarking techniques - A review. *International Journal of Scientific Research in Computer Science, Engineering and Information Technology*, *3*(1), 1890–1894.

Antony, R., & Uma, M. (2014). Using digital signature. *International Journal of Computer Network and Security*, *6*(1), 16–21.

Atrey, P., Yan, W., Chang, E., & Kankanhalli, M. (2004) A hierarchical signature scheme for robust video authentication using secret sharing. *International Multimedia Modelling Conference*, 330-337. 10.1109/MULMM.2004.1265004

Atrey, P., Yan, W., & Kankanhalli, M. (2007). A scalable signature scheme for video authentication. *Multimedia Tools and Applications*, *34*(1), 107–135. doi:10.100711042-006-0074-7

Bansal, M., Yan, W., & Kankanhalli, M. (2003). Article. *Proceedings of IEEE Pacific Rim Conference on Multimedia,* 2, 965-969.

Deepak, C., & Prachi, S. (2018). Digital video watermarking scheme using wavelets with MATLAB. *International Journal of Computers and Applications*, *180*(14), 30–34. doi:10.5120/ijca2018916272

Ding, W., & Yan, W. (2000). Digital image scrambling and digital watermarking technology based on Conway's game. *Journal of North China University of Technology*, *12*(1), 1–5.

Ding, W., Yan, W., & Qi, D. (2001a). Digital image watermarking based on U-system. *Journal of Image and Graphics*, *6*(6), 552–557.

Ding, W., Yan, W., & Qi, D. (2001b). Cox's and Pitas's schemes for digital image watermarking. *Journal of Northern China University of Technology*, *12*(3), 1–12.

Ding, W., Yan, W., & Qi, D. (2002). Digital image watermarking based on discrete wavelet transform. *Journal of Computer Science and Technology*, *17*(2), 129–139. doi:10.1007/BF02962205

Fu, W., Yan, W., & Kankanhalli, M. (2005) Progressive scrambling for MP3 audio. *IEEE International Symposium on Circuits and Systems (ISCAS)*, 5525-5528.

Gupta, M. (2021). *Improving Security for Video Watermarking* [Master's Thesis]. Auckland University of Technology, New Zealand.

Gutub, A., & Al-Shaarani, F. (2020). Efficient implementation of multi-image secret hiding based on LSB and DWT steganography comparisons. *Arabian Journal for Science and Engineering*, *45*(4), 2631–2644. doi:10.100713369-020-04413-w

Gutub, A. (2022a). Boosting image watermarking authenticity spreading secrecy from counting-based secret-sharing. *CAAI Transactions on Intelligence Technology*, cit2.12093. doi:10.1049/cit2.12093

Gutub, A. (2022b). Watermarking images via counting-based secret sharing for lightweight semi-complete authentication. *International Journal of Information Security and Privacy*, *16*(1), 1–18. doi:10.4018/IJISP.2022010118

Gutub, A. (2022c). Adopting counting-based secret-sharing for e-Video watermarking allowing fractional invalidation. *Multimedia Tools and Applications*, *81*(7), 9527–9547. doi:10.100711042-022-12062-4

Harahap, M., & Khairina, N. (2020). Dynamic steganography least significant bit with stretch on pixels neighborhood. *Journal of Information Systems Engineering and Business Intelligence*, *6*(2), 151. doi:10.20473/jisebi.6.2.151-158

Hassan, S., & Gutub, A. (2021). Efficient image reversible data hiding technique based on interpolation optimization Fatuma. *Journal for Science and Engineering, 46*, 8441–8456.

Hassan, F., & Gutub, A. (2022). Improving data hiding within colour images using hue component of HSV colour space. *CAAI Transactions on Intelligence Technology, 7*(1), 56–68. doi:10.1049/cit2.12053

Hsieh, S., Chen, C., & Shen, W. (2014). Combining digital watermarking and fingerprinting techniques to identify copyrights for color images. *The Scientific World Journal, 2014*, 1–14. doi:10.1155/2014/454867 PMID:25114966

Ian, T., Bouridane, A., Kurugollu, F., & Yan, W. (2008) Video watermarking using complex wavelets. In Multimedia Communication Security: Recent Advances (pp. 197-216). NOVA Publisher.

Imen, N. (2018). *A novel blind and robust video watermarking technique in fast motion frames based on SVD and MR-SVD*. Hindawi Security and Communication Networks.

Kheshaifaty, N., & Gutub, A. (2021). *Engineering graphical captcha and AES crypto Hash functions for secure online authentication. Journal of Engineering Research*.

Langelaar, G. C., Setyawan, I., & Lagendijk, R. (2000). Watermarking digital image and video data. *IEEE Signal Processing Magazine, 17*(5), 20–46. doi:10.1109/79.879337

Li'skiewicz, M., Reischuk, R., & Wölfel, U. (2017). Security levels in steganography insecurity does not imply detectability. *Theoretical Computer Science*, 1–15.

Liu, F., & Yan, W. (2014). *Visual cryptography for image processing and security: Theory, methods, and applications*. Springer. doi:10.1007/978-3-319-09644-5

Mohd, W., Nasir, A., Muhammad, H., & Sahib, K. (2018) On combining MD5 for image authentication using LSB substitution in selected pixels. In *Proceedings of International Conference on Engineering and Emerging Technologies* (pp. 1-6). Academic Press.

Muthumanickam, S., & Arun, C. (2018). Performance analysis of 2 levels DWT-SVD based non-blind and blind video watermarking using range conversion method. *Microsystem Technologies*, 1–9.

Natarajan, M., & Govindarajan, Y. (2015). A study of DWT-SVD based multiple watermarking scheme for medical images. *International Journal of Network Security, 17*(5), 558–568.

Nurul, K., Muhammad, K., & Juanda, H. (2018). The authenticity of image using Hash MD5 and steganography least significant bit. *International Journal of Information System & Technology*, *2*(1), 1–6.

Pallavi, M. (2018). Digital watermarking system for video authentication. *International Journal of Advanced Research in Computer and Communication Engineering*, 1–4.

Po-Chyi, S., Chin-Song, W., Fan, C., Ching-Yu, W., & Ying-Chang, W. (2017). A practical design of digital watermarking for video streaming services. *Journal of Visual Communication and Image Representation*, *42*, 161–172. doi:10.1016/j.jvcir.2016.11.018

Pradhan, A., Sekhar, K., & Swain, G. (2018). Digital image steganography using LSB substitution, PVD, and EMD. *Mathematical Problems in Engineering*, *2018*, 1–12. doi:10.1155/2018/1804953

Sahib, K., Muneeza, W., Tawab, K., Nasir, A., & Muhammad, H. Z. (2018) Column level image authentication technique using hidden digital signatures. In *Proceedings of International Conference on Automation and Computing* (pp. 1-6). Academic Press.

Sahu, A., & Gutub, A. (2022). Improving grayscale steganography to protect personal information disclosure within hotel services. *Multimedia Tools and Applications*, *81*(21), 30663–30683. doi:10.100711042-022-13015-7

Saqer, W., & Barhoom, T. (2016). Steganography and hiding data with indicators-based LSB using a secret key. Engineering, Technology &. *Applied Scientific Research*, *6*(3), 1013–1017.

Tasheva, A., Tasheva, Z., & Nakov, P. (2017) Image-based steganography using modified LSB insertion method with contrast stretching. *Proceedings of International Conference on Computer Systems and Technologies*.

Thompson, I., Bouridane, A., Kurugollu, F., & Yan, W. (2008). *Video watermarking using complex wavelets*. Nova Science Publishers.

Wahid, M., Ahmad, N., Zafar, M. H., & Khan, S. (2018) On combining MD5 for image authentication using LSB substitution in selected pixels. In *Proceedings of International Conference on Engineering and Emerging Technologies* (pp. 1-6). 10.1109/ICEET1.2018.8338621

Weir, J., & Yan, W. (2011). A comprehensive study of visual cryptography. *Springer Transactions on DHMS, 6010*, 70–105.

Yan, W. (2019). *Introduction to Intelligent Surveillance: Surveillance Data Capture, Transmission, and Analytics*. Springer London. doi:10.1007/978-3-030-10713-0

Yan, W., & Qi, D. (2001). Mapping-based watermarking of 2D engineering drawings. *International Conference on CAD/Graphics*, 464 – 469.

Yan, W., & Weir, J. (2010). *Fundamentals of Media Security*. Bookboon.

Chapter 3

Visual Watermark Identification From the Transparent Window of Currency by Using Deep Learning

Duo Tong
Auckland University of Technology, New Zealand

Wei Qi Yan
Auckland University of Technology, New Zealand

ABSTRACT

Banknote identification plays an increasingly important role in financial fields due to the diffusion of automatic bank systems in terms of vending machines. Nowadays, YOLOv5 has become the state-of-the-art detector of visual objects because of its relatively outperformed accuracy with a high speed of computing. In this chapter, the squeeze-excitation (SE) attention module is mingled with the terminal of the backbone in YOLOv5 to further improve visual watermark recognition of paper banknotes. The main contribution of this chapter is that the excellent precision reaches 99.99% by utilizing the novel model YOLOv5+SE.

DOI: 10.4018/978-1-6684-4945-5.ch003

INTRODUCTION

Despite the escalating commence of electronic currency, nowadays, banknotes remain galore owing to the indispensability in circulation, which means currency issuers have still confronted the menace of forging. With the prevalence of automated systems such as vending machines, currency recognition has become increasingly significant in a number of financial sectors such as currency exchange centers, shopping malls, banking systems and ticket counters (Mittal, 2018). Meanwhile, fraud techniques have been increasingly, resulting in the light of recognizing fake currency (Zhang & Yan, 2018; Yan, 2021). Besides, numerous nations suffer from the forged currency on a large scale due to its ease of printing (Trinh et al., 2020). Hence the identification of counterfeit currency has become one of the most redhot topics.

As a genre of image classifications in the computer vision, currency recognition is defined as the process of identifying the denomination and the authenticity of currency (Singh et al., 2010). In order to effectively determine its credibility, it is necessary for banknotes to be inspected for several specialized security features involving serial number, puzzle number, the color-changing bird, raised ink and transparent window. There are a vast variety of methods to detect currency that majorly consists of digital image processing, machine learning, and deep learning algorithms.

In recent years, deep learning has boomed in image classification and detection areas. As a kind of machine learning methods, they take use of a neural network framework consisting of multiple layers that are mainly constructed to perform classification tasks directly from sounds, images, and textures. Deep learning approaches exceed conventional machine learning algorithms in precision and accuracy, though they require much data and training time. Another contributing factor of deep learning for being a popular technology in computation is that the complexity is increasingly declined with the enhancement of data and the layers of a neural network. There are various deep learning architectures in terms of VGG (Simonyan & Zisserman, 2015; Russakovsky et al., 2015), YOLOv5 (Jocher, 2020), Faster R-CNN (Ren, et al., 2015), AlexNet (Krizhevsky et al., 2017) and GoogleNet (Szegedy et al., 2015), which are utilized to find patterns from training data.

A state-of-the-art algorithm is selected to perform this task in this chapter. YOLOv5 is an appropriate model because of its excellent performance on object detection, acceptable precision, the first implementation on currency recognition with an attention mechanism.

Therefore, the focus of this research project is on visual watermark recognition of paper currencies through implementing deep learning algorithms involving YOLOv5 and its variants (YOLO-SE), which comprises of the SE attention block. Remarkably, the experiments have the huge size of the dataset to improve the precision and generalization ability. Hence, data augmentation consisting of cropping, flipping, rotation, colour modification, and noise addition was implemented.

This book chapter aims to achieve currency identification based on the transparent window whose phases are separated into data collection, data augmentation, denomination recognition and the analysis of the outcomes. The contributions in this research are majorly summarized into three-folds: The construction of comprehensive samples, the proposal of YOLOv5-SE, and the result analysis.

First of all, regarding the requirement of dataset in deep learning, the samples in this experiment involve the front and back sides, the changes of location, size, and others. As a result, we create a relatively full-scale dataset, which is beneficial for the experiments.

Also, YOLOv5-SE, the amalgamation of YOLOv5 and Squeeze-and-Excitation (SE) attention mechanism, is proposed to identify currency watermarks. Moreover, we compare YOLOv5 and YOLOv5-SE, analyse the likely reasons according to the experimental outcomes and the analysis from existing research work, which effectively evaluate the advantages and disadvantages. Last but not least, we conduct complementary experiments to attest the relationship between the depth of networks and noises and performance in this case.

In this chapter, following related work, methodology will be iterated. The result analysis will be explicated which leads to the final conclusion of this book chapter.

Figure 1. The security features of currency. The highlighted window is the target for object detection.

RELATED WORK

The process of currency identification includes banknote recognition and verification (Frosini et al., 1996). Throughout the pertinent historical work, there are various successful methods to identify currency. In 2014, MATLAB platform was applied to recognize the credibility of currencies by utilizing red, green and blue components for segment as well as the standard deviation for evaluation (Alekhya et al., 2014).

The recognition of currency also took use of MATLAB based on PCA (principal component analysis) and LBP (local binary patterns) for the objectives of training and matching, respectively (Gautam, 2020). The images taken by the digital camera under ultraviolet light were converted into grayscale ones. Based on image processing achieved by MATLAB, the division of multiple parts by cropping, the intensity of each feature was calculated to confirm the incredibility of currency. The system acquires a high accuracy of 100% when testing the images from the dataset. Nevertheless, it fails to identify the hidden features involving latent images and watermarks. The given six features are not precisely extracted because of the variance of the size for each currency note, either.

Another method was presented to detect currency based on the features extracted from frequency domain, which applied the spatial characteristics in banknote images to accomplish the task (Shah et al., 2015). The classifying process involves four phases in terms of the preprocessing for the optimal, the implementation of a two-dimensional discrete wavelet transforms, the extraction of coefficient statistical moments from the approximate efficient matrix and the utilization of serial number extraction through the deployment of OCR to detect fake currency.

Both image processing and machine learning are considered effective solutions for currency detection (Upadhyaya et al., 2018). *k*-means algorithm was employed to cluster similar characteristics and an SVM classifier was taken into account to train the classifier for currency recognition (Kamal et al., 2015). In 2019, HMM was employed as a robust currency detection algorithm (Kamble et al., 2019). The proposed method is utilized to differentiate paper currency from various nations via modelling the texture features as a random process. To assess the performance of the algorithm, beyond 100 denominations from distinct countries were involved in the experiment, whose outcomes indicated 98% precision for currency detection.

Deep learning-based models have been also applied to currency identification. The features of currency are extracted by utilizing convolutional neural network (CNN) under the framework of single shot multi-box detector (SSD) (Zhang & Yan, 2018; Yan, 2021). Currency recognition with transfer learning having an extensive CNN pre-trained on enormous natural images was implemented to classify images from new classes (Mittal, 2018). CNN was applied to identify folded currency which involves angles, folding, damages and standard images (Jiao et al., 2018). Deep

CNN was implemented as a feature extractor in currency identification without digital image processing which affirms the existence of security notes (Bharati & Pramanik, 2020).

Resulting from the necessity of being trained separately in every single component, object detection approaches such as R-CNN are complicated, slow, and difficult to be optimized (Redmon et al., 2016). These restrictions motivate the emergence of YOLO algorithms, which was influenced by GoogLeNet model for excellent performance. Different from other models, such as two-stage algorithms that segment an image into the parts or segments, YOLO, as the name described, scans an image once to predict objects (Onyango, 2018). It treats object detection as a regression issue ranging from image pixels to the coordinates of bounding boxes as well as the probabilities of classes (Redmon et al., 2016). YOLO aims to detect objects by precisely predicting the bounding box, including the instance, and localizing it according to the bounding boxes. Currently, YOLO family has the updated versions from one to five.

YOLO structure has become one of the most popular models in visual object detection owing to its superiority to other traditional algorithms. First and foremost, since only neural networks are required to be run based on input images to predict objects at test time in lieu of a complicated pipeline, which performs extremely fast, the mean average precision (mAP) is over two times higher than other models (Redmon & Farhadi, 2017). Secondly, while predicting objects, YOLO infers globally from the images, which means, the whole image is taken into consideration in the period of training and testing. The final advantage of YOLO is the high generalization, which is applied to a new field or unexpected inputs.

Attention mechanism, which mimics human cognition, not only highlights the position that we need to focus on but also presents interests as well (Woo et al., 2018). In accordance with attention, the modules are generally classified into vanilla attention and self-attention. Since all useful information from the input sequence must be compressed into a fixed-length vector, a standard encoder-decoder suffers from long sentence processing. Correspondingly, this shortcoming motivates the generation of vanilla attention that syndicates the standard encoder-decoder and the capability of learning joint alignment as well as translation (Bahdanau et al., 2014).

Self-attention refers to the particular attention mechanism that is related to various positions in a single sequence for the representation, which comprises Source2Token and Token2Token (Vaswani et al., 2017). Source2Token self-attention was applied to show the significance of each token to a gamut of sequences in the representation (Lin et al., 2018). The language translation models fulfil the-state-of-art performance through implementing token2token self-attention (Vaswani et al., 2017).

Inspired by the achievement of self-attention in the NLP area, it has been one of the most predominant methods in computer vision. This kind of attention-based algorithms are mainly grouped into the altered transformers, the integration of convolutional neural networks, and a pure attention network.

Firstly, there are numerous research projects associated with the transformer applied to image classification. An image transformer, which incorporates self-attention into an autoregressive model, was proposed for image generation (Parmar et al., 2018). By diminishing a number of hand-designed elements, a detection transformer was introduced for end-to-end object detection (Carion et al., 2020). The vision transformer, which treats each image as a sequence of patches, implements the basic encoder with a supplementary learnable classification vector for image recognition (Dosovitskiy et al., 2020). It, nevertheless, has an impediment to pixel-level dense detection, which contributes to the production of the pyramid vision transformer (PVT) (Wang, et al., 2021). The dense prediction transformer was proposed to compensate for the drawback of omitting feature resolution as well as granularity in deeper layers for convolutional networks (Ranftl et al., 2021).

Secondly, it is prevalent for attention modules that incorporate into convolutional networks. Squeeze-and-excitation (SE) demonstrates a vast of potentials in advancing performance by reducing dimensionality (Hu et al., 2018). SE, however, considerably hoists the computational complication, which arises from the capture of dependencies across all channels. Efficient channel attention (ECA) is a complementary approach to solve the problem (Wang, et al., 2020). ECA effectively shows the decline of channel dimensionality while obtaining cross-channel interaction via an extraordinary lightweight way. Both SE and ECA are channel-wise attention block unmatched with the demand of computer vision as the images are considered as the inputs with spatial architecture. Along with bottleneck attention module (Park, et al., 2018), convolutional block attention module (Woo et al., 2018) refines convolutional features through adopting channel and spatial attention.

Although the combination of self-attention and convolutional networks has been widely employed, it is not inextricably bonded with convolutional neural networks in the success of computer vision. Pairwise attention network (PSA), which is a variant of self-attention, is an independent block for image identification (Zhao et al., 2020).

Compared to recurrent neural networks (RNN) and convolutional neural networks (CNN), self-attention is much flexible because it has been modeled either long-range or local dependencies (Shen et al., 2018). Another obvious superiority of self-attention is the ease of being facilitated due to its highly parallelizable computation (Vaswani et al., 2017). Self-attention also has a number of limitations because of the complexity of memory and quadratic computation. In computer vision, the input with considerable spatial dimensions further engenders the tremendous cost of global self-attention implementation.

METHODOLOGY

We choose to manually produce a video through using the camera of the iPhone7s with the resolution of 1080 pixels at 30fps and then split it into digital images by using each frame regarding the requirement of data volume in deep learning. The instances involve $10NZD, $50NZD and $100NZD. Each monetary denomination has front (F) and back (B) sides, hence we have the string labels of six classes (including "10F", "10B", "50F", "50B", "100F" and "100B") in this dataset. To enhance the experimental precision, the opted images must be consistent with the following criteria:

- The images should be in high resolution.
- The currencies must be flat; the transparent window must be completely displayed in each image.
- The object should be displayed in the center of the image and have sufficient space to ensure a complete appearance when cropping and resizing.
- The currencies should be rotated in different angles and distances between the camera and the object when shooting a video.

Data labeling refers to the action of marking visual object on the given images with a bounding box whose four coordinates are stored in the corresponding "XML" file (Lee et al., 2019). The marked images demonstrate the recognizable patterns and tell machines which object will be detected. It plays an imperative role in deep learning as computers have no target to recognize without image annotation. In this chapter, the annotation tool called LabelImg labels the objects within a rectangle. An example is shown in Figure 2.

Figure 2. The example of data labelling

The construction of efficient and robust deep learning networks covets massive high-quality data, particularly in the situation of sharing features amongst the involved classes (Rey-Area et al., 2020). Due to the heavy reliance on big data, deep learning algorithms are able to effectively eschew overfitting, which is defined as the phenomenon if the model perfectly utilizes the training data while it fails to fit supplementary data (Shorten & Khoshgoftaar, 2019).

Data augmentation is a feasible approach to remedy the scarcity of data and class imbalance. Data augmentation aims to bolster the variability of the original data so that the deep learning models acquire higher robustness to the input images collected from various environments (Bochkovskiy et al., 2020). Data augmentation enriched the volume and quality of datasets by encompassing a set of image transformation techniques including geometric and photometric augmentation (Iwana & Uchida, 2021). The former refers to Affine transformations such as rotation, flipping, cropping, scaling, and zooming, while the latter means color modification such as color jittering and manipulation, edge improvement, and PCA. These two types are effective ways to avoid overfitting in deep learning. The samples of image augmentation of this project are shown in Figure 3.

In this chapter, we espouse the conventional augmentations to complete the task of data preparation. The augmentation scheme we applied including flipping, rotating, cropping, color tweak and noise injection. Differentiated from the previous algorithms such as Faster R-CNN, YOLOv5 is a single-stage detector. The frame of YOLOv5 composes of three major components: Backbone, neck, and output, which is described in Figure 4.

Figure 3. The samples of image augmentation

Figure 4. The architecture of YOLOv5

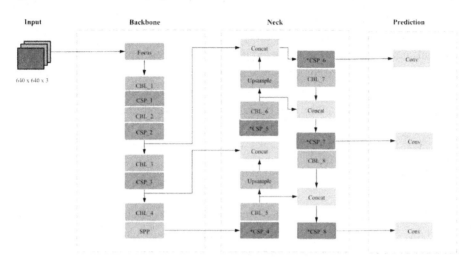

The input image with the resolution of 640×640×3 passes through the focus module in the backbone. It firstly takes use of slicing operations to become the feature map with resolution 320×320×12. Under 32 convolution kernels, it varies to a 320×320×32 one. Next, incorporating CSP networks into DarkNet functions as the main part of the backbone, which is utilized to extract informative features from inputs. It effectively and significantly reduces the duplication of gradient information in the optimization of convolutional neural networks, especially for large-scale backbones. Besides, it combines gradient variance and feature map to decrease the parameters and floating-point operations per second, guaranteeing inference speed and precision, whereas shrinking the model size.

As for the neck, PANet, which is constructed with a bottom-up path based on FPN structure, is responsible for acquiring feature pyramids. From top to bottom, the FPN layer transmits solid semantic features. In the converse direction, the feature pyramid transfers positional features. This design enhances the transmission of low-level features and promotes the accuracy of locations for objects.

The head of YOLOv5, which is as same as the fourth generation, engenders feature maps with three different sizes (18×18, 36×36, 72×72) to predict targets in multiscale including small, medium, and oversized objects.

We modify YOLOv5 model by adding a SE block after the *CSP_4 module. As a computational unit, the process of SE is mainly grouped into squeeze and excitation through the operation of global average pooling and fully connected layers, respectively. Next, it takes use of the self-gating mechanism (sigmoid) to limit the output of FC to interval [0, 1], and finally multiplies this value as the scale to the channels so as to be the input data of the next stage. The principle of this structure is to enhance the important features and cripple the unimportant ones by controlling the size of the scale so as to significantly highlight the extracted features.

Global spatial statistics are squeezed into a channel descriptor by utilizing global average pooling to produce channel-wise information. The information z is produced by spatial dimensions $H \times W$. U indicates the collection of statistics expressive for the full image ($H \times W \times C$). The c-th element of z is computed by eq. (1).

$$z_c = \frac{1}{H \times W} \sum_{i=1}^{H} \sum_{j=1}^{W} u_c(i, j) \tag{1}$$

Two fully connected layers achieve the squeezing process that aims to aggregate the valuable information, followed by the excitation to catch all channel-wise dependencies. The first layer, followed by ReLU, compresses C channels into C/r, r means the percentage of compression) channels to reduce the spate of computation. According to the research conducted (Hu et al., 2018), the SE module achieves a superior tradeoff among precision and complication if r equals 16. Hence, we utilize this value for the experiment. The second full connection is used to restore to C channels, which follows the sigmoid function.

In order to measure loss, YOLO takes use of the sum-squared error between predictions with the highest IoU and ground truth. Its loss function consists of the localization, the confidence (also known as the objectness of boxes) and the classification loss. YOLOv5 adopts GIoU to be the localization loss rather than Intersection over Union (IoU), where IoU is defined as eq. (2).

$$IoU = \frac{|A \cap B|}{|A \cup B|} \tag{2}$$

where A and B are two arbitrary convex shapes, IoU refers to the similarity among A and B, which allows the coordinates to be related to each other and has scale invariance, which overcomes the weakness of smooth L1 loss (Rezatofighi, et al., 2019). However, IoU suffers from the optimization problem if A and B have no intersection.

Alternatively, GIoU is an effective key to address the above issues, which inherits the advantages of IoU in terms of the invariance of scale and all properties of loss metrics (Rezatofighi, et al., 2019). In contrast to IoU, it focuses on overlapping areas and non-overlapping regions, which better reflects the intersection among A and B. The definition of $GIoU$ is shown as eq. (3).

$$GIoU = IoU - \frac{\left| C\left(A \cap B \right) \right|}{\left| C \right|} \tag{3}$$

where C indicates the minimum encompassing convex object. Thus, $GIoU$ is an appropriate replacement for IoU in computer vision tasks, even though it has some explicit restrictions.

In this project, the model evaluation metrics involve three indicators: Precision (P), recall (R) and average precision (mAP). In visual object detection, both precision and recall are the two fundamental assessment criteria. Precision refers to the percentage of accurately recognized objects amongst all detected samples, whilst recall is defined as the proportion of precisely identified objects among all positive instances detected, eq. (4) and eq. (5) are the equations for these two indices, mAP is a comprehensive indicator that takes precision and recall rate into consideration, which is calculated by using the average precision (AP) over the number of classes (M), mAP indicates the performance throughout all classes while AP demonstrates the performance on a given class i. The calculation of mAP is shown as eq. (6).

$$P = \frac{TP}{FP + TP} \tag{4}$$

$$R = \frac{TP}{FN + TP} \tag{5}$$

$$mAP = \frac{1}{M} \sum_{i=1}^{M} AP_i \tag{6}$$

where AP is defined as the region under the precision and recall curve, which is shown as eq. (7).

$$AP = \int_{0}^{1} P\left(R \right) dR \tag{7}$$

RESULT ANALYSIS

Corresponding to the research objectives of this book chapter, three experiments were conducted. To complete the task of currency detection, the secondary work we need to cogitate is the stages of research from data generation, training data and resultant analysis. The experimental implementation can considerably benefit from the basic idea about the specific process of currency identification.

In Figure 5, the first stage is the preparation of data, which is separated into four parts, including shooting a video, the split of images by frames, label marking, and augmentation. The first two actions are applied to acquire original images for the experiment. The next process is for the computers to recognize the inputs, while the final one is to address the scantiness of data and buttress the generalization capability. After that, the outcomes of data augmentation are utilized as the input of the designed model to complete the transparent window recognition of currency, which includes training, feature extraction, dense detection, and the acquisition of the results. Specifically, the features of input images are compressed down through the backbone to complete feature extraction and forwarded to detection neck and head to accomplish feature aggregation and detection, respectively. In particular, we merge localization and classification into one step since YOLOv5 is a one-stage detector in which these two operations for every bounding box are implemented simultaneously.

Figure 5. The phases of the proposed experiments

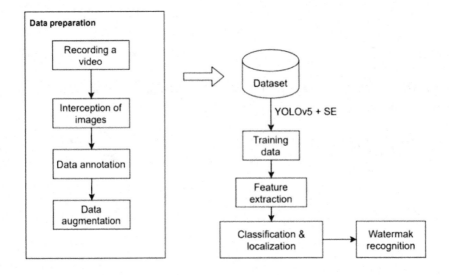

The outcomes of watermark identification are shown in Figure 6. The six classes are represented by bounding boxes with different colors. Specifically, the blue, light green, purple, pink, yellow and green ones show the classes with textual labels "10F", "10B", "50F", "50B", "100F", and "100B". For instance, the string "10F" means the front side of transparent windows for $10NZD. Instead, "10B" depicts the backside of the corresponding currencies. The confidence values are ranging from 0.88 to 0.92.

Figure 6. The results of currency watermark detection

(a) 10NZD_Front	(c) 50NZD_Front	(e) 100NZD_Front
(b) 10NZD_Back	(d) 50NZD_Back	(f) 100NZD_Back

As we all know, the only variance among different versions of YOLOv5 is the depth of networks. Therefore, we implemented the experiments, the comparison is shown in Table 1, pertaining to YOLOv5s, YOLOv5m, YOLOv5l and the updated versions that amalgamate the SE module. Table 1 indicates that YOLOv5l-SE obtains the outperforming outcomes on GIoU loss, accuracy, and mAP with the toll of training time. In other words, with the addition of SE block, each model costs longer time on training while other evaluating results such as GIoU and accuracy become superior.

For the state-of-the-art architectures, the SE module generates crucial performance promotion with the minimal expenditure on computation, which is consistent with our experimental results that more satisfying accuracy and loss value are acquired with the sacrifice of the executing speed (Hu et al., 2018). Throughout utilizing global information, SE attention mechanism explicitly models dynamic and nonlinear dependencies among channels (Hu et al., 2018). Thereby, the new model eases the process of learning and dramatically hikes the representative ability of the network. These are the main reasons for the superiority of the proposed algorithm. However, due to the high accuracy rate of the basic model, the attention-based algorithm has little space to improve the performance, hence the betterment of each evaluation criteria is not apparent.

As implied in the outcomes of all the modified models, by enhancing depth of networks, the model performs better except for training time. YOLOv5l-SE takes the longest time to train data compared to other models, attributing to that the deeper networks can extract much features so that it can promote the overall performance but will lead to much more computational costs and overhead.

Table 1. The outcomes of multiple models

Models	Training Time(s)	GIoU Loss	Precisions	mAP@0.5
YOLOv5s	439.56	0.02282	0.9972	0.9959
YOLOv5s-SE	461.16	0.02227	0.9980	0.9960
YOLOv5m	666.72	0.02066	0.9989	0.9959
YOLOv5m-SE	673.56	0.02047	0.9990	0.9960
YOLOv5l	1004.4	0.01995	0.9988	0.9958
YOLOv5l-SE	1100.72	0.01950	0.9990	0.9961

CONCLUSION

The main objective of this research project is to detect the watermark of paper currency based on deep learning because we integrate the SE attention module in YOLOv5 as the detector. Fortunately, the proposed model presents satisfactory outcomes.

Throughout the corresponding operations, we conclude that the attention-based model outperforms the unmodified on precision, mAP and GIoU with the exchange of time consumptions. The other finding is that the overall performance will be promoted by enhancing network layers meanwhile training time will be longer.

REFERENCES

Alekhya, D., Prabha, G., & Rao, G. (2014). Fake currency detection using image processing and other standard methods. *International Journal of Research in Computer and Communication Technology, 3*, 128–131.

Bahdanau, D., Cho, K., & Bengio, Y. (2014) Neural machine translation by jointly learning to align and translate. *Proceedings of International Conference on Learning Representations.*

Bharati, P., & Pramanik, A. (2020). Deep learning techniques - R-CNN to Mask R-CNN: A survey. In *Proceedings of Computational Intelligence in Pattern Recognition* (pp. 657–668). Springer. doi:10.1007/978-981-13-9042-5_56

Bochkovskiy, A., Wang, C., & Liao, H. (2020). *YOLOv4: Optimal speed and accuracy of object detection.* CoRR abs/2004.10934.

Carion, N., Massa, F., Synnaeve, G., Usunier, N., Kirillov, A., & Zagoruyko, S. (2020). End-to-end object detection with transformers. In *Proceedings of European Conference on Computer Vision* (pp. 213 - 229). Springer.

Chambers, J., Yan, W., Garhwal, A., & Kankanhalli, M. (2014). Currency security and forensics: A survey. *Multimedia Tools and Applications, 74*(11), 4013–4043. doi:10.100711042-013-1809-x

Dosovitskiy, A., Beyer, L., Kolesnikov, A., Weissenborn, D., Zhai, X., Unterthiner, T., Dehghani, M., Minderer, M., Heigold, G., Gelly, S., Uszkoreit, J., & Houlsby, N. (2020). An image is worth 16×16 words: Transformers for image recognition at scale. *Proceedings of ICLR.*

Frosini, A., Gori, M., & Priami, P. (1996). A neural network-based model for paper currency recognition and verification. In *Proceedings of IEEE Transactions on Neural Networks* (pp. 1482 - 1490). IEEE Press. 10.1109/72.548175

Gautam, K. (2020). Indian currency detection using image recognition technique. In *Proceedings of International Conference on Computer Science, Engineering and Applications* (pp. 1 - 5). 10.1109/ICCSEA49143.2020.9132955

Hu, J., Shen, L., & Sun, G. (2018). Squeeze-and-excitation networks. In *Proceedings of IEEE Conference on Computer Vision and Pattern Recognition* (pp. 7132 - 7141). IEEE.

Iwana, B., & Uchida, S. (2021). An empirical survey of data augmentation for time series classification with neural networks. *PLoS One, 16*(7), e0254841. doi:10.1371/journal.pone.0254841 PMID:34264999

Jiao, M., He, J., & Zhang, B. (2018). Folding paper currency recognition and research based on convolution neural network. In *Proceedings of International Conference on Advances in Computing, Communications and Informatics* (pp. 18 - 23). 10.1109/ICACCI.2018.8554772

Jocher, G. (2020). *YOLOv5, Code repository, 2020.* https://github.com/ultralytics/yolov5

Kamal, S., Chawla, S. S., Goel, N., & Raman, B. (2015). Feature extraction and identification of Indian currency notes. In *Proceedings of National Conference on Computer Vision, Pattern Recognition, Image Processing and Graphics* (pp. 1 - 4), IEEE Press. 10.1109/NCVPRIPG.2015.7490005

Krizhevsky, A., Sutskever, I., & Hinton, G. (2017). ImageNet classification with deep convolutional neural networks. *Communications of the ACM, 60*(6), 84–90. doi:10.1145/3065386

Lee, Y., Im, D., & Shim, J. (2019). Data labeling research for deep learning based fire detection system. In *Proceedings of International Conference on Systems of Collaboration Big Data, Internet of Things & Security* (pp. 1 - 4). 10.1109/SysCoBIoTS48768.2019.9028029

Lin, Z., Feng, M., Santos, C., Yu, M., Xiang, B., Zhou, B., & Bengio, Y. (2017). A structured self-attentive sentence embedding. *Proceedings of ICLR.*

Ma, X., & Yan, W. (2021). Banknote serial number recognition using deep learning. *Multimedia Tools and Applications, 80*(12), 18445–18459. doi:10.100711042-020-10461-z

Mittal, S., & Mittal, S. (2018). Indian banknote recognition using convolutional neural network. In *Proceedings of International Conference on Internet of Things: Smart Innovation and Usages* (pp. 1 - 6). 10.1109/IoT-SIU.2018.8519888

Onyango, L. (2018). *Convolutional neural network to enhance stock taking.* University of Nairobi.

Park, J., Woo, S., Lee, J., & Kweon, I. (2018). BAM: Bottleneck attention module. *Proceedings of BMVC.*

Parmar, N., Vaswani, A., Uszkoreit, J., Ukasz, K., Shazeer, N., & Ku, A. (2018). Image transformer. *Proceedings of International Conference on Machine Learning (ICML).*

Ranftl, R., Bochkovskiy, A., & Koltun, V. (2021). Vision transformers for dense prediction. *Proceedings of ICCV.*

Redmon, J., Divvala, S., Girshick, R., & Farhadi, A. (2016). You Only Look Once: Unified, real-time object detection. In *Proceedings of IEEE Conference on Computer Vision and Pattern Recognition* (pp. 779 - 788). 10.1109/CVPR.2016.91

Redmon, J., & Farhadi, A. (2017). YOLO9000: Better, faster, stronger. In *Proceedings of IEEE Conference on Computer Vision and Pattern Recognition* (pp. 7263 - 7271). IEEE.

Ren, S., He, K., Girshick, R., & Sun, J. (2015). Faster R-CNN: Towards real-time object detection with region proposal networks. arXiv preprint arXiv:1506.01497. doi:10.4018/IJDCF.2018070105

Ren, Y., Nguyen, M., & Yan, W. (2018). Real-time recognition of series seven New Zealand banknotes International. *Journal of Digital Crime and Forensics*, *10*(3), 50–66. doi:10.4018/IJDCF.2018070105

Rey-Area, M., Guirado, E., Tabik, S., & Ruiz-Hidalgo, J. (2020). FuCiTNet: Improving the generalization of deep learning networks by the fusion of learned class-inherent transformations. *Information Fusion*, *63*, 188–195. doi:10.1016/j.inffus.2020.06.015

Russakovsky, O., Deng, J., Su, H., Krause, J., Satheesh, S., Ma, S., Huang, Z., Karpathy, A., Khosla, A., Bernstein, M., Berg, A. C., & Fei-Fei, L. (2015). ImageNet large scale visual recognition challenge. *International Journal of Computer Vision*, *115*(3), 211–252. doi:10.100711263-015-0816-y

Szegedy, C., Liu, W., Jia, Y., Sermanet, P., Reed, S., Anguelov, D., Erhan, D., Vanhoucke, V., & Rabinovich, A. (2015). Going deeper with convolutions. In *Proceedings of IEEE Conference on Computer Vision and Pattern Recognition* (pp. 1 - 9). IEEE.

Shen, T., Zhou, T., Long, G., Jiang, J., & Zhang, C. (2018). Bi-directional block self-attention for fast and memory-efficient sequence modeling. *Proceedings of ICLR*.

Shorten, C., & Khoshgoftaar, T. (2019). A survey on image data augmentation for deep learning. *Big Data*, *6*(1), 60. doi:10.118640537-019-0197-0

Simonyan, K., & Zisserman, A. (2015). Very deep convolutional networks for large-scale image recognition. *Proceedings of International Conference on Learning Representations*.

Singh, S., Tiwari, A., Shukla, S., & Pateriya, S. (2010). Currency recognition system using image processing. *International Journal of Engineering Applied Sciences and Technology*.

Trinh, H., Vo, H., Pham, V., Nath, B., & Hoang, V. (2020). Currency recognition based on deep feature selection and classification. In *Proceedings of Asian Conference on Intelligent Information and Database Systems* (pp. 273 - 281), Springer. 10.1007/978-981-15-3380-8_24

Upadhyaya, A., Shokeen, V., & Srivastava, G. (2018). Analysis of counterfeit currency detection techniques for classification model. In *Proceedings of International Conference on Computing Communication and Automation* (pp. 1 - 6), IEEE Press. 10.1109/CCAA.2018.8777704

Vaswani, A., Shazeer, N., Parmar, N., Uszkoreit, J., Jones, L., Gomez, A. N., Kaiser, L., & Polosukhin, I. (2017). Attention is all you need. Proceedings of Advances in Neural Information Processing Systems.

Wang, G., Wu, W., & Yan, W. (2017). The state-of-the-art technology of currency identification: A comparative study. *International Journal of Digital Crime and Forensics*, 9(3), 58–72. doi:10.4018/IJDCF.2017070106

Wang, Q., Wu, B., Zhu, P., Li, P., Zuo, W., & Hu, Q. (2020). ECA-Net: Efficient channel attention for deep convolutional neural networks. In *Proceedings of IEEE/ CVF Conference on Computer Vision and Pattern Recognition* (pp. 11531 - 11539). 10.1109/CVPR42600.2020.01155

Wang, W., Xie, E., Li, X., Fan, D.-P., Song, K., Liang, D., Lu, T., Luo, P., & Shao, L. (2021). Pyramid vision transformer: A versatile backbone for dense prediction without convolutions. In *Proceedings of ICCV* (pp. 568-578). 10.1109/ ICCV48922.2021.00061

Woo, S., Park, J., Lee, J. Y., & Kweon, I. (2018). CBAM: Convolutional block attention module. In *Proceedings of ECCV* (pp. 3 - 19). Academic Press.

Yan, W., & Chambers, J. (2013). An empirical approach for digital currency forensics. *IEEE International Symposium on Circuits and Systems (ISCAS)*, 2988-2991. 10.1109/ISCAS.2013.6572507

Yan, W., Chambers, J., & Garhwal, A. (2014). An empirical approach for currency identification. *Multimedia Tools and Applications*, 74(7).

Yan, W. (2021). *Computational Methods for Deep Learning - Theoretic, Practice and Applications*. Springer. doi:10.1007/978-3-030-61081-4

Yan, W. (2019). *Introduction to Intelligent Surveillance Surveillance Data Capture, Transmission, and Analytics*. Springer. doi:10.1007/978-3-030-10713-0

Zhang, Q., & Yan, W. (2018). Currency detection and recognition based on deep learning. In *Proceedings of IEEE International Conference on Advanced Video and Signal Based Surveillance* (pp. 1 - 6). 10.1109/AVSS.2018.8639124

Zhang, Q., Yan, W., & Kankanhalli, K. (2019). Overview of currency recognition using deep learning. *Journal of Banking and Financial Technology*, *3*(1), 59–69. doi:10.100742786-018-00007-1

Zhao, H., Jia, J., & Koltun, V. (2020). Exploring self-attention for image recognition. In *Proceedings of IEEE/CVF Conference on Computer Vision and Pattern Recognition* (pp. 10073-10082). IEEE.

Chapter 4

A New Efficient Crypto–Watermarking Method for Medical Images Security Based on Encrypted EPR Embedding in Its DICOM Imaging

Boussif Mohamed

(iD) https://orcid.org/0000-0003-3198-7605
University of Tunis El Manar, Tunisia

Mnassri Aymen
University of Tunis El Manar, Tunisia

ABSTRACT

Digitalization of media has exploded in recent years. It has resulted in the rise of private data hacking, which has been increased by the growth of the data exchange system, i.e., the Internet, as well as the simple access to storage media. New approaches, such as watermarking in (C. Iwendi et al., 2020; D. Datta et al, 2021; Randhir Kumar et al,2021), are being used to combat these hackers. The application of image watermarking technologies to medical images, as proposed in (Nazari, M., et al, 2021; Thanki, R, 2021; Manoj K., 2020), is the focus of this research. In this chapter, we propose a new robust blind crypto-watermarking solution for medical imaging or DICOM file (Digital Imaging and Communications in Medicine) security based on masking (or hide) electronic patient information (patient name, patient ID, patient age...) in its medical imaging, then, erases them from the tag of the DICOM. Before being included into medical imaging, DICOM patient information, or EPR,

DOI: 10.4018/978-1-6684-4945-5.ch004

is encrypted using a modified AES (Advanced Encryption Standard) encryption technique. The image is broken into 8x8 pixel chunks. In each block, we use the 2D-LWT (Lifting wavelet transform), 2D-DCT (discrete cosine transforms), and SVD (singular value decomposition) to insert one bit of the encrypted watermark into the hybrid transform domain. Various attacks, such as noise, filtering, scaling, and compression, are used to test the method. According to the obtained results the watermark (EPR) is imperceptible in the imaging, and the suggested technique has passed the attacks test with success.

INTRODUCTION

The use of telemedicine (Kumar et al., 2017; Lakshmanna et al., 2016) has helped patients distancing in hospitals during the Covid19 (Coronavirus Disease 2019) pandemic and its danger on persons with chronic conditions, as described in (Rajput et al., 2021). Medical data, diagnostics, medical images, and reports are sent between health entities using information and communications technology. The necessity to safe these data has become important as a result of this rapid change. Digital watermarking (Boussif et al., 2017, 2020; Saeid et al., 2022; Gutub, 2022; Hassan et al., 2021; Adnan, 2010), cryptography (Mohamed et al., 2019, 2020; Koppu et al., 2018, 2020; Adnan, 2020; Adnan et al., 2021), and crypto-watermarking (Hureib et al., 2020 ; Noorah et al., 2018) are now widely employed in the network environment to protect intellectual property, and they have become the principal applications for protecting and securing medical images. Ensuring the security of DICOM data must respect the imperceptibility of electronic patient information when hidden in medical imaging. The watermark must be extremely resistant to many forms of attacks. Several approaches for watermarking of medical images have been suggested in the State-Of-The-Art, such as (Mettripun, 2016), where the author developed a robust medical imaging watermarking approach based on DWT (Discrete Wavelet Transform) for patient identification. The context is identical to this chapter. However, he has only employed the DWT transform which making the system vulnerable to some attacks such as geometry transformation. By combining the DCT with the DWT, M. Jamali et al. (2016) presented a robust watermarking approach in Non-ROI (Region of Interest) of the medical images. The insertion was precisely in a specific area of the imaging which resulting a small insertion capacity. B. Kima et al. (2003) was suggested a digital image watermarking scheme that is particularly resistant to geometrical attacks. However, because filtering and compression are widely utilized in DICOM medical imaging, the resistance against these attacks is required. Y. Zolotavkin et al. (2014) suggested a novel QIM (Quantization Index Modulation)-based watermarking approach that is robust to gain attack. However, because medical images are sensitive, imaging quantization is not suitable for DICOM images. To ensure security in Telemedicine, Z. Ali et al. (2018) suggested a unique watermarking scheme based on the Hurst Exponent. C. Manuel et al. (2015) presented a DFT (Discrete Fourier Transform)-based watermarking system for the protecting of medical imaging in hospitals. Rayachoti Eswaraiah et al. (2015) presented a robust image watermarking approach for identifying tampers inside ROI and retrieving the original ROI. Due to a combination of FDCuT (Fast Discrete Curvelet Transform) and DCT, Rohit Thanki et al. (2017) presented a novel watermarking approach. In invariant DWT, Y. Gangadhar et al. (2018) introduced a watermarking strategy for safe medical images. Priya Selvam et al. (2017) suggested a reversible watermarking solution for medical imaging security in telemedicine applications that combines signal processing transformations. A high-capacity watermarking approach for DICOM images has been proposed by Frank Y. Shih et al. (2016).

Proposed watermarking algorithms need improvement by increasing the robustness of the watermark since transmission and storing images in public networks and clouds are exposed to many attacks like noise and compression, respectively, that can remove the watermark. For this issue, in this paper, we propose a novel robust blind crypto-watermarking system for the security of DICOM images in telemedicine. As shown in Figure 1, we encrypt the watermark (DICOM patient information) before inserting it in the imaging. We propose a watermarking algorithm combining the LWT-DCT-SVD transforms to be robust. The AES encrypted data are inserted block by block in the cover image. The objectives can be summarized as follows: 1) Hide the information of patients in the related imaging. 2) Attach imaging with its relative patient. A short version of this chapter that use AES with 128 bits has been presented at an international conference (Boussif, 2021). In this chapter, we use a modified AES to be more suitable with the watermarking process.

There are many approaches in the literature that have propose a watermarking system for DICOM images, which hide patient identities in the imaging, like in our chapter. However, the system will be more efficient if the watermarking is more robust.

The remainder of the paper is laid out as follows. In Section 2, we describe the suggested watermarking scheme along with an explanation of the transforms employed. The findings of the experiments and simulations are then provided in Section 3. In Section 4, we give a comparison analysis in which we compare the suggested technique to existing transform-based methods as well as current State-Of-The-Art. Limitations and future work are discussed in Section 5. In Section 6, we give the conclusion.

Figure 1. The presented crypto-watermarking approach

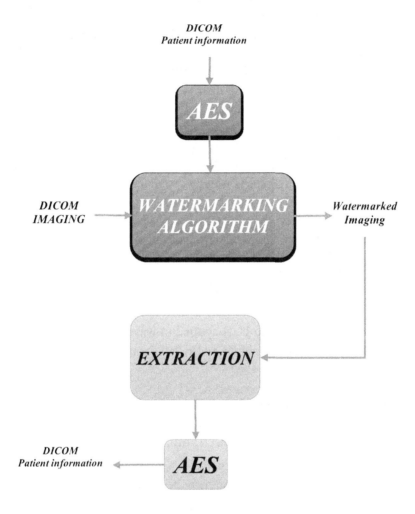

THE PROPOSED WATERMARKING APPROACH

This section delves into the specifics of the proposed DICOM medical imaging security model. As a result, brief descriptions of the signal processing and mathematical transformations employed in the watermarking system, such as the Lifting Wavelet Transform (LWT), Discrete Cosine Transform (DCT), and Singular Value Decomposition (SVD), are offered initially. we merely show the proposed watermarking approach. And since the AES encryption method is conventional and known, we only describe the modification that we applied on it.

The Lifting Wavelet Transform or LWT

A lifting wavelet, as depicted in Figure 2, is a wavelet transformation implementation that differs from that accomplished by filter banks. It is a procedure that is optimized in terms of the number of operations to execute, i.e., time complexity, and memory use, i.e., space complexity. Calculating the LWT, for example, takes half the time it takes to calculate the FFT. As illustrated in Figure 2, the approach is to split the signal to be changed first, then enhance its attributes by alternating the prediction and update processes using three steps: Split step: In this step, the input signal E[n] is split into two subsets, each of which has no common elements and is half the length of E[n]. The original signal is usually separated into two subsets: an odd subset Xo[n]=X[2n+1] and an even subset Xe=X[2n]. Predict step: The predict operator designated P predicts the odd signal Xo[n] based on the even signal Xe [n], and the noise or detail are known as D wavelet coefficients or D[n], which are defined as follows:

$$D[n] = X_o[n] - P(X_e[n]) \tag{1}$$

Update step: This step, dubbed U, is applied to wavelet coefficients D[n], and the outcome is the sum of the odd signal Xe [n] and the updated D[n] signal, which is referred to as scale coefficients C[n]:

$$C[n] = X_e[n] + U(D[n]) \tag{2}$$

Figure 4 shows a deconstruction of the 2D lifting wavelet transform of the Lena picture.

Figure 2. Principle of the LWT transform

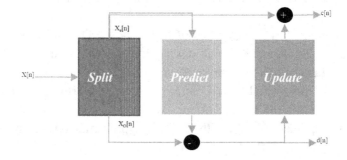

Figure 3. Bands of the DCT transform for a block with 8x8 pixels

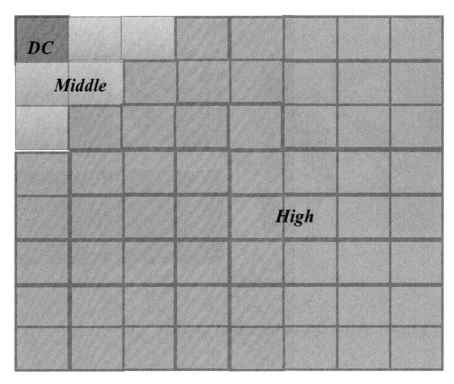

The Discrete Cosine Transform or DCT

The Discrete Cosine Transform (DCT) is similar to the Discrete Fourier Transform (DFT). The projection kernel in the DCT, however, is cosine. As a result, it generates stringent real coefficients, as opposed to the DFT, which uses a complex exponential kernel and generates complex coefficients. The DCT is one of the DFT's subfunctions. It is one of the most widely used signal processing methods, particularly in digital watermarking. As illustrated in Figure 3, the DCT coefficients of an 8x8 image may be separated into three frequency bands: lower, medium, and higher. Because of their high resistance to modification, middle-frequency bands are favored for watermarking. It performs better in the face of strength attacks like compression and filtering.

Figure 4. 2D lifting wavelet transform of gray Lena: (a), (b), (c), and (d) are the LL sub band, the LH sub band, the HL sub band, and the HH sub band, of the LWT, respectively

Original Lena

(a)   (b)

(c)   (d)

The Singular Value Decomposition or SVD

Singular value decomposition (SVD) is a matrices linear algebra technique. It is an essential tool for factoring rectangular matrices that are real or complex. Applications for it include meteorology, statistics, and signal processing. Assume that A is an MxN matrix with coefficients in the field K, where K is either R or C. The form is then factorized as follows:

$$A = USV$$ (3)

U is a unitary MxM matrix on K, and S is an MxN matrix. Only in the diagonal do its coefficients have positive real values (Note all other coefficients are null, and the diagonal coefficients always have a decreasing order). A unitary NxN matrix on K, V is the adjoint matrix of V. The singular value decomposition of the matrix M is the term used to describe this factorization.

Figure 5. The proposed watermarking and extraction algorithms. S and Sw are the original and the watermarked diagonal coefficients matrices, respectively. The U*Sw*V' is the inverse transformation of the SVD.

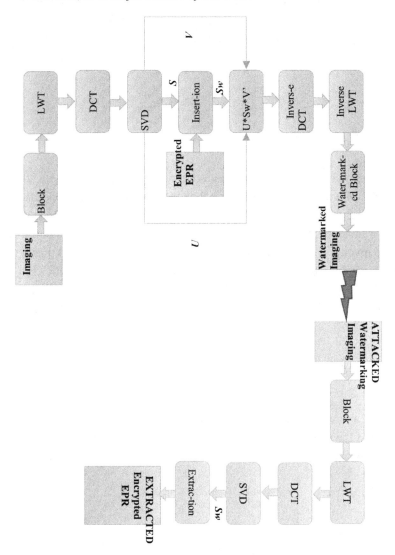

The Proposed Insertion/Extraction Processes: The Watermarking Method

The suggested technique processes the imaging in blocks, as seen in Figure 5. A block is 8x8 pixels in size. We start by calculating the 2-D-LWT coefficient for each block. Then, we transformed the 4x4 LL coefficient of the LWT using the 2-D-DCT method. Using the SVD transformation of the four middle coefficients (matrix of 2x2) of the DCT, we construct the matrices U, S, and V. The insertion is made in the matrix S's S22, the second diagonal coefficient. After inserting the watermark in S22, the coefficient S 11 must continue to be bigger than S 22 in order for the diagonal coefficients' order to stay decreasing. To ensure this, we add π/f to S11.

$$S_{22} = M(S_{22})$$

$$S_{11} = S_{11} + \frac{\pi}{f} \tag{4}$$

The insertion function, shown in equation 5, and the watermarking strength are, respectively, M and f. After performing the insertion, we multiply the matrix U, the watermarked S matrix, and the transposed coefficients V to get the inverse SVD. We use the inverse DCT and replace the watermarked low coefficient. Finally, we utilize the inverse LWT to get the watermarked block. Each block has a single bit embedded in it. Inserting all DICOM patient's data is adequate (or EPR). For instance, we can conceal 4096 bits for a 512x512 picture. The following definitions describe the function of insertion M that enables bit insertion into coefficients:

$$M\left(S_{22}, w\right) = \frac{\pi}{f}\left[\bar{w} + 2Round\left(f\frac{S_{22}}{2\pi}\right)\right] \tag{5}$$

Where f, M, and w, respectively, stand for the watermarking strength, the insertion function, and the watermark bit. The inverse function for removing the watermark from the watermarked image is given by the equation below:

$$w_{ex} = M^{-1}\left(S_{22}^{w}\right) = \cos f \times S_{22}^{w} \tag{6}$$

Where S_{22}^{w} and w_{ex} are the watermarked coefficient and the extracted watermark, respectively. The function that we used in the conversion of the image to blocks is called img2blk:

Table 1. Robustness test of the proposed algorithm august attacks: we use the average value

Attack	Metric	Value	NC	Successful Extracted
Contrast adjustment	Contrast factor	0.5	0.9998	Yes
		2	0.9989	Yes
		2.5	0.9967	Yes
Cropping	pourcent	1/10	0.9345	Yes
		1/8	0.1201	Yes
		1/6	0.8977	Yes
Average Filtering	Block filter size	1x1	1	Yes
		2x2	0.9981	Yes
		3x3	0.9877	Yes
Noise	Density	0.002	1	Yes
		0.005	1	Yes
		0.01	0.9855	Yes
Compression JPEG	Factor quality	100%	1	Yes
		90%	1	Yes
		76%	1	Yes
Gamma correction	-	--	0.9393	Yes
Gain	--	10	1	Yes
		30	1	Yes
		50	1	Yes
Median Filtering	Block filter size	2x2	1	Yes
		4x4	1	Yes
		5x5	0.9911	Yes
Noise	Density	0.002	1	Yes
		0.005	1	Yes
		0.01	0.9901	Yes
Compression JPEG 2000	Compression ratio	3	1	Yes
		6	1	Yes
		8	0.9981	Yes

```
% here b=8 because we use blocks of 8x8
function y=img2blk(I,bl)
c=size(I);
o=(fix(c(1)/bl),fix(c(2)/bl),bl,bl)=0;
for bi=1:fix(c(1)/bl)
    for bc=1:fix(c(2)/bl)
    for i=1:b
        for j=1:b
            o(bi,bc,i,j)=I((bi-1)*bl+i,(bc-1)*bl+j);
        end
    end
    end
end
y=o;
% y matrix of 4-D where bi and bc are the indices of the block
and i,j are the indices of a pixel in a block
end
```

The inverse function that we are used to convert blocks of image to an image is called blk2img:

```
%here bl=8 because we use blocks of 8x8
function y=blk2img(bI,bl)
c=size(bI);
o(c(1)*b,c(2)*b)=0;
for bk=1:l(1)
    for bc=1:l(2)
    for bi=1:b
        for bj=1:b
            o((bk-1)*bl+bi,(bc1)*bI+bj)=bimg(bk,bc,bi,bj);
        end
    end
    end
end
y=o;
% y return matrix of 2-D an image
End
```

Box 1. Quality evolution of the proposed watermarking system using PSNR with 6 samples

Images	a	b	c	d	e	f	Average
PSNR	57.4141	60.4816	56.8463	59.4139	60.8468	56.0846	57.8463

The Modified AES

We have studied and analyzed the AES in Boussif (2022). Found results and cryptanalysis show that the algorithm is very sensitive in the decryption which make its robustness against noise information is null. Therefore, in this paper, we proposed a modification to AES to be robust against noise information and then suitable for encrypting data before a watermarking process. The state is modified to 8-bit (4x2 bit) instead of 128 divided in a vector of 16 elements each of 8-bit. The key is of 128-bit, however, for each state we use only one element (8 bit) selecting from the 8 elements. The first state is encrypted with the first element (the first 8 bit). The rest of states are encrypted using the next steps:

Increment the position of the element of the AES key to find Ptemp. If the position exceeds 16 we must return to the first element.
Determine the new key state or key element which used for encrypting the current state using the modulo of Ptemp (unsigned integer of 8 bit) and 16, then we add one to find the final key index.

EXPERIMENT RESULTS AND DISCUSSION

Experiments with 50 DICOM images were reviewed on MATLAB tool, but we only offer the average value of these images, which was determined by averaging the results of five tests for each DICOM imaging with various AES encryption keys. Additionally, we provide six examples of DICOM medical images in different modalities, sizes, and depths: MRA is a type of magnetic resonance imaging that has 256x256 pixels and a 16-bit depth. MR is a type of magnetic resonance imaging that has 576x448 pixels and a 12-bit depth. CR imaging with a resolution of 2570x2040 pixels and a 12-bit depth. 12-bit depth, 320x240 pixel magnetic resonance imaging (MRA) modality. MR imaging using a 512x512 pixel resolution and a 12-bit depth. In Figure 6, several examples from our dataset are provided. We employ the peak signal to noise ratio (PSNR) to assess the watermarking distortion of an imaging Iw that has undergone complete watermarking:

$$PSNR\left(I, I_w\right) = 10 Log_{10} \left(\frac{\left[2^{dep} - 1\right]^2}{MSE\left(I, I_w\right)} \right)$$

$$MSE\left(I, I_w\right) = \frac{1}{L} \sum_{k=1}^{L} \left[I\left(k\right) - I_w\left(k\right)\right]^2 \tag{7}$$

L stands for the number of imaging pixels, while dep is an abbreviation for imaging depth. the mean squared error, or MSE. The distortion between the retrieved watermark w ex after applying attacks and the watermark w before insertion is measured using the correlation coefficients NC:

$$NC\left(w, w_{ex}\right) = \frac{Cov\left(w, w_{ex}\right)}{\sigma_w \, \sigma_{w_{ex}}} \tag{8}$$

Where $Cov(x,y)$, and σ_x are the covariance of x and y, and the standard deviation of x, respectively.

$$Cov\left(x, y\right) = \frac{1}{N} \sum_{i=1}^{N} \left(x_i - \bar{x}\right)\left(y_i - \bar{y}\right)$$

$$\sigma_x = \sqrt{E\left[x^2\right] - E\left[x\right]^2}$$

$$E\left[x\right] = \sum_{i=1}^{n} x_i p_i \tag{9}$$

Where $\bar{x}$ and p_i are the average value of x and the probability of x_i, respectively. As shown in Figure 6, there is no visible difference between the watermarked images and the original images, so the watermark is imperceptible. From Table 1, we can conclude that the average PSNR is equal to 58, which emphasizes the performance of the proposed algorithm. The NC of the attacked watermarked images closes to 1. Therefore, the proposed algorithm is robust to different attacks such as contrast adjustment, cropping, filtering, Noise, and jpeg compression. The robustness of the proposed algorithm to various attacks is given in Table 2.

Figure 6. Imperceptivity tests of the watermarking algorithm: (a-f) are the original medical images. (a'-f') are the full watermarked medical images, respectively.

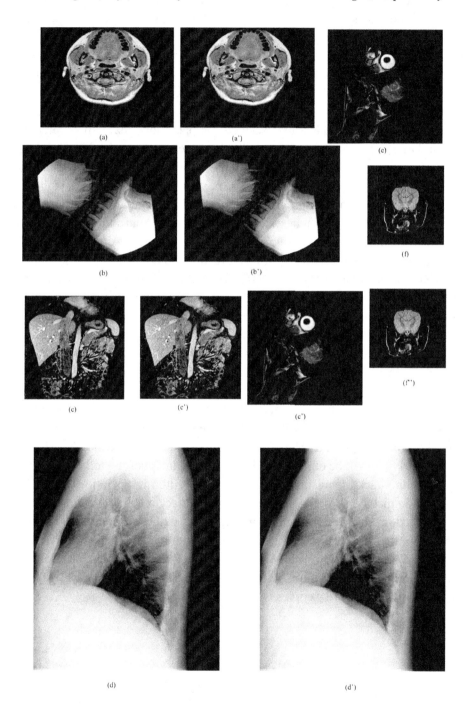

This robustness is one of the fundamental criteria to consider when designing a watermarking algorithm. Indeed, the mark must resist the various attacks, whether intended or not intended, of course, we must except for the digital watermarking of the fragile type. There are many types of attacks which we classified as: 1) unintended attacks: includes manipulations performed by a user that do not initially aim to prevent detection of the mark. These may be degradations due to compression (JPEG, JPEG2000), filtering to reduce noise, format conversion, change of resolution (zoom), etc. In addition, these manipulations can be combined with each other to create more complex attacks. 2) Intended attacks: Includes operations that aim to remove or prevent the correct extraction of the mark. There are two main classifications in the literature detailing more precisely the different attacks of this type where an image can undergo. The first classification is as the next: In this type we have the following four categories: A) Simple attacks: attacks that attempt to damage the inserted mark by manipulating all the data of the watermarked image, without attempting to identify and isolate the mark. This may include filtering, JPEG compression, noise addition, spatial domain quantization and gamma correction. B) Infeasible detection attacks: or synchronization attacks, these are attacks that attempt to make the recovery of the mark impossible or to make the detection process infeasible, mainly by geometric deformations such as scaling (scaling), rotation, shearing, cropping, permutation of pixels, or any other geometric transformation. A characteristic of this type of attack is that the mark remains in the watermarked and attacked images: it can typically be recovered using modified detection methods. C) Attacks of ambiguity: or attacks of confusion, attacks of inversion, and attacks of the rigged mark. These attacks attempt to produce an attempt to confuse by producing fake watermarked images. D) Deep attacks: These are attacks that try to analyze the watermarked images, estimate the mark or original image, and separate the watermarked image into the original image and the mark that will be eliminated. This category includes the following attacks: the collusion attack, denoising, certain nonlinear filtering operations and certain compression methods. For a collusion attack, an attacker can use several copies of watermarked images: each of them is watermarked with a different brand from the other. From these copies, the attacker can construct a copy of the original image that does not contain any marks. Stone conjectured that the collusion attack of a digital watermarking algorithm, based on the spread spectrum in the DCT domain, requires only more than 10 copies in order to be effective.

PERFORMANCE AND COMPARISON

In this part, we evaluate the effectiveness of the suggested system by contrasting the outcomes with those of published transform-based watermarking systems and newly published watermarking schemes that were also acquired under the identical circumstances. When compared with the methods suggested in Mettripun (2016), Amornraksa et al. (2006), Pramoun et al. (2012), Tagesse et al. (2016), Harjito et al. (2017), Preda et al. (2015), the robustness of the proposed approach against attacks is shown. Mettripun has suggested a reliable watermarking method for medical images in Mettripun (2016) that makes use of two 2-D discrete wavelet transform levels. An amplitude modulation-based picture watermarking technique was put out by T. Amornraksa et al. (2006). To watermark color images, T. Pramoun et al. (2012) suggested altering the DWT LL subband's coefficients. The idea of DWT+DCT+SVD-based picture watermarking through GA was put out by T. Tagesse et al. (2016). DWT and SVD are the only two transform algorithms used in the effective picture watermarking technique presented by Harjito et al. (2017). Blind picture watermarking has been proposed by R.O. Preda et al. (2015). A level-based picture watermarking technique based on DWT has been proposed by Rita Ch. et al. (2016). An effective picture watermarking method based on projection and the Laplacian pyramid has been presented by Nguyen et al. (2017). The average value of the PSNR watermarked pictures created using the suggested technique is notable when compared to the previous cited methods, as seen in Figure 7. The average NC of the suggested technique is higher than Mettripun (2016), Amornraksa et al. (2006), Pramoun et al. (2012), Preda et al. (2015) and was derived after applying a jpeg attack at different quality factors (see Figure 8). The suggested method's average NC, which was derived after contrast attack at various brightness factors, is more stable than Mettripun (2016), Amornraksa et al. (2006), Pramoun et al. (2012), as can be shown in Figure 9. The suggested method's average NC comparison, produced after the attacks with Gaussian and pepper noise at various noise variance and densities, is more reliable than Mettripun (2016), Amornraksa et al. (2006), Pramoun et al. (2012), Tagesse et al. (2016), Harjito et al. (2017), Preda et al (2015) (see Figure 10 and Figure 11).

Table 2 compares the robustness of the proposed method with recent state-of-the-art for various attacks and with a new average value obtained from 10 testes with different images. For all methods presented in Table 3, the capacity is fixed to 1/64 bpp, and for each attack strength (attached parameter), the table presents the average value. It is shown that the proposed system has a best robustness.

Table 2. Performances comparison with latest state-of-art. We use Lena image. The References are presented in Table 3.

	10	11	12	13	14	15	16	17	18	9	The proposed
PSNR of watermarked image	58	**48**	-	47	58	57	**41**	32	**54**	**39**	58
NC of extracted watermark with "No Attacks"	-		-	1	-	-	-	-	1	1	1
NC of extracted watermark with "Average filtering 3×3"		0.8984	0.9866	0.981	-	-	-	-	-	-	0.9908
NC of extracted watermark with "Average filtering 5×5"		0.6211	-	-	-	-	-	-	-	-	0.9951
NC of extracted watermark with "Median filtering 2×2"		-	-	-	-	0.9618	-	-	-	-	1
NC of extracted watermark with "Median filtering 3×3"		0.9609	0.9865	0.978	0.99	-	-	0.9541	-	-	1
NC of extracted watermark with "Median filtering 5×5"		0.7402	-	-	-	-	-	0.5073	-	-	1
NC of extracted watermark with "Median filtering 5×5"								0.9771	-	-	1
NC of extracted watermark with "Gaussian Noise(0.005)"		0.9531			-	-	-	-	-	-	1
NC of extracted watermark with "Gaussian Noise(0.01)"		0.7031	0.9968	-	0.99	-	-	-	-	-	**0.9821**
NC of extracted watermark with "Histogram equalization"		0.5039	-	0.982	0.98	-	-	0.9972	-	-	0.9986
NC of extracted watermark with "Resizing 512–>256–>512"		0.9004	-	-	0.84	-	-	-	-	-	0.9921

continues on following page

Table 2. Continued

	10	11	12	13	14	15	16	17	18	9	The proposed
NC of extracted watermark with "Salt and pepper noise (0.001)"	-	-	-	-	1	-		-	-	-	1
NC of extracted watermark with "Salt and pepper noise (0.01)"	0.9971	0.9785	0.9868	0.958	-	-		0.9899	-	-	0.9964
NC of extracted watermark with "Jpeg compression (50%)"	-	0.99...	-	0.999	0.99	0.9635		-	-	-	1
NC of extracted watermark with "Jpeg 2000 compression (2:1)"	0.8577	-	-	-	-	-	-	-	-	-	1
NC of extracted watermark with "Gamma Correction (0.1)"	-	-	0.9980	0.998	-	-		-	-	-	1

Figure 7. Performance comparison in term of PSNR between original and watermarked imaging, respectively

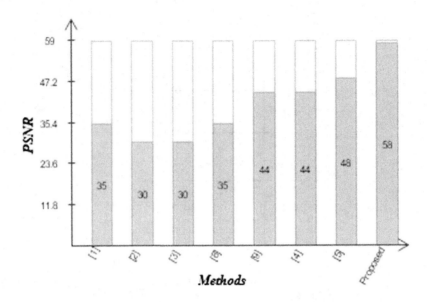

Figure 8. Average NC comparison after applying jpeg attack at various quality factors

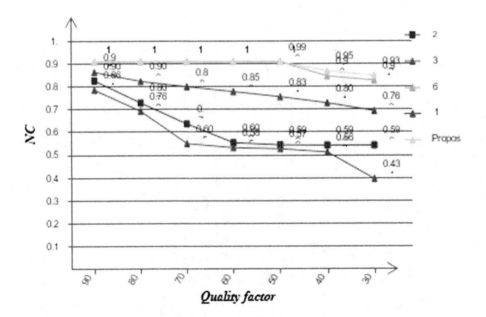

Figure 9. Average NC comparison after applying contrast attack at various brightness factors

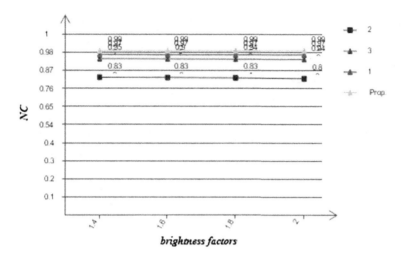

Figure 10. Average NC comparison after applying Gaussian noise attack at various variances

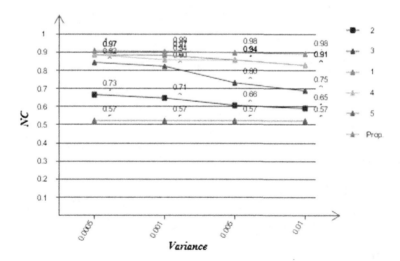

Figure 11. Average NC comparison after applying salt and pepper noise attack at various noise densities

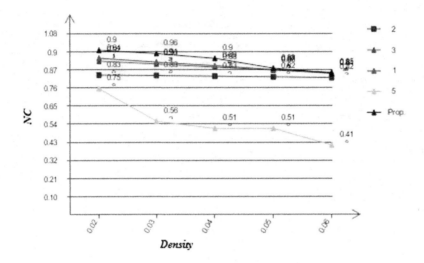

Table 3. References of numbers of method used in the comparison

Method Number	Reference	Method Number	Reference
1	(Mettripun, 2016)	10	(K. Prabha et al,2020)
2	(Amornraksa et al, 2006)	11	(M. F. Kazemi et al, 2020)
3	(Pramoun et al, 2012)	12	(Tanya Koohpayeh Araghi et al, 2018)
4	(Tagesse et al, 2016)	13	(Kwanghyok Mun et al,2021)
5	(Harjito et al, 2017)	14	(Nazari, M. et al, 2021)
6	(Preda et al, 2015)	15	(Thanki, R. et al, 2021)
7	*(Choudhary et al, 2016)*	16	(Manoj K. Singh et al, 2020)
8	*(Nguyen,2017)*	17	(Zhou Z et al, 2021)
9	*(R. Hu et al,2021)*	18	(S. Haddad et al, 2020

LIMITATIONS AND PERSPECTIVES

In the paper, we focus on the robustness of watermarking. For responding to these criteria, we use three transforms, the LWT, the DCT, and the SVD, which makes the system heavy in runtime, compared with other watermarking techniques that use only one or two transformers. Therefore, we must calculate the cookbook that contains the three transformations of the combination of permutations possible of a block image. Then, we can use a deep learning system to learn the three transforms only on blocks of 8x8 pixels, for both transformation LWT-DCT-SVD and ISVD-IDCT-ILWT. Therefore, our future work will minimize the run time or complexity time using the deep learning system.

CONCLUSION

In this paper, we have proposed a robust blind crypto-watermarking algorithm based on hybrid transform (LWT+DCT+SVD) for the security of DICOM medical images. Our objective was to secure medical images in telemedicine using a robust image watermarking method; therefore, we inserted the modified AES-based encrypted patient information in the relative medical imaging. We tested the proposed algorithm by applying various attacks such as noise, filtering, and compression…, where we show that the proposed algorithm is robust against different types of attacks. Finally, we have compared the performance of the proposed method with the state-of-the-art, where we found that our system has the best performance in terms of quality, invisibility, and robustness. The perspective of the work consists of minimizing the run time of the watermarking algorithm to be runnable in low equipment like embedded systems.

ACKNOWLEDGMENT

The authors express their gratitude to the reviewers for their insightful remarks, which helped us improve the article's quality.

REFERENCES

Alanizy, N., Alanizy, A., Baghoza, N., AlGhamdi, M., & Gutub, A. (2018). 3-layer PC text security via combining compression, AES cryptography 2LSB image steganography. *Journal of Research in Engineering and Applied Sciences*, *3*(4), 118–124. doi:10.46565/jreas.2018.v03i04.001

Ali, Z., Hossain, M. S., Muhammad, G., & Aslam, M. (2018). New Zero-Watermarking Algorithm Using Hurst Exponent for Protection of Privacy in Telemedicine. *IEEE Access, Volume*, *6*, 7930–7940. doi:10.1109/ACCESS.2018.2799604

Amornraksa, T., & Janthawongwilai, K. (2006). Enhanced Images Watermarking based on Amplitude Modulation. *Image and Vision Computing, 24*(2), 111–119. doi:10.1016/j.imavis.2005.09.018

Araghi, T. K., Manaf, A. A., Alarood, A., & Zainol, A. B. (2018). Host Feasibility Investigation to Improve Robustness in Hybrid DWT+SVD Based Image Watermarking Schemes. *Advances in Multimedia, 2018*, 1609378. Advance online publication. doi:10.1155/2018/1609378

Boussif, M. (2022). On The Security of Advanced Encryption Standard (AES). *8th International Conference on Engineering, Applied Sciences, and Technology (ICEAST)*, 83-88. 10.1109/ICEAST55249.2022.9826324

Boussif, M., Aloui, N., & Cherif, A. (2017). New Watermarking/Encryption Method for Medical Images Full Protection in mHealth. *Iranian Journal of Electrical and Computer Engineering, 7*(6), 3385–3394.

Boussif, M., Aloui, N., & Cherif, A. (2020). DICOM imaging watermarking for hiding medical reports. *Medical & Biological Engineering & Computing, 58*(11), 2905–2918. doi:10.100711517-020-02269-8 PMID:32979170

Boussif, M., Bouferas, O., Aloui, N., & Cherif, A. (2021), A Novel Robust Blind AES/LWT+DCT+SVD-Based Crypto-Watermarking schema for DICOM Images Security. *IEEE International Conference on Design & Test of Integrated Micro & Nano-Systems (DTS)*. 10.1109/DTS52014.2021.9497916

Cedillo-Hernandez, M., Garcia-Ugalde, F., Nakano-Miyatake, M., & Perez-Meana, H. (2015). Robust watermarking method in DFT domain for effective management of medical imaging. *Signal, Image and Video Processing, 9*(5), 1163–1178. doi:10.100711760-013-0555-x

Choudhary, R., & Parmar, G. (2016). A Robust Image Watermarking Technique using 2-level Discrete Wavelet Transform (DWT). *2nd International Conference on Communication Control and Intelligent Systems (CCIS)*. 10.1109/CCIntelS.2016.7878213

Datta, D., Garg, L., Srinivasan, K., Inoue, A., & Thippa Reddy, G. (2020). An efficient sound and data steganography based secure authentication system. *Computers. Materials & Continua, 67*(1), 723–751. doi:10.32604/cmc.2021.014802

Eswar Kumar, M., Thippa Reddy, G., & Sudheer, K. (2017). Vehicle Theft Identification and Intimation Using GSM & IOT. *IOP Conf. Ser.: Mater. Sci. Eng, 263*, 042062.

Eswaraiah, R., & Reddy, E. S. (2015). Robust medical image watermarking technique for accurate detection of tampers inside region of interest and recovering original region of interest. *IET Image Processing, Volume, 9*(8), 615–625. doi:10.1049/iet-ipr.2014.0986

Gangadhar, Y., Giridhar Akula, V. S., & Chenna Reddy, P. (2018). An evolutionary programming approach for securing medical images using watermarking scheme in invariant discrete wavelet transformation. *Biomedical Signal Processing and Control, 43*, 31–40. doi:10.1016/j.bspc.2018.02.007

Gutub, A. (2022a). Enhancing Cryptography of Grayscale Images via Resilience Randomization Flexibility. *International Journal of Information Security and Privacy, 16*(1), 1–28. doi:10.4018/IJISP.307071

Gutub, A. (2022b). Boosting image watermarking authenticity spreading secrecy from counting-based secret-sharing. *CAAI Transactions on Intelligence Technology*, cit2.12093. doi:10.1049/cit2.12093

Gutub, A. (2022c). Watermarking images via counting-based secret sharing for lightweight semi-complete authentication. *International Journal of Information Security and Privacy, 16*(1), 1–18. doi:10.4018/IJISP.307071

Gutub, A., & Al-Roithy, B. (2021). Varying PRNG to improve image cryptography implementation. *Journal of Engineering Research, 9*(3A). Advance online publication. doi:10.36909/jer.v9i3A.10111

Gutub, A. A.-A. (2010). Pixel indicator technique for RGB image steganography. *Journal of Emerging Technologies in Web Intelligence, 2*(1), 56–64. doi:10.4304/jetwi.2.1.56-64

Haddad, S., Coatrieux, G., Moreau-Gaudry, A., & Cozic, M. (2020). Joint Watermarking-Encryption-JPEG-LS for Medical Image Reliability Control in Encrypted and Compressed Domains. *IEEE Transactions on Information Forensics and Security, 15*, 2556–2569. doi:10.1109/TIFS.2020.2972159

Harjito, B., & Suryani, E. (2017). Robust image watermarking using DWT and SVD for copyright protection. *AIP Conference Proceedings, 1813*, 040003. doi:10.1063/1.4975968

Hassan, F. S., & Gutub, A. (2021). Efficient image reversible data hiding technique based on interpolation optimization. *Arabian Journal for Science and Engineering, 46*(9), 8441–8456. doi:10.100713369-021-05529-3

Hassan, F. S., & Gutub, A. (2022). Improving data hiding within colour images using hue component of HSV colour space. *CAAI Transactions on Intelligence Technology*, 7(1), 56–68. doi:10.1049/cit2.12053

Hu, R., & Xiang, S. (2021). Cover-Lossless Robust Image Watermarking Against Geometric Deformations. *IEEE Transactions on Image Processing*, 30, 318–331. doi:10.1109/TIP.2020.3036727 PMID:33186107

Hureib, E. S., & Gutub, A. A. (2020). Enhancing medical data security via combining elliptic curve cryptography and image steganography. *Int. J. Comput. Sci. Netw. Secur.*, 20(8), 1–8.

Iwendi, C., Jalil, Z., Javed, A. R., Reddy G, T., Kaluri, R., Srivastava, G., & Jo, O. (2020). KeySplitWatermark: Zero Watermarking Algorithm for Software Protection Against Cyber-Attacks. *IEEE Access : Practical Innovations, Open Solutions*, 8, 72650–72660. doi:10.1109/ACCESS.2020.2988160

Jamali, M., Samavi, S., Karimi, N., Soroushmehr, S. M. R., Ward, K., & Najarian, K. (2016). Robust Watermarking in Non-ROI of Medical Images Based on DCT-DWT. *38th Annual International Conference of the IEEE Engineering in Medicine and Biology Society (EMBC)*. 10.1109/EMBC.2016.7590920

Kazemi, M. F., Pourmina, M. A., & Mazinan, A. H. (2020). Analysis of Watermarking Framework for Color Image through a Neural Network-based Approach. *Complex & Intelligent Systems*, 6(1), 213–220. doi:10.100740747-020-00129-4

Kim, B.-S., Choi, J.-G., Park, C.-H., Won, J.-U., Kwak, D.-M., Oh, S.-K., Koh, C.-R., & Park, K.-H. (2003). Robust digital image watermarking method against geometrical attacks. *Real-Time Imaging*, 9(2), 139–149. doi:10.1016/S1077-2014(03)00020-2

Koppu & Viswanatham. (2020). An efficient image system-based grey wolf optimiser method for multimedia image security using reduced entropy-based 3D chaotic map. *International Journal of Computer Aided Engineering and Technology*, 13(3).

Koppu, S., & Viswanatham, V. M. (2018). Medical image security enhancement using two dimensional chaotic mapping optimized by self-adaptive grey wolf algorithm. *Evol. Intel.*, 11, 53–71.

Kumar, R., Tripathi, R., Marchang, N., Srivastava, G., Gadekallu, T. R., & Xiong, N. N. (2021). A secured distributed detection system based on IPFS and blockchain for industrial image and video data security. *Journal of Parallel and Distributed Computing*, 152, 128–143. doi:10.1016/j.jpdc.2021.02.022

Lakshmanna & Khare. (2016). Constraint-Based Measures for DNA Sequence Mining using Group Search Optimization Algorithm. *International Journal of Intelligent Engineering and Systems*, *9*(3).

Lakshmanna, K., Kaluri, R., & Thippa Reddy, G. (2016). An enhanced algorithm for frequent pattern mining from biological sequences. *Int J Pharm Technol*, *8*, 12776–12784.

Mettripun, N. (2016). A Robust Medical Image Watermarking Based on DWT for Patient Identification. *13th International Conference on Electrical Engineering/ Electronics, Computer, Telecommunications and Information Technology (ECTI-CON)*. 10.1109/ECTICon.2016.7561455

Mohamed, B., Aloui, N., & Cherif, A. (2019). Images encryption algorithm based on the quaternion multiplication and the XOR operation. *Multimedia Tools and Applications*, *78*(24), 35493–35510. doi:10.100711042-019-08108-9

Mohamed, B., Aloui, N., & Cherif, A. (2020). Securing DICOM images by a new encryption algorithm using Arnold transform and Vigenère cipher. *IET Image Processing*, *14*(6), 1209–1216. doi:10.1049/iet-ipr.2019.0042

Mun, K., & Son, C. (2019). Design of optimal blind watermarking technique based on MOEA/D. *IET Image Processing*. Advance online publication. doi:10.1049/ iet-ipr.2019.1551

Nazari, M., & Mehrabian, M. (2021). A novel chaotic IWT-LSB blind watermarking approach with flexible capacity for secure transmission of authenticated medical images. *Multimedia Tools and Applications*, *80*(7), 10615–10655. doi:10.100711042-020-10032-2

Nguyen, S. C., Kha, H. H., & Nguyen, H. M. (2017). An Efficient Image Watermarking Scheme Using the Laplacian Pyramid based on Projection. *International Conference on Recent Advances in Signal Processing, Telecommunications & Computing (SigTelCom)*. 10.1109/SIGTELCOM.2017.7849804

Prabha & Sam. (2020). An Effective Robust and Imperceptible Blind Color Image Watermarking using WHT. *Journal of King Saud University - Computer and Information Sciences*, *44*.

Pramoun, T., & Amornraksa, T. (2012). Improved Image Watermarking Scheme based on DWT Coefficients Modification in LL Sub-band. Int. Proc. of IEEE on the 9th Electrical Engineering/Electronics, Computer, Telecommunications and Information Technology (ECTI-CON-2012), 1-4.

Preda, R. O., & Vizireanu, D. N. (2015). Watermarking-based image authentication robust to JPEG compression. *Electronics Letters, 51*(23), 1873–1875. doi:10.1049/el.2015.2522

Rajput, D. S., Basha, S. M., & Xin, Q. (2021). *Providing diagnosis on diabetes using cloud computing environment to the people living in rural areas of India.* J Ambient Intell Human Comput. doi:10.100712652-021-03154-4

Selvam, P., Balachandran, S., Iyer, S. P., & Jayabal, R. (2017). Hybrid transform based reversible watermarking technique for medical images in telemedicine applications. *Optik (Stuttgart), 145*, 655–671. doi:10.1016/j.ijleo.2017.07.060

Shih, F. Y., & Zhong, X. (2016). High-capacity multiple regions of interest watermarking for medical images. *Information Sciences, 367–368*, 648–659. doi:10.1016/j.ins.2016.07.015

Singh, M. K., Kumar, S., Ali, M., & Saini, D. (2020). Application of a novel image moment computation in X-ray and MRI image watermarking. *IET Image Processing.* Advance online publication. doi:10.1049/ipr2.12052

Takore, Kumar, & Devi. (2016). A Modified Blind Image Watermarking Scheme Based on DWT, DCT and SVD domain Using GA to Optimize Robustness. *International Conference on Electrical, Electronics, and Optimization Techniques (ICEEOT).*

Thanki, Borra, Dwivedi, & Borisagar. (2017). An efficient medical image watermarking scheme based on FDCuT–DCT. *Engineering Science and Technology, 20*(4), 1366-1379.

Thanki, R., & Kothari, A. (2021). A. Multi-level security of medical images based on encryption and watermarking for telemedicine applications. *Multimedia Tools and Applications, 80*(3), 4307–4325. doi:10.100711042-020-09941-z

Wang, J., Wan, W. B., Li, X. X., Sun, J. D., & Zhang, H. X. (2020). Color Image Watermarking Based on Orientation Diversity and Color Complexity. *Expert Systems with Applications, 140*, 112868. doi:10.1016/j.eswa.2019.112868

Zhou, Z., Zhu, J., Su, Y., Wang, M., & Sun, X. (2021). Geometric correction code-based robust image watermarking. *IET Image Processing*, 1–10. doi:10.1049/ipr2.12143

Zolotavkin & Juhola. (2014). A New QIM-Based Watermarking Method Robust to Gain Attack. *International Journal of Digital Multimedia Broadcasting.* doi:10.1155/2014/910808

Chapter 5
An Enhancement of Lossless Video Compression Using Two-Layer Approach

Donia Ammous
Laboratory of Electronics and Information Technologies, National Engineering School of Sfax, Tunisia

Amina Kessentini
Laboratory of Electronics and Information Technologies, National Engineering School of Sfax, Tunisia

Naziha Khlif
Laboratory of Electronics and Information Technologies, National Engineering School of Sfax, Tunisia

Fahmi Kammoun
Laboratory of Electronics and Information Technologies, National Engineering School of Sfax, Tunisia

Nouri Masmoudi
Laboratory of Electronics and Information Technologies, National Engineering School of Sfax, Tunisia

ABSTRACT

Several lossless video compression methods have been developed and published in the literature. The authors focused on the hierarchical lossless video compression methods that consist of two layers: The EL layer is used to code the error's information realized by both the transformation and the quantization. The BL layer contains the common chain of the H264/AVC standard's lossy coding. They integrated some features into two-layer lossless video compression in order to enhance their performance. The simulation results demonstrated that, in comparison to earlier work, the approach reduces the total bit of the coded sequence.

DOI: 10.4018/978-1-6684-4945-5.ch005

INTRODUCTION

Video takes an important place in various applications such as multimedia, medical, and security, etc. This is why the quality of the images used has become a primary criterion (Ammous et al., 2019, 2020). Therefore, the evaluation of the quality of the images is a key element of the coding performance definition. In fact, it became necessary to judge the quality of the images processed or produced in many multimedia applications, compared to the initial image at the level of a coding chain. Using lossless video compression, the issue of image quality is resolved. In this paper, we are interested in hierarchical lossless video compression method and we can introduce improvements there. The outline of this chapter was presented in the following sections. In the second section, we listed the lossless video compression methods based on the standard H.264 such as H.264-LS, H.264-LS-DPCM, and the hierarchical technique. In the third section, we explained the progress of the algorithm of our contribution. In the fourth section, we described the structure of the code JM of the standard H.264 / AVC and we provided the results of the proposed method. Our conclusions were made in the paper's final section.

STATE OF THE ART LOSSLESS VIDEO COMPRESSION METHODS

The first version of the standard H.264 / AVC lossless coding (H.264-LS) is a technique of PCM (pulse code modulation) where original sequence samples are sent directly to entropy coding without performing the steps of prediction, transformation, and quantization. A lot of research tried to introduce improvements to this method of H.264 - LS to improve its performance. In fact, H.264-LS-DPCM (Differential Pulse Code Modulation) is an improved lossless coding method of the H.264-LS standard. In this version, the prediction process is done with the DPCM technique instead of the prediction based on the blocks. For more precision in the prediction step, the DPCM concept is applied where each sample is predicted by its immediate neighbouring samples.

The two-layer coding methods were proposed to further improve the performance of the standard H.264 based on the lossless coding (H.264-LS-DPCM). These methods were based on the ordinary lossy video coding of the standard H.264 with another layer to compensate the lossy bitstream. Thus, combining the powerful lossy coding tools into the lossless coding system would be more efficient.

Jun-RenDing's Method

In general, the transformation and the quantization cannot be used for the lossless coding of images and videos, such as JPEG-LS, H.264-LS. If we want to transmit a bit-stream, which can provide lossless and lossy images at the same time for different clients, JPEG-LS or H.264-LS cannot offer such a capability. To solve this problem of universal access, Jun-Ren Ding et al. (2008) proposed a lossless video coding method based on the lossy coding of the standard H.264 as shown in Figure 1. They can control the lossy video compression bit stream by checking quantization parameters (QP). For lossless applications, they use the existing entropy coding to code the difference between the original and reconstructed images after running the inverse DCT and the inverse quantization obtained from the lossy bitstream. As shown in Figure 1, the D bitstream is used to represent the results of coding of the difference of the images after the execution of CABAC. The authors can achieve lossless compression through a combination of D bitstream and lossy bitstream (Ding et al., 2008).

Figure 1. Diagram of the block of the proposed H.264-LS based on the lossy video coding of the standard H.264
Source: Ding et al. (2008)

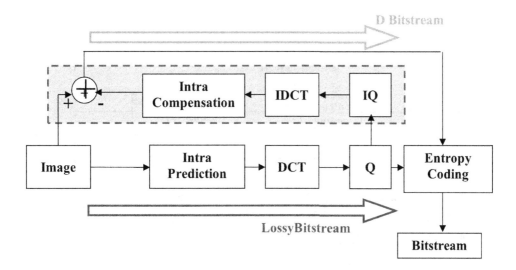

Wei-Da-Chien Method

First Version

The quantization and the transformation engender a distortion. But in return, these two procedures can significantly reduce the flow. That is why a new method was developed. It maintains the power of the lossy coding in terms of the compression ratio: it is a two-layer structure based on the ordinary H.264 / AVC standard (Chien et al., 2011). This new architecture also called hierarchical lossless coding system. In the hierarchically lossless coding scheme, the flow of bits coded by the second layer is used to compensate the distortions in the coded bitstream of the first layer to reconstruct the original video (see Figure 2). The first Base Layer (BL) is the lossy coding system of the H.264 / AVC, and the second Enhancement Layer (EL) is the lossless entropy coding system used to code the error made by the DCT and the quantization.

This technique is based on 2 layers. A base layer generates a lossy compression bitstream and the other layer corrects the latter by the second bitstream to obtain a final bitstream that allows lossless reconstruction (Ding et al., 2008; Ammous et al., 2014; Chien et al., 2014; Heindel et al., 2014, 2016; Wang et al., 2011).

Figure 2. Detailed diagram of lossless hierarchical coding
Source: Chien et al. (2011)

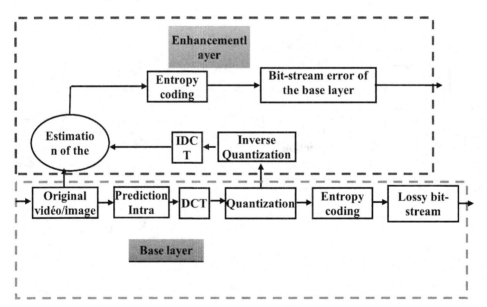

Wei Da Chien's layer EL contains four parts: inverse quantization, inverse transformation, estimation of the distortion and entropy coding.

Second Version

Direct application of the transformation and quantization processes, which would result in errors, is not allowed in lossless video coding. The spatial redundancies bit-coded can be significantly reduced, though, by the transformation and quantization processes. In order to increase compression effectiveness and application flexibility, a two-layer hierarchical lossless coding system with the Rice coder for residual error coding in the enhancement layer and the H.264 / AVC coder in the base layer was developed. To explore the optimal quantization, it is necessary to redesign the enhancement layer (Chien et al., 2014). Indeed, the base layer provides a good performance of lossy coding, and the enhancement layer corrects the errors caused by the base layer. Finally, We-Da-Chien et al. realized the lossless video by combining bitstreams of base layer and enhancement layer in the proposed coding architecture.

We-Da-Chien et al. proposed an effective lossless video coding system with the architecture of coding in two layers to simultaneously provide lossless and lossy video. The difference of this method with the method of Jun-Ren Ding et al. The first is the use of the rice coder with respect to a CABAC entropy coding and secondly the addition of the QP selection module.

Three primary parts make up the proposed two-layer lossless video coding system depicted in Figure 3: (1) H.264/AVC coding; (2) a QP-adaptive rice coder; and (3) the QP selection method. The following diagram discusses the specific descriptions of these three elements:

Method of Li-Li Wang et al.

In the proposed algorithm of Li-Li Wang et al., two contributions were made. First, rather of employing prediction based on blocks as a whole, samples in a macroblock (MB) or block are hierarchically predicted. Four groups are particularly taken from the samples in a macroblock or block. Following the prediction of the samples for the first group using the directional intra prediction approach, the samples for the remaining groups are predicted using the samples from the first group as a guide. As a result, since the samples can be reliably predicted using closer references, the information in the residual block can be decreased.

Figure 3. Two-layer lossless hierarchical coding system proposed by Wei-Da-Chien et al. (2014)

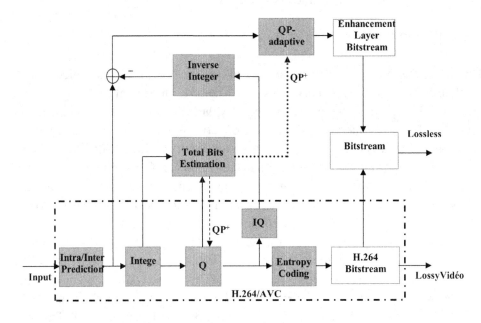

Two coding modes that are created to effectively code the resulting residual block are another contribution. A better mode of coding can be chosen according to the optimization of the debit RO (rate optimization). Additionally, a suggestion was made to enhance the CAVLC method of entropy coding, which is more effective, to code the flags of coding schemes for an MB (Wang et al., 2011).

The block diagram of the coding scheme selection process is shown in Figure 4 (Wang et al., 2011). There are in fact two coding systems: the schemes of coding in one and in two layers, conceived to code the residual. The residual coefficients are directly scanned and encoded using the CAVLC method for entropy coding in the single-layer coding scheme. While both lossy and lossless coding techniques are used in the two-layer coding architecture. In the lossy coding procedure, the residual block is first transformed and quantized to obtain the QDCT coefficients. Entropy coding is used to scan and encode the QDCT coefficients. In contrast, the inverse quantization and inverse DCT are applied to the QDCT coefficients in the lossless coding process to produce the reconstructed residual block r '. The entropy coding was scanned and coded the difference between the original residual block r and the reconstructed residual block r '. A crucial issue during coding is choosing between the two candidate schemas for a better coding scheme.

Figure 4. Choosing a coding system based on the optimization of the flow
Source: Wang et al. (2011)

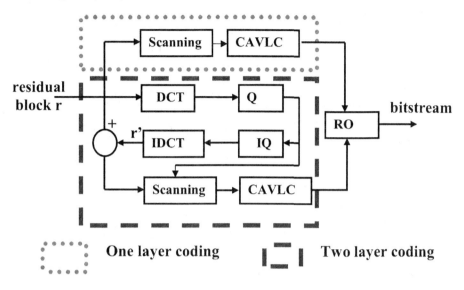

Method of Seung-Hwan Kim et al.

In the method TRC (two-layered residual coding), the first layer FRC (first-layer residual coder) use the residual coding of the conventional H.264 / AVC standard, which consists of stages of transformation and quantization with a parameter of quantization (QP). The second layer SRC (second-layer residual coder) adopts a BPC (bit plane coding) method (Kim et al., 2011).

The TRC method consists of three steps. The structure of the TRC method is illustrated in the Figure 5 (see the first step in yellow, the second step in blue and the third step in red). The input image is coded in three stages: 1) intra prediction of the H.264 / AVC standard; 2) DCT, quantization, inverse DCT, and inverse quantization in the first layer FRC; and 3) the method of coding BPC of the second layer SRC. Indeed, after intra prediction of the lossy coder H.264 / AVC, an advanced scheme was proposed for the coding of the residuals. It constituted by two residual coders in cascade. The residual coder of the first layer is processed via a transformation and a quantization with a given quantization parameter. The residual coder of the second layer is a method of coding BPC (bit plane coding). They are detailed below.

The following coding specifications were defined for the proposed TRC and the reference software H.264 / AVC (Suehring et al., 2016):

Figure 5. Structure of the TRC method
Source: Kim et al. (2011)

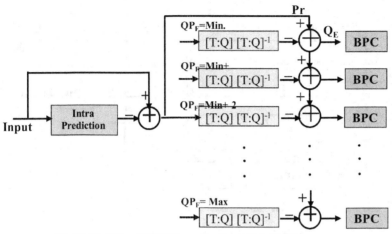

. $|T:Q| \ |T:Q|^{-1}$ = |DCT/Quantization| |Inv.DCT
. BPC : bit-plane coding, Pr : Prediction residual, Q_E : Quantization error

1. ProfileIDC= 244 (high 4: 4: 4).
2. IntraPeriod = 1 (only intra coding).
3. QPISlice = 0.
4. SymbolMode = 0 ou 1 (0: CAVLC, 1: CABAC).
5. QPPrimeYZeroTransformBypassFlag = 1 (lossless).
6. The number of coded images = 100.
7. Min. QPF =10, Max. QPF = 40, Δ = 2 (As illustrated in the Figure 5).

Method of Qi Zhang et al.

Schlockermann (2003) indicates the possibility of observing the residual image as granular noise. The granular noise is not important in the video SD and does not even less perceptible in the low-resolution videos such as CIF and QCIF. Nevertheless, these superficial variations in HD video have been observed. The approach of Qi Zhang et al. seeks to eliminate redundancy by exploiting the spatial and temporal correlation of granular noise.

The block diagram in Figure 6 represents the HD lossless video coding scheme. A denoising technique divides the input image into two parts. These two components can then each be independently coded. They are integrated again into the decoder unit.

Therefore, the proposed lossless video compression method is based on residual image prediction and coding RIPC (residual image prediction and coding) (Zhang et al., 2009). Indeed, two different prediction schemes are made for content and granular noise, and their residues are encoded by a different entropy coding (as shown in Figure 6).

In the first prediction scheme, for an input image F, a lossy video coding process is used first with a given QP. The extracted noise image noted by N is then the difference between the reconstructed image F' and the original image F. Finally, entropy coding as CABAC is applied to the images N. There is a compromise between the bits assigned to the coding of F' and the coding of N, depending on QP selected.

Concerning the second part of residual image, a combination of spatial and temporal prediction methods was used to perform a prediction by blocks (Dai et al., 2008) in the residual image. Then, the prediction errors were coded by Exp_Golomb codes.

Unlike other lossless or lossy coding systems, the RIPC system can produce lossless and lossy coding results without hardware modification. It can also achieve adaptability with minor modifications.

Figure 6. Lossless coding for HD content
Source: Zhang et al. (2009)

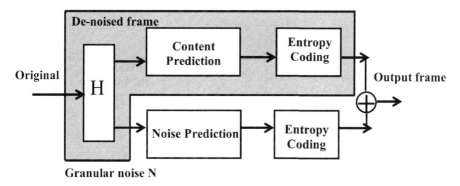

PROPOSED METHOD

Presentation

We introduce improvements mainly on the EL layer of the Wei-Da-Chien method (first version). We propose an approach that includes three steps. For that purpose, we add three blocks "difference of images", "order of the coefficients" and "Huffman coding". Indeed, the coding chain of the standard H.264 / AVC generates two outputs: the reconstructed image and the lossy bitstream BL. First, we calculate the difference between the lossy reconstructed image (of the BL layer) and the original image to correct the lossy bitstream (see part of algorithm 1 in the appendix). Secondly, we integrate a code of ordering of the coefficients according to a criterion of appearance of the distortions follows in the code of difference in the code JM. Figure 7 gives a detailed overview of this system.

This code's goal can be summed up as follows: The loss of the data exists mainly in the boundaries of blocks 4×4 of the image (effect of blocks). The idea is to schedule the coefficients of the difference image before sending them to the Huffman coding. For the luminance component, the boundary coefficients of the 4×4 blocks are sent first. The coefficients of the two chrominance components are sent with a similar scheduling secondly. Finally, the rest of the coefficients ("cores" of blocks 4×4) is transmitted.

Figure 7. The general structure of hierarchical lossless video coding improvement
src[i,t] represent the source image
rec[i,t] denote the reconstructed image
diff[i,t] indicate the difference image
diff_ord[i,t] is referred the ordered difference image

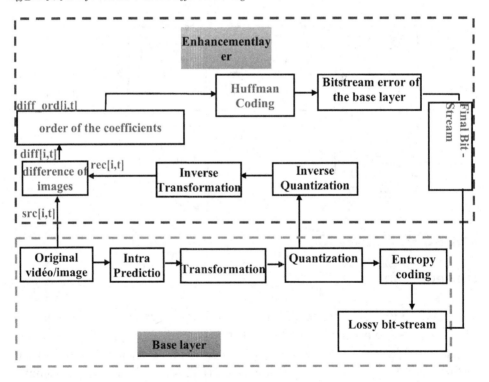

Progress of the Algorithm

The algorithm of the sequencing of the coefficients of the reconstructed image is made in two big different parts (see Figure 8):

Sequencing of the coefficients situated on the border of the image.
Sequencing of the coefficients situated in the core of the image.

The algorithm for ordering the coefficients of the reconstructed image is done in two large parts (see Figure 8):

- Scheduling of the coefficients located in the image boundary.
- Scheduling of the coefficients located in the core of the image.

Each scheduling part consists of three parts:

- Order the luma coefficients.
- Order the chroma coefficients U.
- Order the chroma coefficients V.

Figure 8. General structure of order

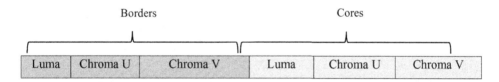

The algorithms of orders of the three components are identical in the case of borders. Similarly, these algorithms are identical in the case of cores.

The algorithm of order of the borders consists of four cases (see part of algorithm 2 in the appendix):

- Horizontal high.
- Horizontal low.
- Vertical left.
- Vertical right.

The proposed algorithm is performed on a block 4×4 of an image of format CIF in Figure 9.

Figure 9. Partitioning of the block 4×4 in four cases

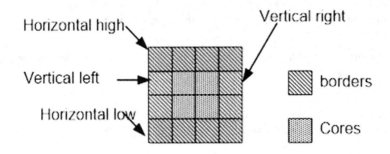

The algorithm of order uses a matrix of size 352×288 to facilitate the implementation for programmers.

Since we work on CIF format 352 × 288 and the scheduling is done by block 4×4, this image is composed in 88 blocks horizontally and in 72 blocks vertically. The algorithm of order of the boundary coefficients is done in four steps (see Figure 10).

Figure 10. Progress of algorithm of order of the coefficients on the borders

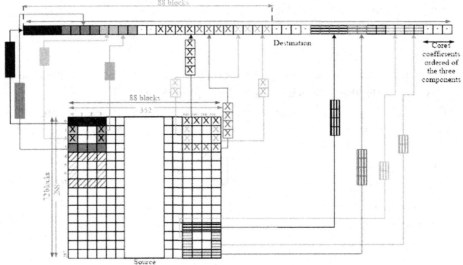

We fix two counters that correspond to the x and y coordinates associated with the lines and columns of the image to move and indicate the current position in the image. We begin by transferring the first 12 pixels of four cases from the source to the destination according to the order mentioned in the Figure 9.

This chain is repeated until the end of 88 blocks of the line 0. Then, we increment the line 1 and we make a transfer in the same way the 12 pixels to finish the pixels of 88 blocks. We store the results at the destination in the same way until the end of all lines that means until we reach line 287.

The algorithm for ordering the coefficients of the cores is done in another way. We realize a scanning line by line and we store the coefficients from the source to the destination by transferring four pixels block by block and line by line until the end of all the image coefficients (see Figure 11).

Figure 11. Progress of algorithm of order of the coefficients of the cores

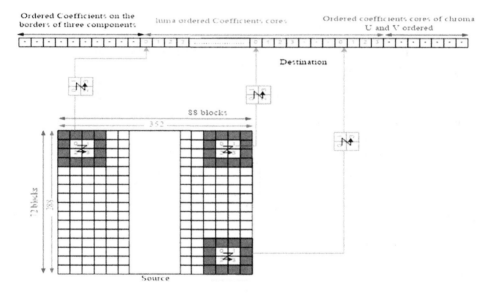

Finally, we make a concatenation between the border ordering coefficients and the cores scheduling coefficients to form an ordered difference image. This image will be applied to the input of the Huffman coder (Ou et al., 2016; Wei et al., 2011). We implemented the Huffman coding, which serves to realize the binary codes of the obtained symbols and subsequently generate the bitstream of the enhancement layer (EL).

The Huffman coding algorithm (Huffman, 1952) is named after its inventor, David Huffman, who developed this algorithm in 1950. The Huffman algorithm is a solution to the problem of elaboration of codes. This method allows a statistical analysis of the symbols composing the source file in order to obtain a lossless compression of the data.

The principle of the Huffman method is to associate the most probable symbols with the shortest binary words.

Example

Consider the example of a message of our ordered image «0 3 -3 1 -8 -1 -1 6 -3 -5 -4 -1 -1 -4 5 8 -1 3 -2 3 -1 -1 -2 3 4 5 7.......». The frequency distribution of the symbols is as follows: $f(-)=123637$; $f(1)=103693$; $f(0)=62778$; $f(2)=59781$; $f(3)=32444$; $f(4)=18926$; $f(5)=12016$; $f(6)=7357$; $f(7)=4707$; $f(8)=2932$; $f(9)=1766$. We build then the binary tree of Huffman according to the following 3 steps:

Step 1

Rank the symbols in descending order of their frequencies of appearance. The frequency table is given in Table 1.

Table 1. Frequencies of appearance

Caractères	Frequency of Occurrence
-	123637
1	103693
0	62778
2	59781
3	32444
4	18926
5	12016
6	7357
7	4707
8	2932
9	1766

Step 2

Group sequentially the pairs of lower probability symbols. The procedure is summarized in Figure 12. We obtain a tree structure called: "Huffman Tree structure".

Figure 12. Huffman tree structure

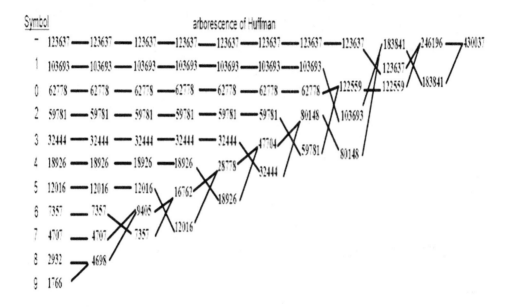

Step 3

Code with back return from the last group, and by adding a 0 or a 1 to differentiate previously grouped symbols. To obtain the codes, it is enough to browse the tree from the studied pattern to the end of the path by piling the binary symbols encountered on the path. The search results are given in Figure 13.

We notice that the compacted file contains 1170128 bits (32444×3 + 18926×4 + 12016×5 + 7357×6 + 1766×8 + 2932×8 + 4707×7 + 103693×2 + 59781×3 + 62778×3 + 123637×2 = 1170128) against 3440296 bits for the original file.

Figure 13. Huffman tree structure with codes

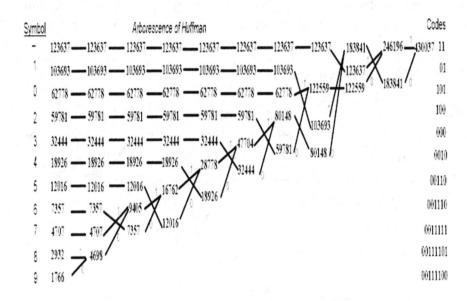

EXPERIMENTAL RESULTS AND DISCUSSION

JM Software

The JVT group has created a reference software JM (Joint Model) whose sources are freely downloadable on its site (Suehring, 2015; Brouard, 2010). It is written in C language. In order to experiment the features of JM, many parameters can be modified in their configuration file, such as the number of images to be coded, the intra \ inter mode, the number of reference frames, the choice of entropy coding (CABAC or CAVLC), the partitioning modes of a macroblock, the quantization step (QP), etc. In this work, we used the JM 18.3 version to validate the proposed algorithm.

We performed a detailed analysis of the software JM of the standard H.264 / AVC (see Figure 14). This analysis aims at understanding globally the progress of each module of the coding chain and then to extract data from the JM (in other terms the input image of the filtering module).

Figure 14. Structure of the JM code

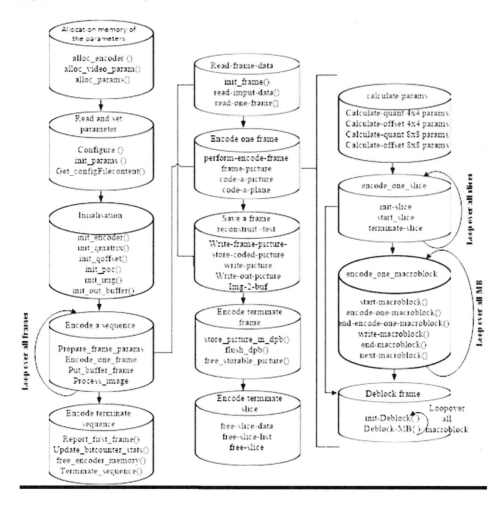

Principle of the Huffman Coding Algorithm

We add three blocks on the EL layer of the Wei-Da-Chien method "difference of images", "order of the coefficients", and "Huffman coding".

In order to get this bitstream, we created a project that consists of three steps related to the Huffman coder:

Step 1

Calculate the appearance probabilities of each character in the ordered image (see Table 2). In the ordered difference image, we got eleven symbols (0, 1, 2, 3, 4, 5, 6,

7, 8, 9, -). For a given symbol, we associate the corresponding value of the ASCII table (American Standard Code for Information Interchange). For example, if we count the occurrences of the number 7 in this file, then we will have: counter [7] = counter [55].

Table 2. The probability of appearance of the symbols

Symbols	Frequency of Appearance
3	32444
4	18926
5	12016
6	7357
9	1766
8	2932
7	4707
1	103693
2	59781
0	62778
-	123637

The establishment of the frequency table is shown in Figure 15.

Step 2

Génération binary codes according to these frequencies using the Huffman coding (see Table 3).

Step 3

Build the bitstream. A part of progress of the bitstream construction algorithm is summarized in part of algorithm 3 of the appendix.

After the implementation of this project, we did some tests to compare our results with the works of the state of the art. Table 4 summarizes the found results.

Our method provides better results than H.264 / AVC_LS _DPCM. We find these results because the two-layer structure maintains the two blocks of transformation and quantization to take advantage of their compression ratio and corrects the errors made of the base layer by a second bitstream.

Figure 15. Flowchart of the symbol counting function

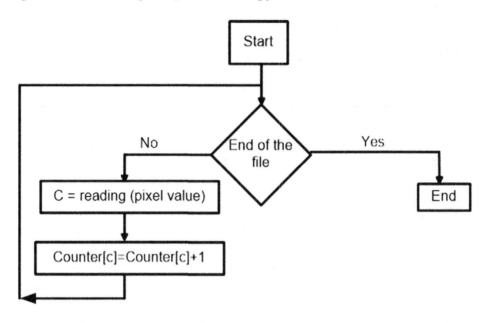

Table 3. The binary codes of the symbols

Symbols	Corresponding Binary Code
3	000
4	0010
5	00110
6	001110
9	00111100
8	00111101
7	0011111
1	01
2	100
0	101
-	11

On the other hand, H.264 / AVC_LS _DPCM transmitted the values of the prediction block directly to the entropy coding and these values are very large and strongly correlated (see Table 4).

Table 4. Comparison of the two-layer structure with H.264/AVC_LS _DPCM (Wei et al., 2009)

Sequences (50 Frames)	H.264/AVC_LS_DPCM (Kilobytes)	Method of Wei Da Chien (Kilobytes)	Our Method (Kilobytes)
Foreman	7955	7707	4608
Mobile	11611	10573	7216
Akiyo	6432	5944	3764
FootBall	7929	7515	5247
WaterFall	10213	9453	6881

During the first step of the CAVLC coding, that is to say the coding of the number of non-zero coefficients, the CAVLC is based on arrays that it chooses them according to a selection parameter N. This parameter depends on the neighboring blocks at the top and left of the current block (Nu and NL). On the other hand, the Huffman coding does not use the neighboring blocks, it deals only with the current coefficients that is the 11 symbols in our case (0-9 and the sign (-).

Based on the fact that the binary codes in the VLC arrays are variable lengths, it can be predicted, thus that the size of bitstream coded by CAVLC is more important than that obtained by the Huffman coding (see Tables 5-8 in the Appendix). Therefore, our method achieves better results than that of Wei Da Chien because the binary codes of Huffman are smaller than those of CAVLC (see Table 3).

CONCLUSION

The loss of information is the most important criterion for compression algorithms, because it directly affects the image or video debit and quality. That is why a great deal of research focused on the study of lossless compression: it ensures a decrease in the bitrate without degrading the visual quality.

This manuscript addressed the hierarchical lossless video coding for the standard H.264/AVC. The enhanced method provides reduction of total bits compared to previous works.

REFERENCES

Ammous, D., Kammoun, F., & Masmoudi, N. (2020, September). Analysis of Coding and Transfer of Arien Video Sequences from H. 264 Standard. In *5th International Conference on Advanced Technologies for Signal and Image Processing (ATSIP)* (pp. 1-5). IEEE. 10.1109/ATSIP49331.2020.9231819

Ammous, D., Kammoun, F., & Masmoudi, N. (2014, December). Improved Hierarchical lossless video coding. In *International Conference on Sciences and Techniques of Automatic Control and Computer Engineering (STA)* (pp. 525-530). IEEE.

Ammous, D., Khlif, N., Kammoun, F., & Masmoudi, N. (2019, December). Encryption of lossless coded videos. In *International Conference on Internet of Things, Embedded Systems and Communications (IINTEC)* (pp. 226-230). IEEE.

Brouard, O. (2010). *Pré-analyse de la vidéo pour un codage adapté. Application au codage de la TVHD en flux H. 264* [Doctoral dissertation]. Université de Nantes.

Chien, W. D., Liao, K. Y., & Yang, J. F. (2014). H. 264-based hierarchical two-layer lossless video coding method. *IET Signal Processing*, *8*(1), 21–29. doi:10.1049/iet-spr.2013.0088

Chien, W. D., Liao, K. Y., & Yang, J. F. (2011, December). H. 264-based Hierarchical Lossless Coding System with New Intra Prediction Method. In *International Conference on Intelligent Computation and Bio-Medical Instrumentation* (pp. 171-174). IEEE. 10.1109/ICBMI.2011.63

Dai, Y., Zhang, Q., Tourapis, A., & Kuo, C. C. J. (2008, October). Efficient block-based intra prediction for image coding with 2D geometrical manipulations. In *15th IEEE International Conference on Image Processing* (pp. 2916-2919). IEEE.

Ding, J. R., Chen, J. Y., Yang, F. C., & Yang, J. F. (2008, March). Two-layer and adaptive entropy coding algorithms for H. 264-based lossless image coding. In *IEEE International Conference on Acoustics, Speech and Signal Processing* (pp. 1369-1372). IEEE.

Heindel, A., Wige, E., & Kaup, A. (2016). Low-complexity enhancement layer compression for scalable lossless video coding based on HEVC. *IEEE Transactions on Circuits and Systems for Video Technology*, *27*(8), 1749–1760. doi:10.1109/TCSVT.2016.2556338

Heindel, A., Wige, E., & Kaup, A. (2014, October). Sample-based weighted prediction for lossless enhancement layer coding in SHVC. In *IEEE International Conference on Image Processing (ICIP)* (pp. 3656-3660). 10.1109/ICIP.2014.7025742

Huffman, D. A. (1952). A method for the construction of minimum-redundancy codes. *Proceedings of the IRE, 40*(9), 1098–1101. doi:10.1109/JRPROC.1952.273898

Kim, S. H., Kang, J. W., & Kuo, C. C. J. (2011). Improved H. 264/AVC lossless intra coding with two-layered residual coding (TRC). *IEEE Transactions on Circuits and Systems for Video Technology, 21*(7), 1005–1010. doi:10.1109/TCSVT.2011.2133170

Ou, X., Yang, L., Zhang, G., Guo, L., Wu, J., & Tu, B. (2016). Improved Adaptive Transform for Residue in H. 264/AVC Lossless Video Coding. *Automatika: časopis za automatiku, mjerenje, elektroniku, računarstvo i komunikacije, 57*(4), 1045-1055.

Schlockermann. (2003). *Film grain coding in H.264/AVC.* JVTI034d2.doc.

Suehring, K. (2015). *H. 264/AVC reference software.* http://iphome. hhi. de/suehring/ tml/

Suehring, K., & Li, X. (2016). JVET common test conditions and software reference configurations. *Jurnal Veteriner*, B1010.

Wang, L. L., & Siu, W. C. (2011). Improved lossless coding algorithm in H. 264/AVC based on hierarchical intra prediction and coding-mode selection. *Journal of Electronic Imaging, 20*(4), 043001. doi:10.1117/1.3644573

Wei, S. T., Shen, S. R., Liu, B. D., & Yang, J. F. (2009, November). Lossless image and video coding based on H. 264/AVC intra predictions with simplified interpolations. In *16th IEEE International Conference on Image Processing (ICIP)* (pp. 633-636). IEEE.

Wei, S. T., Tien, C. W., Liu, B. D., & Yang, J. F. (2011). Adaptive truncation algorithm for Hadamard-transformed H. 264/AVC lossless video coding. *IEEE Transactions on Circuits and Systems for Video Technology, 21*(5), 538–549. doi:10.1109/TCSVT.2011.2129030

Zhang, Q., Dai, Y., & Kuo, C. C. J. (2009, May). Lossless video compression with residual image prediction and coding (RIPC). In *IEEE International Symposium on Circuits and Systems* (pp. 617-620). IEEE. 10.1109/ISCAS.2009.5117824

APPENDIX

Part of the Algorithm 1

```
/////////////////////////////source image /////////////////////////
//////////////
for(i = 0 ; i < 304128 ; i++)
     {
     tab[i]= * (external_buffer_src + i);
     fprintf(Test,"%d ",tab[i]);
     ///printf("%d ",tab[i]);
/*if (i==1759)
     {fprintf(Test, "verficatio= %d ",i);}*///verification
     }
/////////////////////////////source image /////////////////////////
//////////////
////////////////////////inverse quantized transformed image
////////////////
for(i=0;i<p_Vid->height;i++)
  {
for (j=0; j<p_Vid->width; j++)
          {
               m[(i*(p_Vid->width)+j)]=p_Vid->enc_picture-
>imgY[i][j] ;    }}
for(i=0;i<p_Vid->height_cr;i++)
  {
for (j=0; j<p_Vid->width_cr; j++)
          {
               m[101376+(i*(p_Vid->width)+j)]=p_Vid->enc_
picture->imgUV[0][i][j];    }}
for(i=0;i<p_Vid->height_cr;i++)
  {
for (j=0; j<p_Vid->width_cr; j++)
          {
               m[(2*101376)+(i*(p_Vid->width)+j)]=p_Vid->enc_
picture->imgUV[1][i][j];    }}
for(i=0;i<304128;i++)
{fprintf(essai2,"%d ",m[i]);
/*if (i==1759)
     {fprintf(essai2, "verficatio= %d ",i);}*///verification
```

```
}
fclose(essai2);
/////////////////////////inverse quantized transformed image
/////////////////
////////////////////////////////image difference unordered
/////////////////
fp_residu = fopen(im_residu, "a+");//amina
for(ir = 0 ; ir < 304128 ; ir++)
{
residu_vect[ir] = tab[ir] - m[ir];
    fprintf(fp_residu, "%d ",residu_vect[ir]);//residu_
vect[ir]:coefficient non ordonnée
    /*if (ir==1759)
    {fprintf(fp_residu, "verficatio= %d ",ir);}*///
verification

}
fclose(fp_residu);
/////////////////////////////image difference unordered
/////////////////
```

Part of the Algorithm 2

```
for (x=0; x<MBX; x++)
    {
        comp = 4*x ;//x denotes the number of the current
block on the line of the image that contains 88 block ie block
0, block 1, block 2 .............. block 87
            jr = 4*4*88*y; //y denotes the number of the current
block on the column of the image which contains 72 block ie
block 0, block 1, block 2 ............... block 71
    /// horital one
        for (i=0; i<4; i++)
        {
        residu_ord[j] = residu_vect[i + comp +jr];
        fprintf(fp_residu_ord, "%d",residu_ord[j]);
            j++;
        }
    //horizontal bas
        for (i=0; i<4; i++)
```

```
        {
        residu_ord[j] = residu_vect[352*3+i + comp +jr];
        fprintf(fp_residu_ord, "%d",residu_ord[j]);
           j++;
        }
        //gauche
        for (i=1; i<3; i++)
        {
        residu_ord[j] = residu_vect[352*i + comp + jr ];
        fprintf(fp_residu_ord, "%d",residu_ord[j]);
           j++;
        }
        // droite
    for (i=1; i<3; i++)
        {
        residu_ord[j] = residu_vect[352*i + 3 + comp +jr  ];
        fprintf(fp_residu_ord, "%d",residu_ord[j]);
        j++;
        }
//    fprintf(fp_residu_ord, " fin MBX %d \n ", x);
```

Part of the Algorithm 3

```
dec_val1= (unsignedchar*)malloc(sizeof(unsignedchar) *
(size1));
bin_val1= (unsignedchar*)malloc(sizeof(unsignedchar) *
(size2));
fichier1 = fopen("partie2.txt","r");
        fichier2 = fopen("correction_2.txt","a+");
        fichier3 = fopen("verification2.txt","a+");
        getchar();//donia
    do
    {
        for(jj=0;jj<304128;jj++)
                    {
                     fread(&dec_val1[jj],1,(size*1.45),fic
hier1);
                            if(dec_val1[jj]==49)
                                    {    printf ("valeur=%d",
dec_val1[jj]);
```

```
fprintf (fichier3, "valeur=%d", dec_val1[jj]);
                              for (i = 0; i < 2; ++i)
                               {
                              bin_val1[k] = arr1[i];
                              //printf("bin_val1[%d]=%d,
arr1[%d]=%d", k, bin_val1[k], i, arr1[i]);
/*printf("%d", bin_val1[k]);*///essai1
fprintf(fichier2,"%d", bin_val1[k]);//donia
                              //  fprintf(fichier2,"bin_
val1[%d]=%d", k, bin_val1[k]);//donia
                k++;

                                             }

//getchar();//donia
                               }
```

Table 5. Codes of Tot_Coeff and T1s

T1s	Tot_Coeff	$0 \le nC < 2$	$2 \le nC < 4$	$4 \le nC < 8$	$nC \ge 8$
0	0	1	11	1111	000011
0	1	000101	001011	001111	000000
1	1	01	10	1110	000001
0	2	00000111	000111	001011	000100
1	2	000100	00111	01111	000101
2	2	001	011	1101	000110
0	3	000000111	0000111	001000	001000
1	3	00000110	001010	01100	001001
2	3	0000101	001001	01110	001010
3	3	00011	0101	1100	001011
0	4	0000000111	00000111	0001111	001100
1	4	000000110	000110	01010	001101
2	4	00000101	000101	01011	001110
3	4	000011	0100	1011	001111
0	5	00000000111	00000100	0001011	010000
1	5	0000000110	0000110	01000	010001
2	5	000000101	0000101	01001	010010
3	5	0000100	00110	1010	010011
0	6	0000000001111	000000111	0001001	010100
1	6	00000000110	00000110	001110	010101
2	6	0000000101	00000101	001101	010110
3	6	00000100	001000	1001	010111
0	7	0000000001011	00000001111	0001000	011000
1	7	0000000001110	000000110	001010	011001
2	7	00000000101	000000101	001001	011010
3	7	000000100	000100	1000	011011
0	8	0000000001000	00000001011	00001111	011100
1	8	0000000001010	00000001110	0001110	011101
2	8	0000000001101	00000001101	0001101	011110
3	8	0000000100	0000100	01101	011111
0	9	00000000001111	000000001111	00001011	100000
1	9	00000000001110	00000001010	00001110	100001
2	9	0000000001001	00000001001	0001010	100010
3	9	00000000100	000000100	00110	10011
0	10	00000000001011	000000001011	000001111	100100

continues on following page

Table 5. Continues

Tls	Tot_Coeff	$0 \leq nC < 2$	$2 \leq nC < 4$	$4 \leq nC < 8$	$nC \geq 8$
1	10	000000001010	000000001110	00001010	100101
2	10	00000000001101	000000001101	00001101	10010
3	10	0000000001100	00000001100	0001100	100111
0	11	00000000000111	000000001000	000001011	101000
1	11	000000000001110	000000001010	000001110	101001
2	11	00000000001001	000000001001	00001001	101010
3	11	00000000001100	00000001000	00001100	101011
0	12	000000000001011	0000000001111	000001000	101100
1	12	000000000001010	0000000001110	000001010	101101
2	12	000000000001101	0000000001101	000001101	101110
3	12	0000000000100	000000001100	00001000	101111
0	13	0000000000001111	0000000001011	0000001101	110000
1	13	000000000000001	0000000001010	000000111	110001
2	13	000000000001001	0000000001001	000001001	110010
3	13	000000000001100	0000000001100	000001100	110011
0	14	0000000000001011	0000000000111	0000001001	110100
1	14	0000000000001110	00000000001011	0000001100	110101
2	14	0000000000001101	0000000000110	0000001011	110110
3	14	000000000001000	0000000001000	0000001010	110111
0	15	0000000000000111	00000000001001	0000000101	111000
1	15	0000000000001010	00000000001000	0000001000	111001
2	15	0000000000001100	0000000000001	0000000110	111011
3	15	0000000000001100	0000000000001	0000000110	111011
0	16	0000000000000100	00000000000111	0000000001	111100
1	16	0000000000000110	00000000000110	0000000100	111101
2	16	0000000000000101	0000000000101	0000000011	111110
3	16	0000000000001000	00000000000100	0000000010	111111

Table 6. NZ Coeff codes according to VLC tables

VLC 0		VLC 1		VLC 2		VLC 3		VLC 4		VLC 5		VLC 6	
Code	NZ Coeff	Code	NZ Coeff	Code	NZ Coeff	Code	NZ Coeff	Code	NZ Coeff	Code	NZ Coeff	Code	NZ Coeff
1	1	1x	±1	1xx	±1 à ±2	1xxx	±1 à ±4	1xxxx	±1 à ±8	1xxxxx	±1 à ±16	1xxxxxx	±1 à ±32
01	-1	01x	±2	01xx	±3 à ±4	01xxx	±5 à ±8	01xxxx	±9 à ±16	01xxxxx	±17 à ±32	01xxxxxx	±33 à ±64
001	2	001x	±3	001xx	±5 à ±6	001xxx	±9 à ±12	001xxxx	±17 à ±24	001xxxxx	±33 à ±64	…	…
0001	-2	0001x	±4	0001xx	±7 à ±8	0001xxx	±13 à ±15	0001xxxx	±25 à ±32	…	…	…	…
00001	3	00001x	±5	00001xx	±9 à ±10	00001xxx	±17 à ±19	…	…	…	…	…	…
000001	-3	000001x	±6	000001xx	±11 à ±12	…	…	…	…	…	…	…	…
0000001	4	0000001x	±7	…	…	…	…	…	…	…	…	…	…
00000001	-4	…	…	…	…	…	…	…	…	…	…	…	…
…	…	…	…	…	…	…	…	…	…	…	…	…	…

133

Table 7. Tot_Zeros codes according to Tot_Coeff for blocks 4x4

Tot_Zeros	Tot_Coeff														
	1	2	3	4	5	6	7	8	9	10	11	12	13	14	15
0	1	111	0101	00011	0101	000001	000001	000001	000001	00001	0000	0000	000	00	0
1	011	110	111	111	0100	00001	00001	0001	000000	00000	0001	0001	001	01	1
2	010	101	110	0101	0011	111	101	00001	0001	001	001	01	1	1	
3	0011	100	101	0100	111	110	100	011	11	11	010	1	01		
4	0010	011	0100	110	110	101	011	11	10	10	1	001			
5	00011	0101	0011	101	101	100	11	10	001	01	011				
6	00010	0100	100	100	100	011	010	010	01	0001					
7	000011	0011	011	0011	011	010	010	001	00001						
8	000010	0010	0010	011	0010	0001	0001	000000							
9	0000011	00011	00011	0010	00001	001	001								
10	0000010	00010	00010	00010	0001	000000	000000								
11	00000011	000011	000001	00001	00000										
12	00000010	000010	00001	00000											
13	000000011	000001	000000												
14	000000010	000000													
15	000000001														

Table 8. Codes of Run_Before

Run_Before	Zeros_Left						
	1	**2**	**3**	**4**	**5**	**6**	**>6**
0	1	1	11	11	11	11	111
1	0	01	10	10	10	000	110
2	-	00	01	01	011	001	101
3	-	-	00	001	010	011	100
4	-	-	-	000	001	010	011
5	-	-	-	-	000	101	010
6	-	-	-	-	-	100	001
7	-	-	-	-	-	-	0001
8	-	-	-	-	-	-	00001
9	-	-	-	-	-	-	000001
10	-	-	-	-	-	-	0000001
11	-	-	-	-	-	-	00000001
12	-	-	-	-	-	-	000000001
13	-	-	-	-	-	-	0000000001
14	-	-	-	-	-	-	00000000001

Chapter 6
Efficient Speech Recognition System Based on an Improved MFCC Features Using LWT

Mnasri Aymen
University of Tunis El Manar, Tunisia

Oussama Boufares
University of Tunis El Manar, Tunisia

ABSTRACT

Creating a system that can hear and respond accurately like a human is one of the most critical issues in human-computer interaction. This inspired the creation of the automatic speech recognition system, which uses efficient feature extraction and selection techniques to distinguish between different classes of speech signals. In order to improve the ASR (automatic speech recognition), the authors present a new feature extraction method in this study which is based on modified MFCC (mel frequency cepstral coefficients) using lifting wavelet transform LWT (lifting wavelet transform). The effectiveness of the proposed approach is verified using the datasets of the ATSSEE Research Unit "Analysis and Processing of Electrical and Energy Signals and Systems." The experimental investigations have been carried out to demonstrate the practical viability of the proposed approach. Numerical and experimental studies concluded that the proposed approach is capable of detecting and localizing multiple under varying environmental conditions with noise-contaminated measurements.

DOI: 10.4018/978-1-6684-4945-5.ch006

INTRODUCTION

The quickest, most natural, and most popular way for people to communicate is through speech. A speech signal is seen as a complex signal that not only transmits a message but also contains details about the speaker's personality, including gender, age, language, dialect, and emotional state. Speaking to a machine is one of the techniques to improve and speed up human-computer contact, which has developed as a result of technological advancement. As a result, during the past few decades, academics have investigated many ways to improve the effectiveness of spoken communication through systems like speaker and voice recognition. To develop a speech recognition system that can hear and reply naturally like a human is one of the industry's top. This has given rise to the crucial and difficult field of Automatic Speech Recognition (ASR) in recent years. The accuracy, speed, and intimacy of daily interactions between people and machines can all be improved through speech recognition. ASR has seen extensive use recently, including in the design of automobiles, smart phones, video games, internet call centers, and emergency medical situations.

The field of voice recognition faces numerous obstacles despite the availability of numerous techniques. For instance, the extraction and selection of effective features typically has an impact on the classification accuracy in speech emotion identification problems.

The performance of current voice control systems is acceptable under well-controlled conditions of use (no echo, absence of noise, etc.). These details are strongly linked to the difficulty and complexity of the planned activity. Currently, the recognition rate of isolated words obtained in laboratories (noise constraints considered non-existent) in mono-speaker mode reaches 99%. On the other hand, as soon as the voice control systems move in a real environment (the conditions for learning and using a system are different), the recognition rate deteriorates rapidly. Deterioration in performance is dependent on the level and type of noise. These systems are therefore, on the whole, not very robust to environmental fluctuations, even if these may seem weak to the human ear. In addition, a recognition system will generally be integrated into a dedicated device (voice recognition, GPS control,) Of course, the acceleration of the recognition should not lead to a significant drop in the performance of the recognition systems. The latest American experiments on real-time speech recognition have however shown remarkable drops in system performance when the operation of the latter is constrained by time. These results thus validate the need for effective methods that reduce the recognition time without incurring performance losses in real environments. Several techniques have been proposed to increase the robustness of ASR systems, in real environments (various sound environments). The recognition machine needs a specific algorithm that can be used with feature extraction and classification methods in order to recognize speech features. There are many feature extraction techniques, which requires choosing the right technique for a particular type of speech signal (Mohan et al., 2014). Mel frequency cepstral coefficients (MFCC) and linear predictive coding (LPC) and linear predictive cepstral coefficients (LPCC) are the three most frequently used techniques to analyze speech signals (Gaikwad et al., 2011). The main reason why the MFCC approach is preferred is that the speech recognition system finds it accurate (Gaikwad et al., 2011, 2017). There has already been research on the MFCC algorithm's development, and one of the changes made was to incorporate a median filter (Attawibulkul et al., 2017). The study produced system accuracy that was higher than that of traditional MFCC techniques. Analyzing the MFCC algorithm's windowing procedure is another approach of conducting research for the advancement of the MFCC method (Gaikwad et al., 2017). MFCC has decent accuracy, but precision still needs to be further enhanced to get the best outcomes. The study of the creation of a machine algorithm for the recognition of Indonesian speech using the MFCC approach is crucial to be carried out in the light of these considerations. It was expected that by integrating MFCC and PCA the system accuracy would improve, and the feature data size would decrease (Jhawar et al., 2016). The foundation of a language is a vowel (Jhawar et al., 2016). In reality, many feature extraction techniques involve wavelet transforms, as demonstrated by Jhawar et al. (2016)'s study of Indonesian voice recognition. Six different wavelet types were compared to the recognition system's accuracy in the study. The outcomes demonstrated that, when compared to other types, the Haar type of wavelet produces the best performance. However, Wavelet transformation, a feature extraction technique, can also be used to denoise speech signals. In their study on denoising employing wavelet implementation in electromagnetic signals by comparing to various thresholding selection procedures (Safta et al., 2017; Mnassri et al., 2019).

This paper proposed a novel extract feature, called modified and improved Time-Frequency features Cepstral features, based on LWT this method using wavelet transformation used on MFCC feature extraction in Arabic speech recognition system. The method process focused on identifying the type of the wavelet transform appropriate for the MFCC feature extraction method to generate the optimal speech recognition system accuracy.

ASR ARCHITECTURE

Feature extraction, feature selection (reduction), and classification are the three main components of speech recognition. The most crucial part of the feature extraction process is the ASR because effective features for emotion recognition are unclear as well as vocal variety. The studies show that a voice signal is produced by the vocal tract's output, which is stimulated by the signal source. Consequently, unique information like the emotional state of the vocal tract can be used to extract the speaker's voice during the utterance and the intriguing source's qualities. Here, we provide a description of the theoretical underpinnings of our research, as well as a survey of the literature, other ASR research' emotional speech datasets, characteristics, and classifiers.

Our study begins with a complete analysis of the original MFCC coefficients and their first (MFCC+Δ) and second (MFCC+$\Delta\Delta$) derivatives. Generally, in automatic speech recognition systems, only the first 20 MFCC coefficients are used. In fact, the proposed idea is based on the exploitation of different numbers of MFCC coefficients in order to find the best combination that gives the maximum recognition rate. Moreover, to improve the objective characterization of a portion of the speech signal, we used the first and second derivatives of the MFCCs coefficients which provides additional information on the dynamics of the temporal variation in the original MFCCs coefficients. Indeed, the combination of the original MFCCs coefficients as well as the vector composed of the MFCCs coefficients and their first derivatives (MFCC+Δ) and their first and second derivatives (MFCC+$\Delta\Delta$) respectively are used for the extraction of the characteristics of the speech signal. Finally, a comparative study is presented in order to verify their improvement in the proposed algorithm. On the other hand, we have used in this work the support vector machine (SVM) as a classification algorithm for the recognition of isolated words, the SVM method has known a very interesting progress in its principle, its implementation, and its extension to multi-class problems. As a result, various applications have experienced great success with the use of SVMs such as face recognition, handwriting recognition. There are two main reasons for its use: first, the SVM training process is guaranteed to converge to the global minimum of the associated cost function. Second, SVMs exhibit a higher generalization ability.

The Proposed Feature Extraction Approach

The feature extraction method plays a vital role in the speech recognition task. Indeed, some of the classical analysis methods may suffer from lack of data and be poorly estimated. These imperfections present in some poorly modeled areas can cause recognition failure. This results in a loss of information due to the fact that the parameters are limited in terms of extracting the information contained in the signal. The general principle of the combination of the acoustic parameters consists in concatenating additional parameters in a vector of acoustic parameters resulting from a traditional method of analysis which aims to reinforce the effectiveness and to increase the robustness of the systems in the various test conditions.

Figure 2 gives the steps for calculating the LWTMFCC coefficients.

Figure 1. Automatic speech recognition system algorithm

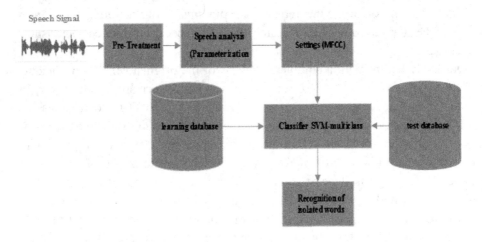

Figure 2. The proposed parametrization algorithm LWTMFCC

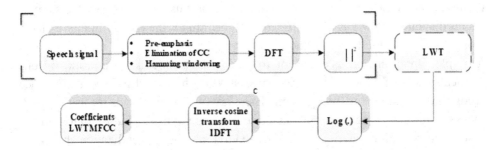

Mel-Frequency Cepstral Coefficients Extraction

The calculation principle of MFCCs is based on psychoacoustic research on the perception and pitch of different frequency bands by the human ear. The fast Fourier transform (FFT: fast Fourier transform) passes through a one-scale, non-linear filter bank (Mel Scale), which mainly takes into account the fact that the perception of the intervals changes according to the zone of the spectrum in which the heights that compose them belong. The main advantage of these coefficients is to extract relevant information in limited number by relying on both speech perception (Mels scale) and both on production (Cepstral theory) (Alcaraz Meseguer et al., 2009).

Figure 3. Relationship between frequency scale and mel scale

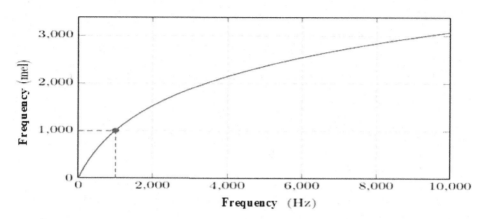

MFCCs are based on the mel scale. A mel is a unit of measurement of the perceived pitch or frequency of a tone. In 1940, Stevens and Volkman assigned 1000 mels at 1000 Hz, and asked participants to change the frequency until they perceived that the pitch had changed in proportion from the reference tone. Threshold frequencies were marked, resulting in a mapping between the actual frequency scale (in Hz) and the perceived frequency scale (in mel). A popular formula for converting from frequency scale to mel scale is:

$$f_{mel} = 1127 \ln(1 + \frac{f_{Hz}}{700}) \tag{1}$$

Where f_{mel} is the frequency in mels and f_{Hz} is the normal frequency in Hz. MFCCs are often calculated using a filter bank of M filters, each has a triangular shape and is evenly spaced on the mel scale. Each filter is defined by:

$$H_m[k] = \begin{cases} 0 & k < f[m-1] \\ \dfrac{k - f[m-1]}{f[m] - f[m-1]} & f[m-1] < k \le f[m] \\ \dfrac{f[m+1] - k}{f[m-1] - f[m]} & f[m] \le k < f[m+1] \\ 0 & k \ge f[m+1] \end{cases} \tag{2}$$

Given the DFT of the input signal with N as the sample size:

141

$$X[k] = \sum_{n=0}^{N-1} x[n] e^{-j2\Pi kn/N} \tag{3}$$

Let's set $f_{\min}$ and $f_{\max}$ the lowest and highest frequencies of the filter bank in Hz and F_s the sample rate. $M+2$ Boundary points (m= -1, 0, ..., M) are evenly spaced between $f_{\min}$ and $f_{\max}$ on the mel scale

$$f[m] = \frac{N}{F_s} B^{-1}(B(f_{\min}) + m \frac{B(f_{\max}) - B(f_{\min})}{M+1}) \tag{4}$$

Although the traditional cepstrum uses the inverse discrete Fourier transform (IDFT), mel frequency cepstrum is normally implemented using the discrete cosine transform

$$\hat{x}[n] = \sum_{m=0}^{M-1} S[m] \cos\left[(m + \frac{1}{2})\frac{\Pi n}{M}\right] \quad n= 0,1,...,M{-}1 \tag{5}$$

Typically, the number of letters ranges from 20 to 40, and the number of retained coefficients is 13. Some research has shown that the performance of speech recognition and speaker identification systems peaks with 32 to 35 filters. Many speech recognition systems eliminate the zero coefficient from MFCCs because it is the average signal power. The main steps for calculating MFCCs parameters is presented in Figure 4.

Figure 4. Calculation of MFCC coefficients

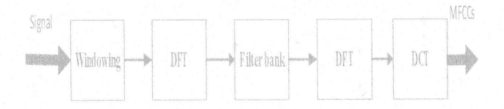

The Lifting Wavelet Transform or LWT

A lifting wavelet is a wavelet transformation implementation that differs from that accomplished by filter banks. It is a procedure that is optimized in terms of the number of operations to execute and memory use. Calculating the LWT, for example, takes half the time it takes to calculate the FFT (Lei et al., 2012). the approach is to split the signal to be changed first, then enhance its attributes by alternating the prediction and update processes: Split step: In this step, the input signal E[n] is split into two subsets, each of which has no common elements and is half the length of E[n]. The original signal is usually separated into two subsets: an odd subset Xo[n]=X[2n+1] and an even subset Xe=X[2n]. Predict step: The predict operator designated P predicts the odd signal Xo[n] based on the even signal X e [n], and the mistakes are known as wavelet coefficients or D[n], which are defined as follows:

$$D[n] = X_o[n] - P(X_e[n]) \tag{6}$$

Update step: This step, dubbed U, is applied to wavelet coefficients D[n], and the outcome is the sum of the odd signal Xe [n] and the updated D[n] signal, which is referred to as scale coefficients C[n]:

$$C[n] = X_e[n] + U(D[n]) \tag{7}$$

The purpose of the LWTMFCC analysis is to estimate the wavelet packet decomposition coefficients. These coefficients are compressed before being analyzed by linear prediction. This last step is actually a spectral compression technique which modifies the short-term power spectrum before its approximation by an autoregressive model.

Classification Method

The development of an automatic system capable of speech recognition with the minimum possible errors is an application that requires the contribution of several factors. Indeed, in addition to an excellent technique for extracting the relevant parameters from the speech signal, the phase of the classification must be granted to a classifier with a large

- Ability to discriminate. For this our choice is fixed on the SVMs models. The main reason for using SVMs is due to their following advantages:

- These are discriminant methods that allow the construction of non-linear classification surfaces, however most of the other methods used in the field of automatic speech recognition are limited to linear solutions,
- These are adaptive methods that allow systems to evolve according to the characteristics of the task they have to perform, especially in the case of incremental learning in real ASR applications.
- These are methods based on statistical estimation techniques from examples of known classes (supervised classification techniques)
- Excellent results are obtained by these methods in speaker verification and image processing which are two areas very close to automatic speech recognition.

Most SVM algorithms can only handle a two-class problem. There are several extensions of a binary classification SVM to multi-class classification tasks (classes, $k^3 3$). Recently, hierarchical methods for multi-class SVMs start from the dataset, divide the data hierarchically into two subsets until each subset consists of only one class. Indeed, in our work we have used two methods which are the most popular: "one against all" and "one against one". Indeed the general idea of classification by SVMs is to associate each voice command of our database with a clearly determined class using the two methods "one against all" and "one against one": or the strategy 'one against all' will build eleven different classifiers where the ith class separates the ith class from the rest, and the 'one against one' strategy builds 11 (11-1) /2= 55 classifiers, using all the binary combinations of the eleven classes. Figures 5 and 6 summarize the approach followed for learning the machine vector support with the two strategies: "one against one" (Liu et al., 2017) and "one against all" (Liu et al., 2005).

The recognition procedure consists in determining the class to which the candidate word belongs. The word to be recognized is represented by an acoustic vector, which will be presented to the machine vector support model. The class of the word to be recognized (winning class) is the most voted class that maximizes the decision function.

EXPERIMENT RESULTS AND DISCUSSION

We evaluated the performance of the proposed LWTMFCC method in the noisy environment by different types of environmental noise (white Gaussein noise: white, real noise: babble, colored noise: pink. The results of the proposed method are compared by two speech denoising methods: Wiener filter and spectral subtraction.

Figure 5. Learning SVM with the strategy: "one against one"

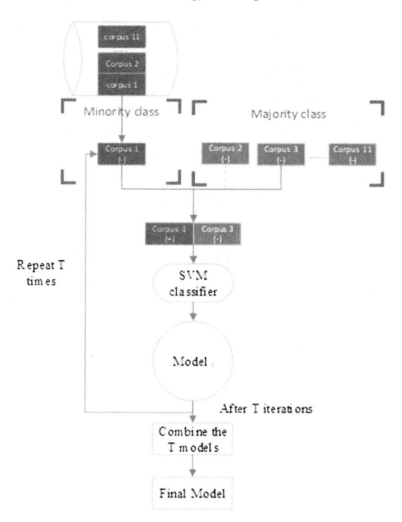

The parameters of the noise reduction techniques used are:

- For spectral subtraction (SS).
  A Hamming window of length 512 with 50% overlap and a DFT of order 512.
- For Wiener filter denoising.
  A Hamming window of length 512 with 50% overlap and a DFT of order 512.

Figure 6. Learning SVM with the strategy: "one against all"

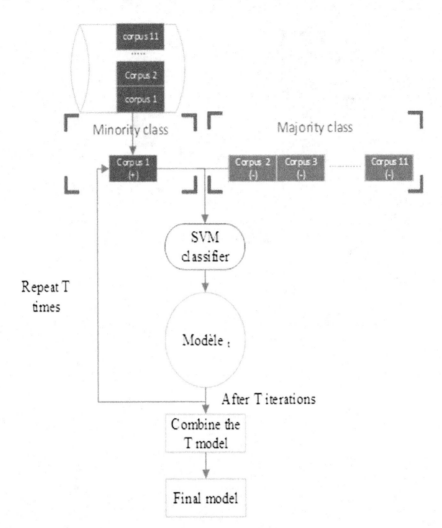

We have built our own speech database which contains eleven Arabic words (yamin, yassar, amam, asraa, khalfa, waraa, istader, takadam, istamer, tawakaf, tarajaa). We used Audacity software (V.1.3) to record vocabulary sound files.

In addition, the database contains 30 occurrences of each of the eleven commands under favorable conditions with the voices of two men and one woman. We will use two thirds of this base for learning and the rest for the recognition test. The voices were recorded in a soundproof chamber using a condenser microphone that was comfortably attached so that the distance to the lips remained constant during the speech. Each element of the speech corpus is recorded at a 16KHz sampling rate and tagged with the corresponding word. Finally, the sound files representing the vocabularies are saved in (. wav) format. Table 1 provides more details on the sample data used in our research.

Figure 7-9 show the performance of our recognition system in the noisy environment in terms of recognition rate with the different noise reduction techniques compared to our proposed method.

Table 1. Speech database used

Pronunciation	Arabic Script
Takadam	تقدم
Amam	امام
Istamer	استمر
Asraa	اسرع
Yassar	يسار
Yamin	يمين
Istader	استدر
Tawakaf	توقف
Tarajaa	تراجع
Khalfa	خلف
Waraa	وراء

Figure 7. Recognition rate of different denoising methods: 'white noise'

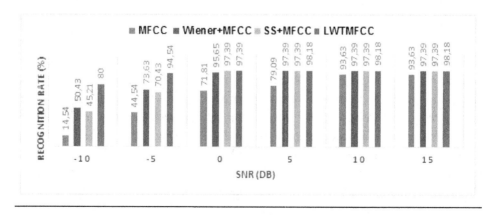

Figure 8. Recognition rate of different denoising methods: 'babble noise'

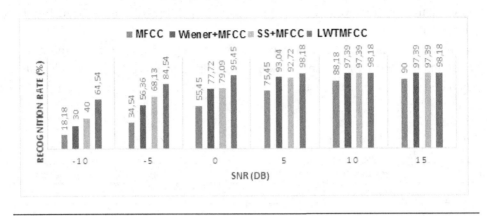

Figure 9. Recognition rate of different denoising methods: 'pink noise'

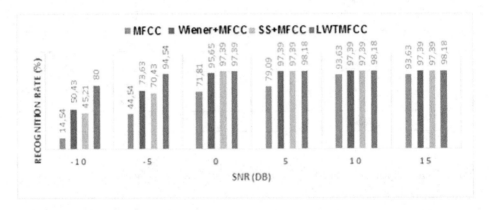

The results obtained allow us to say that: the insertion of a denoising module based on (ss) and (wiener) upstream of the recognition system improves the recognition rate in a noisy environment for SNR values below 0 db. The values of the recognition rates obtained after denoising approach the rates of the signals without noise for SNR values greater than 0 db. denoising techniques significantly improve the recognition rate, especially for SNR 0db, 5db and 10db the denoising method with thresholding offers good performance by increasing the rate by at most 28.18% compared to the wiener filter technique and more than 16% compared to the spectral subtraction technique when the system becomes perturbed for an snr -5db for "babble" type noise In summary, the proposed LWT/MFCC parametrization techniques provide the best recognition rates in both clean and noisy environments and also provide robustness for the recognition task.

CONCLUSION

In this study, a new feature extraction method using adaptive time-frequency coefficients is proposed to improve the accuracy of speech recognition. In the proposed method, we have tried to find a set of features that improve the speech recognition accuracy in different environments. To achieve this goal, the validity of the proposed method is experimentally compared to other speech denoising methods on the same data sets. When the experimental results are reviewed, this study shows that the proposed feature extraction is effective in characterizing and recognizing speech in various environments, compared to other works.

REFERENCES

Alcaraz Meseguer, N. (2009). *Speech analysis for automatic speech recognition* [Master's thesis]. Institutt for elektronikk og telekommunikasjon.

Attawibulkul, S., Kaewkamnerdpong, B., & Miyanaga, Y. (2017). Noisy speech training in MFCC-based speech recognition with noise suppression toward robot assisted autism therapy. In *2017 10th Biomedical Engineering International Conference (BMEiCON)* (pp. 1-5). IEEE. 10.1109/BMEiCON.2017.8229135

Gaikwad, S., Gawali, B., Yannawar, P., & Mehrotra, S. (2011). Feature extraction using fusion MFCC for continuous marathi speech recognition. In *2011 Annual IEEE India Conference* (pp. 1-5). IEEE. 10.1109/INDCON.2011.6139372

Hidayat, R., & Ikawijaya, W. (2015). Wavelet based feature extraction for the vowel sound. In *2015 International Conference on Information Technology Systems and Innovation (ICITSI)* (pp. 1-4). IEEE. 10.1109/ICITSI.2015.7437702

Jhawar, G., Nagraj, P., & Mahalakshmi, P. (2016). Speech disorder recognition using MFCC. In *2016 International Conference on Communication and Signal Processing (ICCSP)* (pp. 0246-0250). IEEE. 10.1109/ICCSP.2016.7754132

Lei, B., Soon, Y., Zhou, F., Li, Z., & Lei, H. (2012). A robust audio watermarking scheme based on lifting wavelet transform and singular value decomposition. *Signal Processing*, *92*(9), 1985–2001. doi:10.1016/j.sigpro.2011.12.021

Liu, Y., Bi, J. W., & Fan, Z. P. (2017). A method for multi-class sentiment classification based on an improved one-vs-one (OVO) strategy and the support vector machine (SVM) algorithm. *Information Sciences*, *394*, 38–52. doi:10.1016/j.ins.2017.02.016

Liu, Y., & Zheng, Y. F. (2005). One-against-all multi-class SVM classification using reliability measures. In *Proceedings 2005 IEEE International Joint Conference on Neural Network* (Vol. 2, pp. 849-854). IEEE. 10.1109/IJCNN.2005.1555963

Mnassri, A., Bennasr, M., & Adnane, C. (2019). A robust feature extraction method for real-time speech recognition system on a raspberry Pi 3 board. *Engineering, Technology & Applied Scientific Research*, 9(2), 4066–4070.

Mohan, B. J. (2014). Speech recognition using MFCC and DTW. In 2014 international conference on advances in electrical engineering (ICAEE) (pp. 1-4). IEEE.

Safta, M., Svasta, P., & Dima, M. O. (2017). Wavelet signal denoising applied on electromagnetic traces. In *2017 IEEE 23rd International Symposium for Design and Technology in Electronic Packaging (SIITME)* (pp. 399-402). IEEE. 10.1109/SIITME.2017.8259934

Saste, S. T., & Jagdale, S. M. (2017). Emotion recognition from speech using MFCC and DWT for security system. In 2017 international conference of electronics, communication and aerospace technology (ICECA) (Vol. 1, pp. 701-704). IEEE. doi:10.1109/ICECA.2017.8203631

Chapter 7
Convergence Analysis for Identification of Multivariable Delayed Systems

Yamna Ghoul
National Engineering School of Sfax, Tunisia

Naoufel Zitouni
National Engineering School of Tunis, Tunisia

ABSTRACT

Identification of system is one of the most important steps in industrial process automation studies. The modeling of a process aims to establish a representation linking the variables of the process, either from an approach of understanding the phenomena involved or from a mathematical processing of the data collected on the process. The object of identification is to estimate the parameters of the models thus obtained. In this chapter, the convergence of a prediction error method applied for the identification of multivariable delayed systems is proven. Indeed, a multivariable system with multiple time delays is used. Then a convergence study is given. A numerical example based on a thermostatic mixing valves process is finally introduced to prove the robustness of the proposed scheme.

INTRODUCTION

Identification of system is one of the most important steps in industrial process automation studies.

DOI: 10.4018/978-1-6684-4945-5.ch007

The modeling of a process aims to establish a representation linking the variables of the process, either from an approach of understanding the phenomena involved, or from a mathematical processing of the data collected on the process.

The object of identification is to estimate the parameters of the models thus obtained.

The keystone of the study of an industrial process resides essentially in the quality and relevance of this representation which doesn't happen without some theoretical and practical difficulties.

Very often, the exact models of the installations studied, when they exist, are very complex. Indeed, they involve a large number of variables, they can be represented by a number of sub-models and are rarely described by linear equations, or differential equations with linear coefficients. Thus, the quality of the representation will be improved if there are precise, reliable and consistent identification methods taking account of these characteristics.

On the other hand, it is well known that time delays are unavoidable in the operation of many industrial process models (Ligang et al., 2015; Liu et al., 2013). As a result, the identification of time delay models is indeed a problem of considerable importance which deserves special attention in virtually all disciplines of science and engineering (Leylaz et al., 2022, 2021; Jiu & Qiu, 2019; Na et al., 2014; Zheng et al., 2015; Beauduin, 2017; Bedoui et al., 2013).

Indeed, several studies have previously been conducted on the issue. In (Bedoui et al., 2013), the problem of simultaneous identification of linear discrete time delay multivariable systems has been addressed by using the least square approach. In Atitallah et al. (2016) an optimization approach based on an hierarchical scheme to estimate the time delay and the parameters of Wiener time-delay systems has been proposed.

In Chandrasekaran and Chidambaram (2012), the closed-loop identification of multivariable delayed systems having time delays has been presented based on optimization method using the combined step-up and step-down responses.

In Bedoui et al. (2012), an algorithm for simultaneous identification of unknown time delays and parameters of interconnected discrete-time delay multivariable systems has been proposed. The developed algorithm consists in constructing a linear-parameter formulation by using a generalized vector observation of each subsystem and using the recursive least squares approach to solve the obtained system.

In this research work, the prediction error method (PEM) is used. The identification method is implemented by using an implicit filtering procedure in order to generate the input/output time derivatives. Then, a convergence analysis of the proposed method is presented under some conditions.

The offered work is divided into six portions: In Section II, a description of the problem statement is presented. Section III presents an instance for the proposed scheme. In Section IV, a convergence analysis of the presented technique is proven under some conditions. We present then in Section V a real process to confirm the validity of the developed method. In the final section, the main achievements are summarized.

PROBLEM STATEMENT

Consider the following delayed multivariable process in the continuous time domain:

$$y(t) = \frac{Q_1(s)}{P(s)} e^{-h_1 s} x_1(t) + \ldots + \frac{Q_r(s)}{P(s)} e^{-h_r s} x_r(t). \tag{1}$$

$x(t) = [x_1(t) \ldots x_r(t)]$ and $y(t)$ indicate, respectively, the input vector and the output of the process. $e^{-h_j s}$ is the time delay operator between the output and the j-th corresponding input.

Equation (1) can then be expressed as:

$$y(t) = \frac{Q_1(s)}{P(s)} x_1(t - h_1) + \ldots + \frac{Q_r(s)}{P(s)} x_r(t - h_r), \tag{2}$$

$Q_j(s)$ and $P(s)$ are presented in the following forms:

$$Q_j(s) = q_{j0} + q_{j1} s + \ldots + q_{j m_j} s^{m_j}, \tag{3}$$

$$P(s) = 1 + p_1 s + \ldots + p_n s^n \tag{4}$$

The estimated output is contaminated by a distribution noise such that:

$$\hat{y}(t) = y(t) + e(t). \tag{5}$$

The vector containing the estimated parameters and the estimated time delays is defined as:

$$\hat{\Gamma}^T = \left[\hat{\theta}, \hat{h}\right]^T. \tag{6}$$

Such that

$$\hat{\theta}^T = [\hat{p}^T, \hat{q}_1^T, ..., \hat{q}_r^T],\tag{7}$$

with

$$\begin{aligned}\hat{p}^T &= [\hat{p}_1, ..., \hat{p}_n],\\\hat{q}_j^T &= [\hat{q}_{j1}, ..., \hat{q}_{jm_j}],\end{aligned}\tag{8}$$

$$\hat{h}^T = [\hat{h}_1, ..., \hat{h}_r].\tag{9}$$

The considered process described in (2) is depicted in Figure 1.

Figure 1. Multivariable delayed process

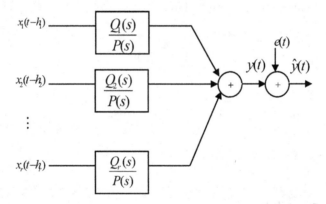

PROPOSED METHOD

The cost function is:

$$\vartheta(\hat{\Gamma}) = \int_0^t \varepsilon^2(t)dt.\tag{10}$$

The predicted output error is computed by:

$$\varepsilon(t) = y(t) - \hat{y}(t).\tag{11}$$

The estimated output can be written in the classical form as follows:

$$\hat{y}(t) = \varphi^T(t, \hat{h})\hat{\theta}. \tag{12}$$

$\varphi^T(t, \hat{h})$ is the observation vector computed in the following manner:

$$\varphi^T(t, \hat{h}) = [-\varphi^T_{[y]}(t), \varphi^T_{[x_1]}(t), ..., \varphi^T_{[x_r]}(t)]. \tag{13}$$

By using the prediction error method, we compute:

$$\hat{\Gamma}^{(j+1)} = \hat{\Gamma}^{(j)} + \Delta\hat{\Gamma}^{(j)}, \tag{14}$$

with

$$\Delta\hat{\Gamma}^{(j)} = -\alpha \left[\frac{\partial\vartheta^2\left(\hat{\Gamma}^{(j)}\right)}{\partial\hat{\Gamma}^2} + \lambda I \right]^{-1} \left[\frac{\partial\vartheta\left(\hat{\Gamma}^{(j)}\right)}{\partial\hat{\Gamma}} \right]. \tag{15}$$

Then we obtain:

$$\hat{\Gamma}^{(j+1)} = \hat{\Gamma}^{(j)} - \alpha \left[\frac{\partial\vartheta^2\left(\hat{\Gamma}^{(j)}\right)}{\partial\hat{\Gamma}^2} + \lambda I \right]^{-1} \left[\frac{\partial\vartheta\left(\hat{\Gamma}^{(j)}\right)}{\partial\hat{\Gamma}} \right]. \tag{16}$$

The gradient is:

$$\frac{\partial\vartheta\left(\hat{\Gamma}^{(j)}\right)}{\partial\hat{\Gamma}} = -\int_0^t \varepsilon(t) \frac{\partial\hat{y}(t)}{\partial\hat{\Gamma}} dt, \tag{17}$$

The hessian is:

$$\frac{\partial\vartheta^2\left(\hat{\Gamma}^{(j)}\right)}{\partial\hat{\Gamma}^2} = \int_0^t \left[\frac{\partial\hat{y}(t)}{\partial\hat{\Gamma}} \right] \left[\frac{\partial\hat{y}(t)}{\partial\hat{\Gamma}} \right]^T dt. \tag{18}$$

We use the sensitivity function:

$$\frac{\partial \hat{y}(t)}{\partial \hat{\Gamma}} = \left[\frac{\partial \hat{y}(t)}{\partial \hat{\theta}}, \frac{\partial \hat{y}(t)}{\partial \hat{h}} \right]^T . \tag{19}$$

Taking the first derivative of $\hat{y}(t)$ with respect to $\hat{\theta}$, we have:

$$\frac{\partial \hat{y}(t)}{\partial \hat{\theta}} = \left[\frac{\partial \hat{y}(t)}{\partial \hat{p}_1} \cdots \frac{\partial \hat{y}(t)}{\partial \hat{p}_n} \cdots \frac{\partial \hat{y}(t)}{\partial \hat{q}_{11}} \cdots \frac{\partial \hat{y}(t)}{\partial \hat{q}_{n1}} \cdots \frac{\partial \hat{y}(t)}{\partial \hat{q}_{1m_1}} \cdots \frac{\partial \hat{y}(t)}{\partial \hat{q}_{nm_r}} \right]^T . \tag{20}$$

$\dfrac{\partial \hat{y}(t)}{\partial \hat{h}}$ is computed as:

$$\frac{\partial \hat{y}(t)}{\partial \hat{h}} = \left[\frac{\partial \hat{y}(t)}{\partial \hat{h}_1} \cdots \frac{\partial \hat{y}(t)}{\partial \hat{h}_r} \right]^T . \tag{21}$$

CONVERGENCE ANALYSIS

The convergence of the proposed prediction error (PEM) identification method is theoretically established in the following.

Theorem

The convergence of the proposed scheme is guarantee if $E\left\{ \Delta \hat{\Gamma} \right\} = 0$.

Proof

In the vicinity of the optimum such that $\lambda \to 0$, the following $\Delta \hat{\Gamma}^{(J)}$ is obtained from (15):

$$\Delta \hat{\Gamma}^{(J)} = -\alpha \left[\frac{\partial \vartheta^2 \left(\hat{\Gamma}^{(J)} \right)}{\partial \hat{\Gamma}^2} \right]^{-1} \left[\frac{\partial \vartheta \left(\hat{\Gamma}^{(J)} \right)}{\partial \hat{\Gamma}} \right] . \tag{22}$$

If we replace $\dfrac{\partial \vartheta \left(\hat{\Gamma}^{(j)} \right)}{\partial \hat{\Gamma}}$ and $\dfrac{\partial \vartheta^2 \left(\hat{\Gamma}^{(j)} \right)}{\partial \hat{\Gamma}}$ by its expressions given in (17) and (18), $\Delta \hat{\Gamma}^{(j)}$ becomes:

$$\Delta \hat{\Gamma}^{(j)} = \alpha \left[\int_0^t \left[\frac{\partial \hat{y}(t)}{\partial \hat{\Gamma}} \right] \left[\frac{\partial \hat{y}(t)}{\partial \hat{\Gamma}} \right]^T \right]^{-1} \left[\int_0^t \varepsilon(t) \frac{\partial \hat{y}(t)}{\partial \hat{\Gamma}} \, dt \right] \tag{23}$$

So:

$$E\left\{ \Delta \hat{\Gamma} \right\} = E \left\{ \left[\int_0^t \left[\frac{\partial \hat{y}(t)}{\partial \hat{\Gamma}} \right] \left[\frac{\partial \hat{y}(t)}{\partial \hat{\Gamma}} \right]^T \right]^{-1} \right\} \times E\left\{ \varepsilon(t) \frac{\partial \hat{y}(t)}{\partial \hat{\Gamma}} \right\}. \tag{24}$$

The proposed method is based on an implicit filtering procedure which is used to to generate the (filtered) input/output time derivatives of the differential equation model. Indeed, the used filter intrinsically allows data filtering and thus simplifies the use of the method on a practical case.

Indeed we can obtain:

$$\frac{\partial \hat{y}(t)}{\partial \hat{\Gamma}} = \frac{1}{P} \hat{\varphi}^T(t, \hat{h}) \tag{25}$$

Equation (24) is the rewritten as follows:

$$E\left\{ \Delta \hat{\Gamma} \right\} = E \left\{ \left[\left[\frac{1}{P} \hat{\varphi}^T(t, \hat{h}) \right] \left[\frac{1}{P} \hat{\varphi}^T(t, \hat{h}) \right]^T \right]^{-1} \right\} \times E\left\{ \varepsilon(t) \frac{1}{P} \hat{\varphi}^T(t, \hat{h}) \right\}. \tag{26}$$

From the expression of the error in (11):

$$\varepsilon(t) = y(t) - \hat{y}(t) = \varphi^T(t, h)\Gamma - \varphi^T(t, \hat{h})\hat{\Gamma} \tag{27}$$

Equation (26) is rewritten in the following formula by replacing the expression of the prediction error given in (27).

$$E\left\{\Delta\hat{\Gamma}\right\} = E\left\{\left[\left[\frac{1}{P}\hat{\varphi}^T(t,\hat{h})\right]\left[\frac{1}{P}\hat{\varphi}^T(t,\hat{h})\right]^T\right]^{-1}\right\}y(t)\times E\left\{\left[\varphi^T(t,h)\Gamma - \varphi^T(t,\hat{h})\hat{\Gamma}\right]\frac{1}{P}\hat{\varphi}^T(t,\hat{h})\right\}.$$

(28)

At the convergence, we have:

$$\Gamma = \hat{\Gamma}$$

(29)

It derives then:

$$E\left\{\left[\varphi^T(t,h)\Gamma - \varphi^T(t,\hat{h})\hat{\Gamma}\right]\frac{1}{P}\hat{\varphi}^T(t,\hat{h})\right\} = 0$$

(30)

Finaly,

$$E\left\{\Delta\hat{\Gamma}\right\} = E\left\{\left[\frac{\partial\hat{y}(t)}{\partial\hat{\Gamma}}\right]\left[\frac{\partial\hat{y}(t)}{\partial\hat{\Gamma}}\right]^T\right\}\times E\left\{\varepsilon(t)\frac{\partial\hat{y}(t)}{\partial\hat{\Gamma}}\right\} = 0$$

(31)

The Theorem is proved.

SIMULATION EXAMPLE

Consider a thermostatic mixing valves suitable for installation at plumbing fixtures and appliances for the final control of water temperature. The proposed system is designed to be installed at the point of use to assist in the prevention of scalding.

The process is described in Figure 2.

A modelisation of the considered process is given in Figure 3.

The input-output representation of the considered process is expressed as the following equation:

$$\ddot{y}(t) + p_1\dot{y}(t) + p_2 y(t) = q_{11}\dot{x}_1(t-h_1) + q_{12}x_1(t-h_1) + q_{21}\dot{x}_2(t-h_2) + q_{22}x_2(t-h_2).$$

(32)

Figure 2. The thermostatic mixing valves process

Figure 3. A modelisation of the thermostatic mixing valves process

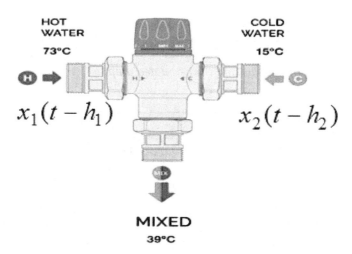

The true values of the parameters and time delays are:

$$p_1=3,\, p_2=2,\, q_{11}=1,\, q_{12}=2,\, q_{21}=2,\, q_{22}=2,\, h_1=8.84s,\, h_2=3.32s$$

Simulation Results

The simulation results in the case of a noise free output and a noisy output, respectively are tabulated in Table 1.

According to Table 1, it is seen that good identification accuracy is obtained by the proposed prediction error method even in the presence of noise.

Table 1. Parameters estimates with the proposed method

	True	Noise Free Output	Noisy Output (e(t) = 0.1rand(1))
p_1	3	3.0097±0.0097	3.0223±0.0223
p_2	2	2.0057±0.0057	2.0299±0.0299
q_{11}	1	1.0195±0.0195	1.0408±0.0408
q_{12}	2	2.0080±0.0080	2.0168±0.0168
q_{21}	2	2.0171±0.0171	2.0356±0.0356
q_{22}	2	2.0132±0.0132	2.0276±0.0276
h_1	8.84	8.8386±0.0014	8.8338±0.0062
h_2	3.32	2.3220±0.0020	2.3376±0.0176

Model Validation

Figure 4 gives the evolution of the true and the estimated outputs.

Figure 4. Evolution of the true and the estimated outputs

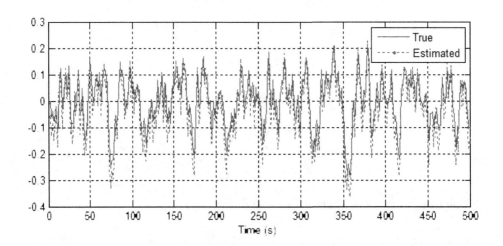

According to Figure 4, it can be shown that a faithful model is obtained.

Another validation of the proposed method is given by computing the error between the real system and estimated model outputs.

It can be noted that the agreement between the estimated model and the real system is good.

Figure 5. Error between the true system and estimated model outputs

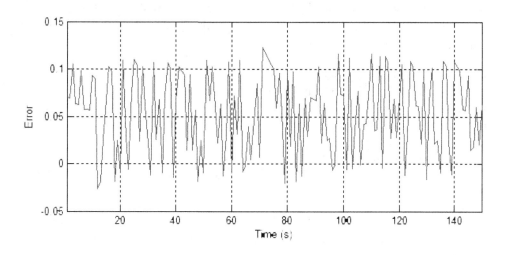

CONCLUSION

In this research work, a prediction error method has been presented to estimate a multivariable delayed system. The convergence of the scheme is proven under some reported conditions. Finally, a thermostatic mixing valves process has been adopted to validate the proposed scheme.

The identification of discrete time multivariable systems with multiple time delays is under investigation.

REFERENCES

Attitallah, A., Bedoui, S., & Abderrahim, K. (2016). System identification: Parameter and time-delay estimation for Wiener nonlinear systems with delayed input. *Transactions of the Institute of Measurement and Control, 40*. Advance online publication. doi:0.1177/0142331216674772

Beauduin, T., & Fujimoto, H. (2017). Identiðcation of system dynamics with time delay: A two-stage frequency domain approach. *IFAC-PapersOnLine, 50*(1), 10870–10875. doi:10.1016/j.ifacol.2017.08.2443

Bedoui, S., Ltaief, M., & Abderrahim, K. (2012).Using a recursive least square algorithm for identification of interconnected linear discrete-time delay multivariable system. *17th International Conference on Methods and Models in Automation and Robotics*. 10.1109/MMAR.2012.6347884

Bedoui, S., Ltaief, M., & Abderrahim, K. (2013). Online Identification of Multivariable Discrete Time Delay Systems Using a Recursive Least Square Algorithm. *Mathematical Problems in Engineering*, *2013*, 1–18. Advance online publication. doi:10.1155/2013/658194

Chandrasekaran, R., & Chidambaram, M. (2012). Closed-Loop Identification of Second-Order Plus Time Delay (SOPTD) Model of Multivariable Systems by Optimization Method. *Industrial & Engineering Chemistry Research*, *51*(28), 9620–9633. doi:10.1021/ie203003p

Jin, F., & Qiu, T. (2019). Adaptive time delay estimation based on the maximum correntropy criterion. *Digital Signal Processing*, *88*, 23–32. doi:10.1016/j.dsp.2019.01.014

Leylaz, Ma, & Sun. (2022). Identification of nonlinear dynamical systems with time delay. *International Journal of Dynamics and Control*, *10*, 1–8. doi:10.1007/s40435-021-00783-7

Leylaz, G., Ma, S. F., & Sun, J. Q. (2021). An optimal model identiðcation algorithm of nonlinear dynamical systems with the algebraic method. *Journal of Vibration and Acoustics*, *143*(2), 1–8. doi:10.1115/1.4048169

Ligang, W. L., Hak-Keung, Z., Yuxin, S., & Zhan. (2015).Time-Delay Systems and Their Applications in Engineering. *Mathematical Problems in Engineering*.

Liu, T., Wang, Q. G., & Huang, H. P. (2013). A tutorial review on process identification from step or relay feedback test. *Journal of Process Control*, *23*(10), 1597–1623. doi:10.1016/j.jprocont.2013.08.003

Na, J., Ren, X., & Xia, Y. (2014). Adaptive parameter identiðcation of linear SISO systems with unknown time-delay. *Systems & Control Letters*, *66*, 43–50. doi:10.1016/j.sysconle.2014.01.005

Yu, L., Qiu, T., & Song, A. M. (2017). A time delay estimation algorithm based on the weighted correntropy spectral density. *Circuits, Systems, and Signal Processing*, *36*(3), 1115–1128. doi:10.100700034-016-0347-y

Zheng, G., Barbot, J. P., & Boutat, D. (2015). Identiðcation of the delay parameter for nonlinear time-delay systems with unknown inputs. *Automatica*, *49*(6), 1755–1760. doi:10.1016/j.automatica.2013.02.020

Chapter 8

Effective Moving Object Detection Using Background Subtraction in Stationary Wavelet Domain

Oussama Boufares
University of Tunis El Manar, Tunisia

Aymen Mnassri
University of Tunis El Manar, Tunisia

Cherif Adnane
University of Tunis El Manar, Tunisia

ABSTRACT

Moving object detection is a fundamental task on smart CCTV systems, as it provides a focal point for further investigation. In this study, an algorithm for moving object detection in video, which is thresholded using a stationary wavelet transform (SWT), is developed. In the detection steps, the authors perform a background subtraction algorithm; the obtained results are decomposed using discrete stationary wavelet transform 2D, and the coefficients are thresholded using Birge-Massart strategy. This leads to an efficient calculation method and system compared to existing traffic estimation methods.

DOI: 10.4018/978-1-6684-4945-5.ch008

INTRODUCTION

A living organism, whether human or animal, can easily distinguish the things around it and categorize them according to each component's understanding of them, but the automated system usually has great difficulty in doing the same. Therefore, the detection of moving objects remains one of the most important challenges of computer vision, which a large number of researchers in this field seek to develop in order to keep pace with technological advances, which depend mainly computer vision systems. In general, there are many methods that can be classified into three main categories: region-based detecting and tracking, model-based detecting and tracking, contour-based detecting and tracking and feature-based detecting and tracking.

Our contribution aims at developing object detection and target tracking using a robust method based on the discrete stationary wavelet transform. We have performed the detection phases using a set of background subtraction, then we have validated the thresholding approach which consists in applying a thresholding on the wavelet coefficients obtained, to truncate the coefficients of low amplitudes obtained. The objective of this step is to locate the moving object in an efficient way by removing any type of noise.

This paper was organized from start to finish as follows. The introduction is presented in the First Section. In the Second Section of the paper, we review a range of techniques for detecting and tracking moving objects. We then detailed our approach to object detection in Section Three. During the Fourth Section we evaluated our approach. The Fifth Section concludes the paper.

RELATED WORKS

Background subtraction approaches generally work to find the absolute difference between the current frame and the background so that relevant changes can be detected. The algorithm's success is dependent on developing an efficient method for modeling and updating the background. Background subtraction works well for extracting all types of objects from videos, but the effectiveness of the approach deteriorates if the background is not static, has lighting fluctuations, and the videos are noisy.

A number of algorithms have been suggested for moving object detection from the standard background subtraction (BS) method and the wavelet transform, which splits frame sequences into detailed and approximate components and performs other operations on only those components. Kavitha et al. (2017) proposed a new method using stationary wavelet transform (SWT) to identify and remove moving shadows based on a threshold defined by wavelet coefficients. The multi-resolution feature of the stationary wavelet transform decomposes the frames into four different bands without losing information. Cheng et al. (2006) based their approach on Discrete Wave Transformation Technology (DWT) as a preprocessing process for detecting and tracking moving objects. 2-D DWT was used to analyze the image into four sub-images (LL, LH, HL and HH). The LL3 range(band) is used for further detection due to Consider low computational costs and noise reduction issues. However, using haar-based DWT distorts the shape of the object. In this study (Chih H. et al, 2014), an improved BS approach based on the Gaussian mixture model (GMM) and wavelet transform (WT) is suggested for the challenge in object detection. Not only can the effect of lighting changes, noise, and shadows be reduced, but dynamic changes to landscapes can also be handled using this method. In Alok et al. (2014), a video surveillance method using the complex wavelet transform and the method based on the approximate median filter for the segmentation of moving objects.

According to the problem of detecting and tracking the moving objects of a video surveillance, the most used techniques deal with a stationary camera (Ismail et al 1998) or closed world representations (Isard et al, 1998) which rely on a fixed background or a specific knowledge on the type of actions taking place, where various difficult cases are not perfectly solved and must be improved such as occlusion, tracking, identification of object, localization and removing shadows of objects.

In this research, we propose an efficient discrete stationary wavelet transform-based method for motion detection. At first, the adaptive BS algorithm detects all the moving objects to get the whole moving area. This step involves computing the absolute values of the difference between the background frame and the current frame, thresholding using SWT-technique, and obtaining the various objects (Mallat et al, (1999). Then in step second, experimental results and some discussions are presented. The last step includes the conclusion of this work. This scheme shows the flowchart of the BS.

PROPOSED ADAPTIVE THRESHOLD USING SWT FOR DETECTION OF MOVING OBJECTS

In this section, an adaptive threshold technique based on SWT is applied to the obtained image using background subtraction to detect moving objects in each frame of a video scene. To better understand the concept of the proposed algorithm, the basic idea of detection using background subtraction is first described. It will then be combined with the stationary wavelet-SWT. As a result, an integrated background subtraction-SWT algorithm for detecting moving objects is obtained.

Figure 1. System block diagram of the BS
Source: Elgammal (2015)

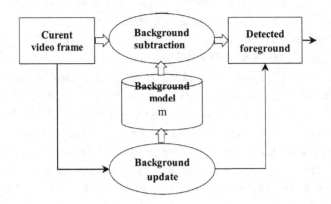

Motion detection methods are basically a process of detecting objects in the monitoring area (Kalpana et al, 2013). Figure 2 summarizes the proposed algorithm for motion detection with background subtraction using an adaptive threshold.

Figure 2. Block diagram of the proposed algorithm

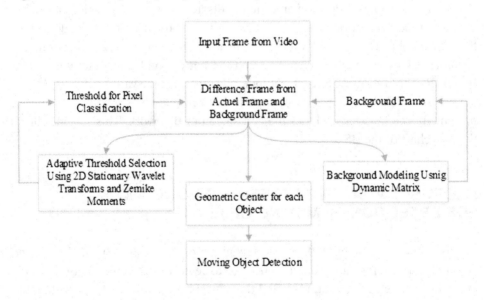

Background Frame Initialization

For video analysis, background reconstruction, also known as background initialization, is an essential process to extract moving objects. Its main purpose is to separate the moving areas according to the current estimation model.

The first goal of building a background model is to fix the number of images. This model can be designed in different ways (Gaussian, fuzzy etc.). In this part, we use the very popular selective averaging method (Sheng-Ke et al, 2007) to obtain the initial background model:

$$B\left(s\right) = \frac{\sum_{m=1}^{N} I_m\left(s\right)}{N} \tag{1}$$

Where B(s) is the initial background of pixel s and I_m(s) is the intensity of pixel s in the mth frame, and N is the number of frames used to design the background model.

Background Subtraction

The technique of background subtraction can be defined as an act of separating out elements in the foreground from the background. This is to be done by creating a foreground mask. The mentioned above technique is a way for detecting objects, which is extracted from static cameras. Background subtraction is important for object tracking. Object tracking uses background subtraction methods, which is one of the most important steps in the object tracking algorithm. The objective of this method is to detect active objects by calculating the absolute difference between the reference frame and the current frame. where each pixel in the current frame at location s in frame f_s, is determined to be foreground if:

$$|f_s - B_s| > \delta. \tag{2}$$

Bs is the background model image δ is the adaptive coefficient threshold determined by SWT. Let consider that $Diff_s$ is the binary foreground of an image.

$$Diff_s\left(k\right) \begin{cases} 1 & for \; \left|f_s\left(k\right) - B_{(s)k-1}\left(k - \gamma\right)\right| > \delta \\ 0 & for \; others \end{cases} \tag{3}$$

Where γ is the time interval each time between the current frame and the previous frame representing the background image. We can differentiate between the foreground image and the background image each time through the proposed algorithm using the complex and represented fixed wavelet.

Image Analysis Using Wavelet Stationary

In this subsection, the obtained image is decomposed into stationary wavelet coefficients by a double-tree stationary wavelet transform. Subsequently, the wavelet coefficients obtained are thresholded. The different types of sub-bands are shown in Table 1.

Table 1. Decomposition of image into four sub-bands using SWT

Diagonal (HH)	Approximation (LL)
Vertical (LH)	Horizontal (HL)

With 2D-SWT, the decomposition of an image into wavelet coefficient is performed as follows: in the first level of decomposition, the image is divided into 4 sub-bands, which each subband image has its own characteristic, namely the HH-band (diagonal detail). HL-band (vertical detail), LH-band-band (horizontal detail) and LL-band(approximation), where H and L show the high and the low-pass filters.

Once the image acquisition is decomposed, the coefficients obtained are determined in the detailed noise suppression sub-bands, and finally the final image is obtained from the reconstruction of the thresholded sub-bands (Chambolle et al., 1998; Alsaidi et al., 2010). The decomposition steps by stationary wavelet transform are as follows:

1. Decompose the image using SWT.
2. Threshold the wavelet coefficients using the selected threshold method.
3. Reconstruct the image using ISWT for the threshold image.

UNIVERSAL THRESHOLD

The universal threshold (Visu Shrink) δ was introduced by Donoho (1995). It is defined as:

$$\delta = \sigma\sqrt{2\ln(N)} \tag{4}$$

Where N is the number of the wavelet coefficients and σ is the noise variance in that image which is calculated from the diagonal sub-band (HH) as:

$$\sigma = MAD(HH) / 0.6745 \tag{5}$$

To estimate the noise level σ, Frank R Hampel showed that the Median Absolute Deviation $MAD(X) = |X–Median(X)|$ converges to 0.6745 times σ as the sample size. After the background subtraction step, we use hard thresholding given as follow:

$$Diff_k = \begin{cases} 1 & for \left| f_k\left(s\right) - B_{k-1}\left(s\right) \right| > \delta \\ 0 & for \, others \end{cases} \tag{6}$$

The hard threshold removes coefficients below a threshold value (δ) which is obtained by the thresholding proposed algorithm.

From the above equation and based on the processed images, the value 1 is black and 0 is white. So, the segmented image gives the moving object a white color with a background always black, and as a result, the moving object is detected with high accuracy.

Background Update

Now, we give a brief introduction to the very popular background refresh algorithm proposed by Tao Y (Graciela R et al, 2016), which is mainly based on dynamic matrix. This algorithm is focused on dynamic matrix D(k) analysis to determine whether or not the pixel belongs to the foreground of the image. Let I (k) represent the frame at time k, and the index s represent the position of the pixel Is(k). The expression (4) of the dynamic matrix D(k) at time k is given by:

$$D_s = \begin{cases} D_s\left(k-1\right) Diff_s\left(t\right) = 0, D_s\left(k-1\right) \neq 0 \\ \rho \qquad Diff_s\left(t\right) = 0 \end{cases} \tag{7}$$

Where λ is the time length to record the pixel's moving state. Once $D_s(k)$ equates to zero, the pixel will be updated into the background with a linear model.

$$B_s(k) = \alpha I_s(k) + (1 - \alpha)I_s(k) \tag{8}$$

Bs is the background image at time k and α is the weight of input frame.

EXPERIMENTAL RESULTS

In this section, we tested our method on a large type of synthetic videos. We also tested it on a number of other methods, including the Mixture of Gaussian GMM algorithm (Lucia et al, 2012) and the Background Estimation Based (MSDE) algorithm (Zivkovic, 2004). While the first test was on carefully selected thresholds so that we could know the capacity of proposed algorithm.

Fixed Thresholds

With these results shown in Figure 3b and obtained after applying our approach consisting in applying an adaptation threshold based on SWT techniques. Where the original images are 3a and 3b represent the detection results of our algorithm, while 3c and 3d are the detection results of moving objects when the threshold value is fixed at 33 and 80. In the video, we can see that the algorithm using fixed thresholds does not give good results. For example, for a high threshold value, motion areas will be falsely detected as foreground objects. It can be seen that our algorithm can perfectly detect and separate moving objects from walking people.

Other Methods

Figure 4 shows four representative frames of the smart room sequence and the traffic sequence, the original frames and the binary mask of moving objects obtained respectively by the proposed algorithm, GMM (Lucia et al., 2012) and MSDE (Sheng-Ke et al., 2007).

In Figure 4a, a person is working in a room. Due to the low quality of the device, some system noise is generated in this footage. As shown in Figure 4d and e, GMM and MSDE approaches generate significant noises due to system noises. The proposed approach applies after calculation of the absolute values of the difference between the background frame and the current image frame, an adaptive threshold using 2D stationary wavelet transforms to calculate the parameter of the probabilities of the background and the foreground. Therefore, the proposed algorithm can detect moving objects and suppress shadows of walking people, as shown in Figure 4f.

Table 2 shows a performance comparison between the proposed algorithm in this paper and the algorithm using different fixed thresholds, the best detection and tracking performance was obtained by our adaptive threshold algorithm.

Figure 3. Detection results of proposed algorithm compared with the method using fixed threshold

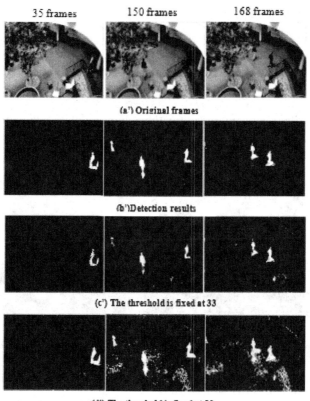

Quantitative Evaluation

To evaluate the performance of proposed algorithm, we used the parameters (precession and recall) for compare our algorithm with the other algorithms the parameters are defined as follows:

$$recall = \frac{Tp}{Tp + \mathrm{F}\,n}$$

$$precession = \frac{Tp}{Tp + Fn}$$

$$F - measure = \frac{2 * recall * precession}{recall + precession}$$

Where Tp is total number of true positive pixels, Fn presents the number of false negative pixels, Fp presents the number of false positive pixels. Table 3 shows the results of accuracy values for Traffic sequence.

Figure 4. Detection results of our algorithm compared with two works introduced: (a) indoor sequence with shadows and (b) sequence with varying illumination

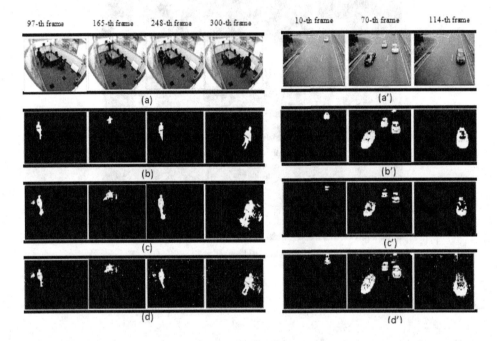

Table 2. The results of objects detection and tracking

Video		c	d	e	Proposed Algorithm
traffic	detection	10	7	5	10
	tracking	7	5	3	9
Correction Rate (%)		70	50	30	90

Table 3. Comparison of different methods for the object detection experiment

Methods	Recall	Precision	F-Measure
Proposed Algorithm	0.79	0.77	0.78
AAPSA (Graciela et al, 2016)	0.74	0.71	0.72
IUTIS (Simone et al., 2017)	0.86	0.61	0.71
SC SBOs (Lucia et al., 2012)	0. 62	0.74	0.67
GMM ZIVKOVIC (Zivkovic, 2004)	0.73	0.52	0.6

From Table 3, it can be seen that the highest recall is obtained by using the IUTIS and our algorithm, but in both cases the precision is far underneath a sufficient level in practice. But by combining these two methods competitive results can be obtained. In fact, state of the art approaches such as IUTIS, SC SBOS and GMM ZIVKOVIC are clearly outperformed and the results are comparable to the approach of AAPSA. But the recall is still insufficient. In contrast, by applying the proposed approach the recall-rate is increased to 79% at a precision of 77%! Considering the complexity of the task the obtained results are quite competitive.

CONCLUSION

We have presented in this paper an object detection method based on the background subtraction method and the stationary wavelet transform. Wavelet analysis is done by extracting new threshold, calculated using wavelet coefficients, is used to classify moving objects. The multiresolution property of SWT allows to reconstruct the image from the subbands without loss of information. The results show that the algorithm is robust, able to better detect moving targets and has wide applicability.

REFERENCES

Alok, K., & Singh, K. (2014). Complex wavelet based moving object segmentation using approximate median filter-based method for video surveillance. *International Advance Computing Conference (IACC).*

Alsaidi, M., & Altaher, M. (2010). A Comparison of Some Thresholding Selection Methods for Wavelet Regression. *International Journal of Mathematics and Computer Science*, 4(2), 105–111.

Chambolle, A., DeVore, R., Lee, N., & Lucier, J. (1998). Nonlinear wavelet image processing: Variational problems, compression, and noise removal through wavelet shrinkage. *IEEE Transactions on Image Processing*, *7*(3), 319–335. doi:10.1109/83.661182 PMID:18276252

Chih-Hsien. (2014). Efficient modified directional lifting-based discrete wavelet transform for moving object detection. *Signal Processing*, 138–152.

Donoho, D. L. (1995). Denoising by soft-thresholding. *IEEE Transactions on Information Theory*, *41*(3), 613–627. doi:10.1109/18.382009

Elgammal, A. A. (2015). *Background Subtraction: Theory and Practice*. Wide Area Surveillance. doi:10.1007/978-3-031-01813-8

Fang-Hsuan, C., & Yu-Liang, C. (2006). Real time multiple objects tracking and identification based on discrete wavelet transform. *Pattern Recognition*, *39*(6), 1126–1139. doi:10.1016/j.patcog.2005.12.010

Graciela, R. & Mario I. (2016) Auto-Adaptive Parallel SOM Architecture with a modular analysis for dynamic object segmentation in videos. *Neurocomputing*, *175*(B), 990–1000.

Isard, M. (1998). A mixed-state condensation tracker with automatic model-switching. *6th International Conference on Computer Vision (IEEE Cat. No.98CH36271)*. 10.1109/ICCV.1998.710707

Ismail, H., David, H., & Larry, S. (1998). A Real-Time System for Detecting and Tracking People in 2 1/2 D. *European Conference on Computer Vision (ECCV)*.

Kalpana, M., Suparshya, S., Susrutha, S., & Habibulla, K. (2013). FPGA implementation of moving object detection in frames by using background subtraction algorithm. *International Conference on Communication and Signal Processing*.

Kavitha, N., & Ruba, K. (2017). Moving shadow detection based on stationary wavelet transform. *EURASIP Journal on Image and Video Processing*, *49*, 1–19.

Lucia, M., & Alfredo, P. (2012). The SOBS algorithm: What are the limits? *Computer Society Conference on Computer Vision and Pattern Recognition Workshops*.

Sasirekha, K., & Thangavel, K. (2014). A novel wavelet-based thresholding for denoising fingerprint image. *International Conference on Electronics, Communication and Computational Engineering (ICECCE)*. 10.1109/ICECCE.2014.7086644

Sheng-Ke, W., Bo, Q., Zheng-Hua, F., & Zong-Shun, M. (2007). Fast shadow detection according to the moving region. *International Conference on Machine Learning and Cybernetics.*

Simone, B., Gianluigi, C., & Raimondo, S. (2017). How Far Can You Get by Combining Change Detection Algorithms? *International Conference on Image Analysis and Processing.*

Zivkovic, Z. (2004). Improved adaptive Gaussian mixture model for back-ground subtraction. *Proc. Int. Conf. Pattern Recognition.*

Chapter 9
Speech Recognition System Implementation of a Method Based on Wave Atom Transform and Frequency–Mel Cepstral Coefficients Using SVM

Walid Mohamed
University of Orleans, Orleans, France

Yosssra Ben Fadhel
University of Tunis El Manar, Tunisia

ABSTRACT

In the field of human-machine interaction, automatic speech recognition (ASR) has been a prominent research area since the 1950s. Single-word speech recognition is widely used in voice command systems, which can be implemented in various applications such as access control systems, robots, and voice-enabled devices. This study describes the implementation of a single-word speech recognition system using wave atoms transform (WAT) and frequency-mel cepstral coefficients (MFCC) on a Raspberry Pi 3 (RPi 3) board. The WAT-MFCC approach is combined with a support vector machine (SVM). The experiment was conducted on an Arabic word database, and the results showed that the proposed WAT-MFCC-SVM method is highly reliable, achieving a detection rate of 100% and a real-time factor (RTF) of 1.50.

DOI: 10.4018/978-1-6684-4945-5.ch009

INTRODUCTION

Speech is a simpler means of communication for people to express their thoughts and feelings. In fact, using it as a means of controlling one's environment is usually tempting. This is why research in Automatic Speech Recognition (ASR) is intensifying and reproducible steps are underway. In fact, several studies have been carried out during the past decades to design an ideal speech recognition system that can understand single-word speech in real time from different speakers and different environments. I was. Nevertheless, achieving this ultimate goal is a continuing requirement for his recently developed ASR system. Additionally, this task is difficult due to the presence of large variations in the speech signal. B. The absence or absence of clear boundaries between words or phonemes and the presence of unwanted noise signals caused by the diversity of speakers and their environment (gender, speaking speed, speaking style, dialect (Norezmi et al., 2017).

There are many applications of ASR systems released to perform a variety of tasks, from the simplest to the most complex Home automation (Rolon-Heredia et al., 2019). Furthermore, the progress recorded in the ASR research field is positively impacting the lives of people with disabilities and the elderly by providing quality support.

There are various perspectives in the literature from which ASR tasks have been considered. Abushariah et al. (2023) discussed some of the challenges of ASR and also gave an overview of many known approaches. In fact, in this work the author considered two feature extraction techniques: Mel-Frequency Cepstrum Coefficients (MFCC) and Predictive Linear Coding Coefficients (LPC). Artificial Neural Networks (ANN), Hidden Markov Models (HMM), Dynamic Time Warping (DTW). Therefore, comparisons were made between many ASR systems based on extracted features and classification techniques. Moreover, many approaches have been cited in Labied et al. (2021) and used as techniques in both the preprocessing and feature extraction stages of ASR systems. In Kothandaraman et al. (2022), the authors presented different perspectives on the structure of ASR systems. In fact, they took into consideration that these systems consist of numerous processing layers. This is because it requires multiple components, leading to a large number of computations. Furthermore, he concludes that with careful selection of appropriate processing layers, the error rate of ASR can now be reduced. In Ibrahim et al. (2017), both ASR and Text-to-Speech (TTS) research areas were discussed by the authors. In the ASR section, we explored various aspects for classifying speech, such as: B. Cepstrum-based feature extraction techniques, data compression and HMM. We also discussed various ways to increase robustness to noise. Presented a discussion in the field of ASR from the perspective of pattern recognition.

Mainly, the ASR system consists of four phases: preprocessing phase, feature extraction phase, classification phase, and language model (Mustafa et al., 2019). In the preprocessing phase, the speech signal is transformed in order to further extract consistent information from the speech signal in the feature extraction phase. In fact, there are common features between the preprocessing and feature extraction phases: B. Pre-emphasis, framing, normalization, denoising, endpoint detection (Tang et al., 2021; Walid et al., 2019). Then, during the feature extraction phase, a number of predefined features are extracted from the processed speech. Therefore, these extracted features should be able to distinguish classes while maintaining robustness against external conditions such as noise. In Huang et al. (2015), Ravi et al. (2021), and Hidayat et al. (2018), the performance of ASR systems can be highly dependent on the feature extraction method chosen, as the classifier used in the classification stage should classify these extracted features efficiently Proven. Ravi et al. (2021). propose various feature extraction techniques, such as MFFC, LPC, and Discrete Wavelet Transform (DWT). For language models, it consists of different kinds of knowledge related to language. B. Semantics and Syntax (de la Fuente Garcia et al., 2020).

In recent decades, creating an ideal ASR system capable of understanding continuous and discrete speech (from different speakers in any environment) in real time has been the focus of much research interest. We are still far from this single decisive goal (Oruh et al., 2022). Real-time applications of ASR include security systems, automation, and robotics. Most language-related applications are taxonomy-based applications. HMM and ANN models are commonly used for classification in ASR systems. HMM models have the disadvantage that the only functions available are probability functions and adjacent frames must be independent. However, these limitations are resolved in the ANN model because each neuron in the hidden layer has an activation function. The ANN algorithm was considered to be a good and highly efficient classifier for pattern recognition (Patange & Alex, 2017). In a sub-database with a vocabulary of 571 words, the Non Negative Matrix (NNM) enabled him to achieve 94% word accuracy versus 88% for his HMM model using low-complexity language structures. became. In contrast, NNM's word accuracy reached 58%, compared to 49% for HMM without linguistic structure. Using the TIMIT database gave poor results for both classifiers, but slightly better for the NNM model (Yao & Cao, 2020). In Chinese speech recognition, the introduction of deep neural network (DNN) reduces character error rate by 20% and outperforms Gaussian Mixture Model (GMM) (Li et al., 2015). In noisy situations, more effective results were obtained using DNN and support vector machine (SVM) classifiers compared to those of the prior art (McLoughlin et al., 2015). Patange and Alex (2017) showed that artificial neural networks (ANNs) are good at recognizing short or isolated words. This is because reconfigurable hardware is faster than software, and implementing neural networks in hardware architecture can be even faster. This is the case for image processing in robotics and pattern recognition applications using neural networks implemented in FPGAs to achieve shorter times and faster response times (Sarić et al., 2020). This configuration used only 33% of the FPGA resources. Neural networks are slower on his FPGA than on a PC, but they are more stable, operating system independent, and cheaper (Shymkovych et al., 2021). By using neural networks, manufactured vehicles become more intelligent. Patel et al. (2015) evaluated a hybrid approach for the Xilinx speech recognition system. This approach is developed based on Multi-Layer Perception (MLP) and shows significant power and area reductions. In Alex et al. (2015), self-organizing feature maps (SOFM) were used to reduce the dimensionality of vector features. Perceptual Linear Predictive (PLP), MFCC, and DWT represent the main features extracted with this approach. Although the dimensionality of the feature vector was greatly reduced, the recognition accuracy was the same as the conventional method. In Patange and Alex (2017), an isolated speech recognition system for spoken words was implemented on the RPi 2. Neural networks used as classifiers and MFCCs as features are the main components that make up this system. In fact, the TIDIGITS corpus achieved 100% accuracy in speaker-dependent speech recognition. However, it was lower for speaker-independent speech recognition. In Alvarez et al. (2016), an embedded isolated word recognition (IWR) system implementation was performed on his STM32F4 discovery platform. The iteration of the system he repeated three times, running in two different scenarios. A very high SNR anechoic chamber and normal environment. We found mean word error rates (WER) of 1.04% and 2.81% in the respective scenarios. The reported real-time factor (RTF) is 1.43, which corresponds to performance levels reported in the literature. Among the solutions proposed in the literature to address the problem of automatic speech recognition (ASR) in embedded systems, they are based on digital signal processing (DSP) (Suryawanshi & Ganorkar, 2014; Alvarez et al., 2016, Wang, 2022) or FPGA (He et al., 2021; Atoui et al., 2020; Belabed et al., 2021). You can also find some implementations based on microcontrollers. Most of them require a communication channel with a remote server that processes the collected data and performs the actual detection (Yuvaraj et al., 2022; Mohamed et al., 2019; Sanjaya et al., 2018). These methods are powerful, but have high latency and high consumption. Again, there are some approximations to a fully microcontroller-based ASR system. In general, these applications use simpler acoustic properties to reduce computational complexity and range from very simple vectors (Küçüktopcu et al., 2019; Lee & Ahn, 2020; Junlin et al., 2019) to more complex and robust vectors (Mnassri et al., 2019; Sugumaran & Prakash, 2015). Finally, other less common implementations rely on dedicated chips to perform the detection process (Rashid et al., 2017; Prongnuch & Sitjongsataporn, 2020; Yin et al., 2021).

In this chapter, we implemented an independent speech recognition system on the RPi 3 board. The proposed system uses Wave Atoms Transform (WAT) and MFCC as extracted features, followed by SVM, MLP, and HMM as classifiers under various noisy conditions on an Arabic database. Was tested with WAT is a type of wavelet-based transform that also includes wavelet packet transform (WPT) and DWT (Lubbad et al., 2019). Furthermore, it is considered a geometric tool used to analyze signals in the presence of noise and uncertainty, providing multiple resolutions in a multiscale tool (Benazzouz & Slimane, 2019). Moreover, time-domain filtering is a simple denoising method applied to corrupted signals (Haridas et al., 2018) to remove high-frequency noise in low-frequency signals. However, this method does not give satisfactory results under real conditions. To solve this problem, we proposed a WAT-MFCC approach to further improve the real-time performance of isolated word recognition systems under various noisy conditions. The remaining sections of this paper are organized as follows. Section 2 presents a proposed method. A real-time implementation of the proposed approach on the RPi 3 board is presented in Section 3. A discussion and analysis of the various results continues in Section 4. Conclusions and perspectives are provided in Section 5.

The Proposed Method

A comprehensive speech recognition system based on WAT and SVM was developed and implemented on a Raspberry PI 3 board to improve real-time recognition accuracy. The system consists of several stages shown in Figure 1.

Figure 1. Block diagram of the proposed speech recognition system

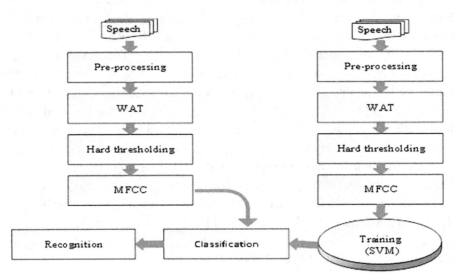

Pre-Processing Speech Stage

Preprocessing consists of his three phases: pre-emphasis, frame-blocking, and windowing.

In the first stage, the aim is to denoise the audio signal at the moment of detection and smooth the spectral shape of its frequencies. In fact, the representation of the pre-emphasis filter in the time domain is

$$y(x) = x(n) - ax(n - 1) \tag{1}$$

Where a can be defined as a predistortion filter constant between 0.9 and 1.0. The second phase is frame blocking. This involves splitting the audio signal into many overlapping frames so that no single signal dropout is found. In fact, all signals must fall into one or two frames during this process. Short-term analysis can be used for this purpose. The third phase of preprocessing is windowing. This can be described as a long tone signal analysis process. In fact, this process applies a FIR (Finite Impulse Response) digital filter to remove aliased waveforms caused by discontinuities in the signal fragments that occur after applying the frame blocking process.

Feature Extraction

Wave Atom Transform (WAT)

The first step in our approach is to decompose the audio signal using Wave Atoms Transform (WAT). This transform is characterized by its ability to transform the time representation of a signal into a time-frequency representation. Furthermore, this domain transformation can reduce redundancy and decorrelate signal samples. In this way a better transmission bit rate can be achieved. In fact, the WAT process is a technique that allows us to concentrate the audio information into a few coefficients (John et al., 2017). Therefore, many coefficients are zero or of negligible magnitude.

Threshold

It is the most important step in recognizing speech in noisy environments. This allows the WAT transform to reject coefficients below a given threshold. There are several methods of thresholding, as follows: B. Hard and soft thresholds, which are commonly used methods. This white paper used a hard threshold given by the following formula:

$$C_{\text{Re}} = \begin{cases} C_{\text{Re}} & if \ \left| C_{\text{Re}} \right| \geq T \\ 0 & otherwise \end{cases} \tag{2}$$

Figure 3. Hard thresholding

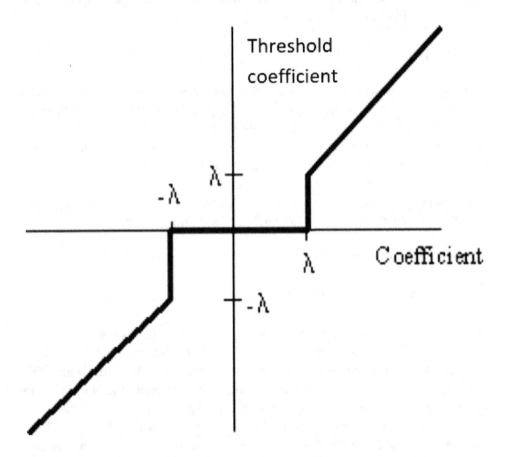

Mel-Frequency Cepstral Coefficients (MFCCs)

Mel-frequency cepstrum coefficients (MFCC) are widely used in automatic speech recognition systems (Hastuty et al., 2021) due to their low estimation complexity and good performance. MFCC representations have been shown to approximate the structure of the human auditory system better than traditional linear and predictive functions. However, the MFCC coefficients are easily affected by local common-frequency random noise to which human perception is largely unaffected. For each frame of the speech signal, the MFCC vector is computed as the spectral power of the windowed signal block is mapped to the mel scale using a triangular filter. The logarithm of the filter bank output is transformed again using the discrete cosine transform (DCT). The relationship between scale Mel and frequency is given by the expression.

$$F(Mel) = 2595 * \log10(1+f/700) \tag{3}$$

In fact, Figure 4 shows a diagram of the MFCC coefficients.

Figure 4. Computation of MFCC coefficients

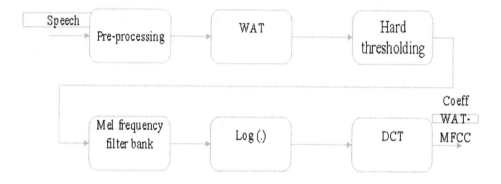

Classification

Support Vector Machine (SVM)

An SVM classifier is a simple and efficient computation of machine learning algorithms that can be used to perform binary classification. The main idea behind using this classifier is to utilize a kernel function to transform the original input set into a high-dimensional feature space. Therefore, this transformation can be used to solve nonlinear problems. In classification problems and pattern recognition, SVM classifiers are widely applied, and with limited training data, this classifier outperforms other algorithms by achieving excellent classification performance (Kerkeni et al., 2018).

The hyper plan resulting from the data separation of the two groups is defined by the formula:

$$f(x) = w^tx + b \tag{4}$$

Where b is a scalar, x is the input coefficient, and w is an m-dimensional vector. SVM determines the hyperplane corresponding to f(x) = 0 for linearly separable data. However, the input samples are mapped into a high-dimensional feature space using the nonlinearly separable case φ function as follows:

$$f(x) = w^t\varphi(x) + b = 0 \tag{5}$$

So, the decision function is defined as:

$$D(x) = \text{sign}(w^t\varphi(x) + b) \tag{6}$$

Recent work aims to extend SVM to multi-class classification applied to real problems. Thus, we reduce the multiclass problem to a composition of several two-class hyperplanes by drawing the boundaries between classes (Jampour & Sardar, 2021). In fact, there are two most common techniques for multiclass classification: one-to-one (OAO) and one-to-one (OAA). The OAA approach is based on a "winner takes all" strategy aimed at creating one his SVM for each class. That is, to classify m classes, one-to-one must create m binary SVM classifiers. This method is more computationally intensive, but less sensitive to imbalanced datasets. In this article, I applied the 'OAA' technique to a Raspberry Pi 3 (RPi3) board using his SVM library in the Python platform (Pisner & Schnyer, 2020).

Figure 5. SVM multiclass classification using one-vs.-rest

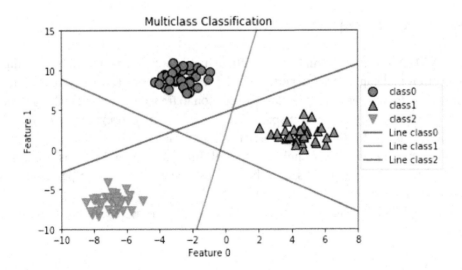

Real-Time Implementation on Raspberry Pi 3 (RPi 3) Board

Database

2/3 of the database was reserved for training and the rest was used for testing. We tested the proposed model on an Arabic database containing 11 spoken Arabic words in different directions (e.g., takadam, tarajaa, 5alfa, amam, asraa, istader, sir, wara, tawakaf, yamine, yassar). These words were repeated 10 times with different SNR values (ranging from -5 to 20 dB).

Materials

Hardware

A Raspberry Pi (RPi) can be defined as a single Linux board computer extended to RPi 2 and RPi 3 versions. The general architecture of the RPi 3 Board Model B is shown in Figure 6.

Figure 6. The general architecture of RPi 3 Board Model B

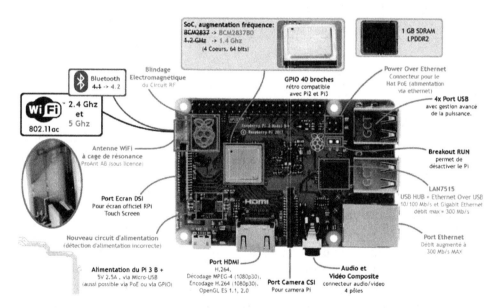

For this work, I used the RPi 3 because it has the following significant advantages: B. High speed 50% faster than RP2 with processor (1.2 KHz) (Gyulyustan & Enkov, 2017), better storage capacity of RAM and expandable memory of external SD card. Compared to the RPi 2, the RPi 3 board includes wireless connectivity with WIFI and Bluetooth integration, making it promising for Internet of Things (IoT) applications. See Table 1 for key technical specifications of the RPi 3 board.

Table 1. Technical specifications of RPi 3 Board Model B

Feature	Type
CPU	1.2 GHz 64-bit quad core ARM Cortex-A53
Memory (SDRAM)	1 GB (shared with GPU)
USB 2.0 Ports	4 (5 with the on-board 5-port USB hub)
Video input	15-pin MIPI camera interface (CSI) connector, used with the Raspberry Pi camera or Raspberry Pi NoIR camera
Video outputs	HDMI (rev 1.3), composite video (3.5 mm TRRS jack)
On-board storage	Micro SDHC slot
On-board network	10/100 Mbit/s Ethernet, 802.11n Wireless, Bluetooth 4.1
Power source	5 V with Micro USB or GPIO header
CPU	1.2 GHz 64-bit quad core ARM Cortex-A53

Software

Raspberry PI 3 Model B supports many programming languages such as C++, Java, and Python. In our work, we implemented the proposed model using Python. This is because it makes data processing faster than other programming languages and includes a rich toolbox.

Results and Analysis

In the clean state, the combination of the SVM algorithm and the WAT-MFCC function gives the best performance in terms of detection accuracy (100%) and real-time factor (RTF=1.50) compared to those obtained with the HMM and MLP algorithms I was able to get Got it. Furthermore, using WAT-MFCC as a feature improved RTF compared to using MFCC alone (1.50 vs. 1.70, respectively) while maintaining high accuracy scores across all tests. In fact, the accuracy and RTF performance results obtained are summarized in Table 2. I should mention that in this paper I only included his RTF results for the algorithm tested in clean conditions, as it did not yield any significant improvement in noisy conditions.

Table 2. Recognition and RTF results for different speech recognition algorithms in clean condition

Algorithm	Recognition Accuracy (%)	RTF
MFCC-SVM	100	1.70
MFCC-HMM	90.90	2.10
MFCC-MLP	93.93	2.70
WAT-MFCC-SVM	100	1.50
WAT-MFCC-HMM	93.93	1.87
WAT-MFCC-MLP	96.96	2.49

Table 3 shows the recognition results obtained with various speech recognition algorithms. From this table, we can conclude that SVM achieved the best detection accuracy under all SNR levels and under all noise conditions. This record was achieved compared to HMM and MLP algorithms. In fact, the best detection accuracy (100%) was achieved at SNRs of 15 and 20 dB. For the MLP and HMM algorithms, it consistently leads to achieving the best 2nd and Her 3rd detection accuracies, respectively, at different SNR levels under different noise conditions. For "cafe" noise with an SNR of 20 dB, the best values for the MLP and HMM algorithms were 96.96% and 93.93%, respectively. We can also see that the detection accuracy improves as the SNR level increases. In all tests, the noise 'traffic jam' had the worst results compared to the noise 'car' and 'café'.

From Tables 2 and 3, it can be said that WAT-MFCC-SVM proves to be efficient in terms of real-time performance in both clean and noisy conditions compared to HM and MLP algorithms. increase. Additionally, the SVM algorithm utilizes a combination of the WAT approach and MFCC coefficients, which significantly contributes to achieving these performances by reducing the amount of noise under test conditions. Table 4 shows some tasks performed in real time using the decoupled speech recognition system. From this table, we can conclude that the proposed model was able to obtain excellent real-time performance compared to other work done on different databases and under different noisy conditions.

Table 3. Recognition results for different speech recognition algorithms in noisy conditions

Type of Noise	Speech Recognition Algorithm	-5db	0db	5db	10db	15db	20db
Traffic jam	WAT-MFCC SVM	**63.63**	**72.72**	**87.87**	**90.90**	**96.96**	**100**
	WAT-MFCC HMM	·54.54	60.6	63.63	69.69	75.75	75.75
	WAT-MFCC MLP	60.6	63.63	66.66	72.72	78.78	84.84
Car	WAT-MFCC SVM	**66.66**	**72.72**	**84.84**	**90.90**	**96.96**	**100**
	WAT-MFCC HMM	60.60	69.69	72,72	72.72	75.75	78.78
	WAT-MFCC MLP	63.63	70.70	72,72	78.78	84.84	87.87
Cafe	WAT-MFCC SVM	**72.72**	**72.72**	**75.75**	**84.84**	**100**	**100**
	WAT-MFCC-HMM	60.60	66.66	69.69	75.75	87.87	93.93
	WAT-MFCC-MLP	63.63	63.63	72.72	78.78	90.90	96.96

CONCLUSION

In this chapter, an implementation of a decoupled speech recognition system was proposed. In this system, his combination of WAT and MFCC with SVM as classifier achieved the best performance in both clean and noisy conditions compared to HMM and MLP algorithms. These performances show recognition accuracy and RTF, with this combination achieving 100% and 1.57 seconds.

Perspectives

As further work, we suggest testing the proposed approach online or offline with other databases, such as the TIMIT database. We also need to implement this approach on other hardware architectures (FPGA, Arduino, etc.) to better see performance progress in real time.

Extend the database and evaluate it with other applications (automotive, medical, transportation), Tested on hybrid recognition modules such as HMM/SVM and HMM/RN Test.

Table 4. Real-time performances obtained with other databases

Database			Feature	Classifier	Accuracy (%)	RTF
Japaneese (Attawibulkul et al., 2017) (10dB)			MFCC	HMM	93.49 (Babble Noise)	2.37
			MFCC +NS		94.84 (Hfchannel Noise)	2.38
Google Speech (Rahat et al., 2018)			Google speech reorganization engine.		Normal environment	
		Bangala			87	
		English			79	
					Calm environment	
		Bangala			85	
		English			90	
					Room environment	
		Bangala			86	
		English			76	
					Wind environment	
		Bangala			70	
		English			70	
Nepali database (Ssarma et al., 2017)			MFCC	HMM	75	-
Indian database (Yağanoğlu et al., 2021)			MFCC	DTW	88	-
Lithuanian database (Adnene et al., 2021)					97.70	-

REFERENCES

Abushariah, A. A. M., Ting, H.-N., Mustafa, M. B. P., Khairuddin, A. S. M., Abushariah, M. A. M., & Tan, T.-P. (2023). Bilingual Automatic Speech Recognition: A Review, Taxonomy and Open Challenges. *IEEE Access : Practical Innovations, Open Solutions, 11*, 5944–5954. doi:10.1109/ACCESS.2022.3218684

Adnene, N., Sabri, B., & Mohammed, B. (2021). Design and implementation of an automatic speech recognition based voice control system. *Conference on Electrical Engineering*.

Ahmed Rahat, S., Imteaj, A., & Rahman, T. (2018). *An IoT based Interactive Speech Recognizable Robot with Distance control using Raspberry Pi*. 2018 2nd Int. Conf. on Innovations in Science, Engineering and Technology (ICISET), Chittagong, Bangladesh.

Alvarez, A. G., Evin, D. A., & Verrastro, S. (2016). Implementation of a Speech Recognition System in a DSC. *IEEE Latin America Transactions, 14*(6), 2657–2662. doi:10.1109/TLA.2016.7555234

Atoui, H., Boughazi, M., & Fezari, M. (2020). Station hybride (DSP/FPGA) pour un système rapide de reconnaissance automatique de la parole. *Synthèse Revue des Sciences et de la Technologie, 26*(2), 33–47.

Attawibulkul, S., Kaewkamnerdpong, B., & Miyanaga, Y. (2017). Noisy Speech Training in MFCC-based Speech Recognition with Noise Suppression Toward Robot Assisted Autism therapy. *The 2017 Biomedical Engineering International Conference (BMEiCON-2017).*

Belabed, T., Coutinho, M. G. F., Fernandes, M. A., Sakuyama, C. V., & Souani, C. (2021). User driven FPGA-based design automated framework of deep neural networks for low-power low-cost edge computing. *IEEE Access : Practical Innovations, Open Solutions, 9*, 89162–89180. doi:10.1109/ACCESS.2021.3090196

Benazzouz, A., & Slimane, Z. E. H. (2019). An automatic muscle activation detection using discrete wavelet and integrated profile: A comparative study. In *Advances in Computing Systems and Applications: Proceedings of the 3rd Conference on Computing Systems and Applications 3* (pp. 169-178). Springer International Publishing. 10.1007/978-3-319-98352-3_18

Bhangale, K. B., & Kothandaraman, M. (2022). Survey of deep learning paradigms for speech processing. *Wireless Personal Communications, 125*(2), 1913–1949. doi:10.100711277-022-09640-y

de la Fuente Garcia, S., Ritchie, C. W., & Luz, S. (2020). Artificial intelligence, speech, and language processing approaches to monitoring Alzheimer's disease: A systematic review. *Journal of Alzheimer's Disease, 78*(4), 1547–1574. doi:10.3233/JAD-200888 PMID:33185605

Gyulyustan & Enkov. (2017). Experimental speech recognition system based on Raspberry Pi 3. *IOSR Journal of Computer Engineering, 19*(3), 107-112.

Haridas, A. V., Marimuthu, R., & Sivakumar, V. G. (2018). A critical review and analysis on techniques of speech recognition: The road ahead. *International Journal of Knowledge-Based and Intelligent Engineering Systems, 22*(1), 39–57. doi:10.3233/KES-180374

Hastuty, A., Muh, B., & Amir, A. (2021). Sistem Pengenalan Ucapan Bahasa Daerah Menggunakan Metode Mel Frequency Cepstral Coefficient (MFCC) dan Adaptive Neuro-Fuzzy Inference System (ANFIS). *Jurnal Sintaks Logika, 1*(2), 76–81.

He, L., Jin, G., & Tsai, S. B. (2021). Design and implementation of embedded real-time English speech recognition system based on big data analysis. *Mathematical Problems in Engineering*, *2021*, 1–12. doi:10.1155/2021/6561730

Hidayat, R., Bejo, A., Sumaryono, S., & Winursito, A. (2018, July). Denoising speech for MFCC feature extraction using wavelet transformation in speech recognition system. In *2018 10th international conference on information technology and electrical engineering (ICITEE)* (pp. 280-284). IEEE. 10.1109/ICITEED.2018.8534807

Huang, H., Xu, H., Wang, X., & Silamu, W. (2015). Maximum F1-score discriminative training criterion for automatic mispronunciation detection. *IEEE/ACM Transactions on Audio, Speech, and Language Processing*, *23*(4), 787–797. doi:10.1109/TASLP.2015.2409733

Ibrahim, Y. A., Odiketa, J. C., & Ibiyemi, T. S. (2017). Preprocessing technique in automatic speech recognition for human computer interaction: An overview. *Ann Comput Sci Ser*, *15*(1), 186–191.

Jamal, N. (2017). Automatic speech recognition (ASR) based approach for speech therapy of aphasic patients: A review. AIP Conference Proceedings, 1883(1). doi:10.1063/1.5002046

Jampour, M., & Sardar, A. K. (2021, April). Facial Expression Recognition using Multi-Feature Concatenation of Local Face Components and Hierarchical SVM. In *2021 5th International Conference on Pattern Recognition and Image Analysis (IPRIA)* (pp. 1-6). IEEE. 10.1109/IPRIA53572.2021.9483543

John, P., Mahesh, T. Y., & Sebastian, B. (2017). ECG signal de-noising, optimization and classification by wave atom transform. *International Conference on Intelligent Computing, Instrumentation and Control Technologies (ICICICT)*. 10.1109/ICICICT1.2017.8342667

John, S. R. A., Mukhedkar, A. S., & Venkatesan, N. (2015). Performance Analysis of SOFM based Reduced Complexity Feature Extraction Methods with back Propagation Neural Network for Multilingual Digit Recognition Networks. *Indian Journal of Science and Technology*, *8*(19), IPL098.

Junlin, Y., Kai, F., & Kaipeng, W. (2019, August). Intelligent recognition mobile platform based on STM32. In *2019 IEEE 3rd International Conference on Circuits, Systems and Devices (ICCSD)* (pp. 153-157). IEEE. 10.1109/ICCSD.2019.8842923

Kerkeni, L., Serrestou, Y., Mbarki, M., Raoof, K., & Mahjoub, M. A. (2018). Speech Emotion Recognition: Methods and Cases Study. *ICAART*, (2), 20. doi:10.5220/0006611601750182

Küçüktopcu, O., Masazade, E., Ünsalan, C., & Varshney, P. K. (2019). A real-time bird sound recognition system using a low-cost microcontroller. *Applied Acoustics*, *148*, 194–201. doi:10.1016/j.apacoust.2018.12.028

Labied, M., & Belangour, A. (2021). Automatic Speech Recognition Features Extraction Techniques: A Multi-criteria Comparison. *International Journal of Advanced Computer Science and Applications*, *12*(8). Advance online publication. doi:10.14569/IJACSA.2021.0120821

Lee, J., & Ahn, B. (2020). Real-time human action recognition with a low-cost RGB camera and mobile robot platform. *Sensors (Basel)*, *20*(10), 2886. doi:10.339020102886 PMID:32438776

Li, X., Yang, Y., Pang, Z., & Wu, X. (2015). A comparative study on selecting acoustic modeling units in deep neural networks based large vocabulary Chinese speech recognition. *Neurocomputing*, *170*, 251–256. doi:10.1016/j.neucom.2014.07.087

Lubbad, M., Alhanjouri, M., & Alhalabi, H. (2019). Robust breast cancer classification using wave atom and back propagation neural networks. *Pertanika Journal of Science & Technology*, *27*(3), 1247–1257.

McLoughlin, Zhang, Xie, Song, & Xiao. (2015). Robust Sound Event Classification Using Deep Neural Networks. *IEEE/ACM Transactions on Audio, Speech, and Language Processing, 23*, 540 - 552.

Mnassri, A., Bennasr, M., & Adnane, C. (2019). A robust feature extraction method for real-time speech recognition system on a raspberry Pi 3 board. *Engineering, Technology & Applied Scientific Research*, *9*(2), 4066–4070.

Mohamed, W., Souha, B., & Adnen, C. (2019). Speech recognition system based on discrete wave atoms transform partial noisy environment. *International Journal of Advanced Computer Science and Applications*, *10*(5).

Mustafa, M. K., Allen, T., & Appiah, K. (2019). A comparative review of dynamic neural networks and hidden Markov model methods for mobile on-device speech recognition. *Neural Computing & Applications*, *31*(S2), 891–899. doi:10.100700521-017-3028-2

Oruh, J., Viriri, S., & Adegun, A. (2022). Long short-term Memory Recurrent neural network for Automatic speech recognition. *IEEE Access : Practical Innovations, Open Solutions*, *10*, 30069–30079. doi:10.1109/ACCESS.2022.3159339

Patange, P. P., & Alex, J. S. R. (2017, March). Implementation of ANN based speech recognition system on an embedded board. In *2017 International Conference on Nextgen Electronic Technologies: Silicon to Software (ICNETS2)* (pp. 408-412). IEEE. 10.1109/ICNETS2.2017.8067968

Patel, S., John, S. R. A., & Venkatesan, N. (2015). Low-Power Multi-Layer Perceptron Neural Network Architecture for Speech Recognition Networks. *Indian Journal of Science and Technology, 8*(20). doi:10.17485/ijst/2015/v8i20/87516

Pisner, D. A., & Schnyer, D. M. (2020). Support vector machine. In *Machine learning* (pp. 101–121). Academic Press. doi:10.1016/B978-0-12-815739-8.00006-7

Prongnuch, S., & Sitjongsataporn, S. (2020). Thai voice-controlled analysis for car parking assistance in system-on-chip architecture. *Advances in Technology Innovation, 5*(4), 203. doi:10.46604/aiti.2020.5597

Rashid, H., Ahmed, I. U., Osman, S. B., Newaz, B., Rasheduzzaman, M., & Reza, S. T. (2017, January). Design and implementation of a voice controlled robot with human interaction ability. In *International Conference on Computer, Communication, Chemical, Materials and Electronic Engineering* (*Vol. 65*, pp. 148-151). Academic Press.

Ravi, D. J. (2021). Robust Perceptual Wavelet Packet Features for Recognition of Continuous Kannada Speech. *Wireless Personal Communications, 121*(3), 1781–1804. doi:10.100711277-021-08736-1

Rolon-Heredia, J. A., Garrido-Arevalo, V. M., & Marulanda, J. (2019). Voice compression using discrete cosine transform and wavelet transform. *Journal of Physics: Conference Series, 1403*(1), 012001. doi:10.1088/1742-6596/1403/1/012001

Sanjaya, W. M., Anggraeni, D., & Santika, I. P. (2018, September). Speech recognition using linear predictive coding (LPC) and adaptive neuro-fuzzy (ANFIS) to control 5 DoF arm robot. *Journal of Physics: Conference Series, 1090*(1), 012046. doi:10.1088/1742-6596/1090/1/012046

Sarić, R., Jokić, D., Beganović, N., Pokvić, L. G., & Badnjević, A. (2020). FPGA-based real-time epileptic seizure classification using Artificial Neural Network. *Biomedical Signal Processing and Control, 62*, 102106. doi:10.1016/j.bspc.2020.102106

Shymkovych, V., Telenyk, S., & Kravets, P. (2021). Hardware implementation of radial-basis neural networks with Gaussian activation functions on FPGA. *Neural Computing & Applications, 33*(15), 9467–9479. doi:10.100700521-021-05706-3

Ssarma, M. K., Gajurel, A., Pokhrel, A., & Joshi, B. (2017). HMM based isolated word Nepali speech recognition. *2017 International Conference on Machine Learning and Cybernetics (ICMLC)*. 10.1109/ICMLC.2017.8107745

Sugumaran, S., & Prakash, V. R. (2015). PSoC based speech recognition system. *International Refereed Journal of Engineering and Science, 4*, 1-7.

Suryawanshi, U., & Ganorkar, S. R. (2014). Hardware Implementation of Speech Recognition Using MFCC and Euclidean Distance. *Int. J. Adv. Res. Electr. Electron. Instrum. Eng., 03*(08), 11248–11254.

Tang, Y., Pino, J., Wang, C., Ma, X., & Genzel, D. (2021). A general multi-task learning framework to leverage text data for speech to text tasks. In *ICASSP 2021-2021 IEEE International Conference on Acoustics, Speech and Signal Processing (ICASSP)* (pp. 6209-6213). IEEE. 10.1109/ICASSP39728.2021.9415058

Walid, M., Bousselmi, S., Dabbabi, K., & Cherif, A. (2019). Real-time implementation of isolated-word speech recognition system on raspberry Pi 3 using WAT-MFCC. *IJCSNS, 19*(3), 42.

Wang, Z. (2022). Audio Signal Acquisition and Processing System Based on Model DSP Rapid Design. *Security and Communication Networks*. doi:10.1155/2022/4593339

Yağanoğlu, M. (2021). Real time wearable speech recognition system for deaf persons. *Computers & Electrical Engineering, 91*, 107026. doi:10.1016/j.compeleceng.2021.107026

Yao, Y., & Cao, Y. (2020). A neural network enhanced hidden Markov model for tourism demand forecasting. *Applied Soft Computing, 94*, 106465. doi:10.1016/j.asoc.2020.106465

Yin, R., Wang, D., Zhao, S., Lou, Z., & Shen, G. (2021). Wearable sensors-enabled human–machine interaction systems: From design to application. *Advanced Functional Materials, 31*(11), 2008936. doi:10.1002/adfm.202008936

Yuvaraj, S., Badholia, A., William, P., Vengatesan, K., & Bibave, R. (2022, May). Speech Recognition Based Robotic Arm Writing. In *Proceedings of International Conference on Communication and Artificial Intelligence: ICCAI 2021* (pp. 23-33). Springer Nature Singapore.

Compilation of References

Abushariah, A. A. M., Ting, H.-N., Mustafa, M. B. P., Khairuddin, A. S. M., Abushariah, M. A. M., & Tan, T.-P. (2023). Bilingual Automatic Speech Recognition: A Review, Taxonomy and Open Challenges. *IEEE Access : Practical Innovations, Open Solutions*, *11*, 5944–5954. doi:10.1109/ACCESS.2022.3218684

Adnene, N., Sabri, B., & Mohammed, B. (2021). Design and implementation of an automatic speech recognition based voice control system. *Conference on Electrical Engineering.*

Ahmed Rahat, S., Imteaj, A., & Rahman, T. (2018). *An IoT based Interactive Speech Recognizable Robot with Distance control using Raspberry Pi.* 2018 2nd Int. Conf. on Innovations in Science, Engineering and Technology (ICISET), Chittagong, Bangladesh.

Alanizy, N., Alanizy, A., Baghoza, N., AlGhamdi, M., & Gutub, A. (2018). 3-layer PC text security via combining compression, AES cryptography 2LSB image steganography. *Journal of Research in Engineering and Applied Sciences*, *3*(4), 118–124. doi:10.46565/jreas.2018.v03i04.001

Alcaraz Meseguer, N. (2009). *Speech analysis for automatic speech recognition* [Master's thesis]. Institutt for elektronikk og telekommunikasjon.

Alekhya, D., Prabha, G., & Rao, G. (2014). Fake currency detection using image processing and other standard methods. *International Journal of Research in Computer and Communication Technology*, *3*, 128–131.

Ali, Z., Hossain, M. S., Muhammad, G., & Aslam, M. (2018). New Zero-Watermarking Algorithm Using Hurst Exponent for Protection of Privacy in Telemedicine. *IEEE Access, Volume*, *6*, 7930–7940. doi:10.1109/ACCESS.2018.2799604

Alok, K., & Singh, K. (2014). Complex wavelet based moving object segmentation using approximate median filter-based method for video surveillance. *International Advance Computing Conference (IACC).*

Alsaidi, M., & Altaher, M. (2010). A Comparison of Some Thresholding Selection Methods for Wavelet Regression. *International Journal of Mathematics and Computer Science*, *4*(2), 105–111.

Alvarez, A. G., Evin, D. A., & Verrastro, S. (2016). Implementation of a Speech Recognition System in a DSC. *IEEE Latin America Transactions*, *14*(6), 2657–2662. doi:10.1109/TLA.2016.7555234

Ammous, D., Kammoun, F., & Masmoudi, N. (2014, December). Improved Hierarchical lossless video coding. In *International Conference on Sciences and Techniques of Automatic Control and Computer Engineering (STA)* (pp. 525-530). IEEE.

Ammous, D., Kammoun, F., & Masmoudi, N. (2020, September). Analysis of Coding and Transfer of Arien Video Sequences from H. 264 Standard. In *5th International Conference on Advanced Technologies for Signal and Image Processing (ATSIP)* (pp. 1-5). IEEE. 10.1109/ATSIP49331.2020.9231819

Ammous, D., Khlif, N., Kammoun, F., & Masmoudi, N. (2019, December). Encryption of lossless coded videos. In *International Conference on Internet of Things, Embedded Systems and Communications (IINTEC)* (pp. 226-230). IEEE.

Amornraksa, T., & Janthawongwilai, K. (2006). Enhanced Images Watermarking based on Amplitude Modulation. *Image and Vision Computing, 24*(2), 111–119. doi:10.1016/j.imavis.2005.09.018

Anjali, S., & Parul, B. (2018). Different video watermarking techniques - A review. *International Journal of Scientific Research in Computer Science, Engineering and Information Technology, 3*(1), 1890–1894.

Antony, R., & Uma, M. (2014). Using digital signature. *International Journal of Computer Network and Security, 6*(1), 16–21.

Araghi, T. K., Manaf, A. A., Alarood, A., & Zainol, A. B. (2018). Host Feasibility Investigation to Improve Robustness in Hybrid DWT+SVD Based Image Watermarking Schemes. *Advances in Multimedia, 2018*, 1609378. Advance online publication. doi:10.1155/2018/1609378

Atoui, H., Boughazi, M., & Fezari, M. (2020). Station hybride (DSP/FPGA) pour un système rapide de reconnaissance automatique de la parole. *Synthèse Revue des Sciences et de la Technologie, 26*(2), 33–47.

Atrey, P., Yan, W., Chang, E., & Kankanhalli, M. (2004) A hierarchical signature scheme for robust video authentication using secret sharing. *International Multimedia Modelling Conference,* 330-337. 10.1109/MULMM.2004.1265004

Atrey, P., Yan, W., & Kankanhalli, M. (2007). A scalable signature scheme for video authentication. *Multimedia Tools and Applications, 34*(1), 107–135. doi:10.100711042-006-0074-7

Attawibulkul, S., Kaewkamnerdpong, B., & Miyanaga, Y. (2017). Noisy speech training in MFCC-based speech recognition with noise suppression toward robot assisted autism therapy. In *2017 10th Biomedical Engineering International Conference (BMEiCON)* (pp. 1-5). IEEE. 10.1109/BMEiCON.2017.8229135

Attawibulkul, S., Kaewkamnerdpong, B., & Miyanaga, Y. (2017). Noisy Speech Training in MFCC-based Speech Recognition with Noise Suppression Toward Robot Assisted Autism therapy. *The 2017 Biomedical Engineering International Conference (BMEiCON-2017).*

Attitallah, A., Bedoui, S., & Abderrahim, K. (2016). System identification: Parameter and time-delay estimation for Wiener nonlinear systems with delayed input. *Transactions of the Institute of Measurement and Control, 40*. Advance online publication. doi:0.1177/0142331216674772

Bahdanau, D., Cho, K., & Bengio, Y. (2014) Neural machine translation by jointly learning to align and translate. *Proceedings of International Conference on Learning Representations.*

Bansal, M., Yan, W., & Kankanhalli, M. (2003). Article. *Proceedings of IEEE Pacific Rim Conference on Multimedia, 2*, 965-969.

Beauduin, T., & Fujimoto, H. (2017). Identiðcation of system dynamics with time delay: A two-stage frequency domain approach. *IFAC-PapersOnLine, 50*(1), 10870–10875. doi:10.1016/j.ifacol.2017.08.2443

Bedoui, S., Ltaief, M., & Abderrahim, K. (2012).Using a recursive least square algorithm for identification of interconnected linear discrete-time delay multivariable system. *17th International Conference on Methods and Models in Automation and Robotics*. 10.1109/MMAR.2012.6347884

Bedoui, S., Ltaief, M., & Abderrahim, K. (2013). Online Identification of Multivariable Discrete Time Delay Systems Using a Recursive Least Square Algorithm. *Mathematical Problems in Engineering, 2013*, 1–18. Advance online publication. doi:10.1155/2013/658194

Belabed, T., Coutinho, M. G. F., Fernandes, M. A., Sakuyama, C. V., & Souani, C. (2021). User driven FPGA-based design automated framework of deep neural networks for low-power low-cost edge computing. *IEEE Access : Practical Innovations, Open Solutions, 9*, 89162–89180. doi:10.1109/ACCESS.2021.3090196

Benazzouz, A., & Slimane, Z. E. H. (2019). An automatic muscle activation detection using discrete wavelet and integrated profile: A comparative study. In *Advances in Computing Systems and Applications: Proceedings of the 3rd Conference on Computing Systems and Applications 3* (pp. 169-178). Springer International Publishing. 10.1007/978-3-319-98352-3_18

Bhangale, K. B., & Kothandaraman, M. (2022). Survey of deep learning paradigms for speech processing. *Wireless Personal Communications, 125*(2), 1913–1949. doi:10.100711277-022-09640-y

Bharati, P., & Pramanik, A. (2020). Deep learning techniques - R-CNN to Mask R-CNN: A survey. In *Proceedings of Computational Intelligence in Pattern Recognition* (pp. 657–668). Springer. doi:10.1007/978-981-13-9042-5_56

Bochkovskiy, A., Wang, C., & Liao, H. (2020). *YOLOv4: Optimal speed and accuracy of object detection.* CoRR abs/2004.10934.

Boussif, M. (2022). On The Security of Advanced Encryption Standard (AES). *8th International Conference on Engineering, Applied Sciences, and Technology (ICEAST)*, 83-88. 10.1109/ICEAST55249.2022.9826324

Boussif, M., Aloui, N., & Cherif, A. (2017). New Watermarking/Encryption Method for Medical Images Full Protection in mHealth. *Iranian Journal of Electrical and Computer Engineering*, *7*(6), 3385–3394.

Boussif, M., Aloui, N., & Cherif, A. (2018). Secured cloud computing for medical data based on watermarking and encryption. *IET Networks*, *7*(5), 294–298. doi:10.1049/iet-net.2017.0180

Boussif, M., Aloui, N., & Cherif, A. (2019). Images encryption algorithm based on the quaternion multiplication and the XOR operation. *Multimedia Tools and Applications*, *78*(24), 35493–35510. doi:10.100711042-019-08108-9

Boussif, M., Aloui, N., & Cherif, A. (2020). DICOM imaging watermarking for hiding medical reports. *Medical & Biological Engineering & Computing*, *58*(11), 2905–2918. doi:10.100711517-020-02269-8 PMID:32979170

Boussif, M., Aloui, N., & Cherif, A. (2020). Securing DICOM images by a new encryption algorithm using Arnold transform and Vigenère cipher. *IET Image Processing*, *14*(6), 1209–1216. doi:10.1049/iet-ipr.2019.0042

Boussif, M., Bouferas, O., Aloui, N., & Cherif, A. (2021). A Novel Robust Blind AES/LWT+DCT+SVD-Based Crypto-Watermarking schema for DICOM Images Security. *IEEE International Conference on Design & Test of Integrated Micro & Nano-Systems (DTS)*, 1-6. 10.1109/DTS52014.2021.9497916

Brouard, O. (2010). *Pré-analyse de la vidéo pour un codage adapté. Application au codage de la TVHD en flux H. 264* [Doctoral dissertation]. Université de Nantes.

Carion, N., Massa, F., Synnaeve, G., Usunier, N., Kirillov, A., & Zagoruyko, S. (2020). End-to-end object detection with transformers. In *Proceedings of European Conference on Computer Vision* (pp. 213 - 229). Springer.

Cedillo-Hernandez, M., Garcia-Ugalde, F., Nakano-Miyatake, M., & Perez-Meana, H. (2015). Robust watermarking method in DFT domain for effective management of medical imaging. *Signal, Image and Video Processing*, *9*(5), 1163–1178. doi:10.100711760-013-0555-x

Chambers, J., Yan, W., Garhwal, A., & Kankanhalli, M. (2014). Currency security and forensics: A survey. *Multimedia Tools and Applications*, *74*(11), 4013–4043. doi:10.100711042-013-1809-x

Chambolle, A., DeVore, R., Lee, N., & Lucier, J. (1998). Nonlinear wavelet image processing: Variational problems, compression, and noise removal through wavelet shrinkage. *IEEE Transactions on Image Processing*, *7*(3), 319–335. doi:10.1109/83.661182 PMID:18276252

Chandrasekaran, R., & Chidambaram, M. (2012). Closed-Loop Identification of Second-Order Plus Time Delay (SOPTD) Model of Multivariable Systems by Optimization Method. *Industrial & Engineering Chemistry Research*, *51*(28), 9620–9633. doi:10.1021/ie203003p

Chien, W. D., Liao, K. Y., & Yang, J. F. (2011, December). H. 264-based Hierarchical Lossless Coding System with New Intra Prediction Method. In *International Conference on Intelligent Computation and Bio-Medical Instrumentation* (pp. 171-174). IEEE. 10.1109/ICBMI.2011.63

Chien, W. D., Liao, K. Y., & Yang, J. F. (2014). H. 264-based hierarchical two-layer lossless video coding method. *IET Signal Processing*, *8*(1), 21–29. doi:10.1049/iet-spr.2013.0088

Chih-Hsien. (2014). Efficient modified directional lifting-based discrete wavelet transform for moving object detection. *Signal Processing*, 138–152.

Choudhary, R., & Parmar, G. (2016). A Robust Image Watermarking Technique using 2-level Discrete Wavelet Transform (DWT). *2nd International Conference on Communication Control and Intelligent Systems (CCIS)*. 10.1109/CCIntelS.2016.7878213

Dai, Y., Zhang, Q., Tourapis, A., & Kuo, C. C. J. (2008, October). Efficient block-based intra prediction for image coding with 2D geometrical manipulations. In *15th IEEE International Conference on Image Processing* (pp. 2916-2919). IEEE.

Datta, D., Garg, L., Srinivasan, K., Inoue, A., & Thippa Reddy, G. (2020). An efficient sound and data steganography based secure authentication system. *Computers. Materials & Continua*, *67*(1), 723–751. doi:10.32604/cmc.2021.014802

de la Fuente Garcia, S., Ritchie, C. W., & Luz, S. (2020). Artificial intelligence, speech, and language processing approaches to monitoring Alzheimer's disease: A systematic review. *Journal of Alzheimer's Disease*, *78*(4), 1547–1574. doi:10.3233/JAD-200888 PMID:33185605

Deepak, C., & Prachi, S. (2018). Digital video watermarking scheme using wavelets with MATLAB. *International Journal of Computers and Applications*, *180*(14), 30–34. doi:10.5120/ijca2018916272

Ding, J. R., Chen, J. Y., Yang, F. C., & Yang, J. F. (2008, March). Two-layer and adaptive entropy coding algorithms for H. 264-based lossless image coding. In *IEEE International Conference on Acoustics, Speech and Signal Processing* (pp. 1369-1372). IEEE.

Ding, W., & Yan, W. (2000). Digital image scrambling and digital watermarking technology based on Conway's game. *Journal of North China University of Technology*, *12*(1), 1–5.

Ding, W., Yan, W., & Qi, D. (2001a). Digital image watermarking based on U-system. *Journal of Image and Graphics*, *6*(6), 552–557.

Ding, W., Yan, W., & Qi, D. (2001b). Cox's and Pitas's schemes for digital image watermarking. *Journal of Northern China University of Technology*, *12*(3), 1–12.

Ding, W., Yan, W., & Qi, D. (2002). Digital image watermarking based on discrete wavelet transform. *Journal of Computer Science and Technology*, *17*(2), 129–139. doi:10.1007/BF02962205

Donoho, D. L. (1995). Denoising by soft-thresholding. *IEEE Transactions on Information Theory*, *41*(3), 613–627. doi:10.1109/18.382009

Dosovitskiy, A., Beyer, L., Kolesnikov, A., Weissenborn, D., Zhai, X., Unterthiner, T., Dehghani, M., Minderer, M., Heigold, G., Gelly, S., Uszkoreit, J., & Houlsby, N. (2020). An image is worth 16×16 words: Transformers for image recognition at scale. *Proceedings of ICLR*.

Elgammal, A. A. (2015). *Background Subtraction: Theory and Practice*. Wide Area Surveillance. doi:10.1007/978-3-031-01813-8

El-Shafai, W., Khallaf, F., El-Rabaie, E. S. M., & El-Samie, F. E. A. (2021). Robust medical image encryption based on DNA-chaos cryptosystem for secure telemedicine and healthcare applications. *Journal of Ambient Intelligence and Humanized Computing, 12*(10), 9007–9035. doi:10.100712652-020-02597-5

Eswar Kumar, M., Thippa Reddy, G., & Sudheer, K. (2017). Vehicle Theft Identification and Intimation Using GSM & IOT. *IOP Conf. Ser.: Mater. Sci. Eng, 263*, 042062.

Eswaraiah, R., & Reddy, E. S. (2015). Robust medical image watermarking technique for accurate detection of tampers inside region of interest and recovering original region of interest. *IET Image Processing, Volume, 9*(8), 615–625. doi:10.1049/iet-ipr.2014.0986

Fang-Hsuan, C., & Yu-Liang, C. (2006). Real time multiple objects tracking and identification based on discrete wavelet transform. *Pattern Recognition, 39*(6), 1126–1139. doi:10.1016/j.patcog.2005.12.010

Frosini, A., Gori, M., & Priami, P. (1996). A neural network-based model for paper currency recognition and verification. In *Proceedings of IEEE Transactions on Neural Networks* (pp. 1482 - 1490). IEEE Press. 10.1109/72.548175

Fu, W., Yan, W., & Kankanhalli, M. (2005) Progressive scrambling for MP3 audio. *IEEE International Symposium on Circuits and Systems (ISCAS), 5525-5528.*

Gaikwad, S., Gawali, B., Yannawar, P., & Mehrotra, S. (2011). Feature extraction using fusion MFCC for continuous marathi speech recognition. In *2011 Annual IEEE India Conference* (pp. 1-5). IEEE. 10.1109/INDCON.2011.6139372

Gangadhar, Y., Giridhar Akula, V. S., & Chenna Reddy, P. (2018). An evolutionary programming approach for securing medical images using watermarking scheme in invariant discrete wavelet transformation. *Biomedical Signal Processing and Control, 43*, 31–40. doi:10.1016/j.bspc.2018.02.007

Gao, X., Mou, J., Xiong, L., Sha, Y., Yan, H., & Cao, Y. (2022). A fast and efficient multiple images encryption based on single-channel encryption and chaotic system. *Nonlinear Dynamics, 108*(1), 613–636. doi:10.100711071-021-07192-7

Gautam, K. (2020). Indian currency detection using image recognition technique. In *Proceedings of International Conference on Computer Science, Engineering and Applications* (pp. 1 - 5). 10.1109/ICCSEA49143.2020.9132955

Graciela, R. & Mario I. (2016) Auto-Adaptive Parallel SOM Architecture with a modular analysis for dynamic object segmentation in videos. *Neurocomputing, 175*(B), 990–1000.

Gupta, M. (2021). *Improving Security for Video Watermarking* [Master's Thesis]. Auckland University of Technology, New Zealand.

Gupta, A., Singh, D., & Kaur, M. (2020). An efficient image encryption using non-dominated sorting genetic algorithm-III based 4-D chaotic maps. *Journal of Ambient Intelligence and Humanized Computing*, *11*(3), 1309–1324. doi:10.100712652-019-01493-x

Gutub, A. (2022a). Boosting image watermarking authenticity spreading secrecy from counting-based secret-sharing. *CAAI Transactions on Intelligence Technology*, cit2.12093. doi:10.1049/cit2.12093

Gutub, A. (2022a). Enhancing Cryptography of Grayscale Images via Resilience Randomization Flexibility. *International Journal of Information Security and Privacy*, *16*(1), 1–28. doi:10.4018/IJISP.307071

Gutub, A. (2022b). Watermarking images via counting-based secret sharing for lightweight semi-complete authentication. *International Journal of Information Security and Privacy*, *16*(1), 1–18. doi:10.4018/IJISP.2022010118

Gutub, A. (2022c). Adopting counting-based secret-sharing for e-Video watermarking allowing fractional invalidation. *Multimedia Tools and Applications*, *81*(7), 9527–9547. doi:10.100711042-022-12062-4

Gutub, A. A.-A. (2010). Pixel indicator technique for RGB image steganography. *Journal of Emerging Technologies in Web Intelligence*, *2*(1), 56–64. doi:10.4304/jetwi.2.1.56-64

Gutub, A., & Al-Roithy, B. (2021). Varying PRNG to improve image cryptography implementation. *Journal of Engineering Research*, *9*(3A). Advance online publication. doi:10.36909/jer.v9i3A.10111

Gutub, A., & Al-Shaarani, F. (2020). Efficient implementation of multi-image secret hiding based on LSB and DWT steganography comparisons. *Arabian Journal for Science and Engineering*, *45*(4), 2631–2644. doi:10.100713369-020-04413-w

Gyulyustan & Enkov. (2017). Experimental speech recognition system based on Raspberry Pi 3. *IOSR Journal of Computer Engineering, 19*(3), 107-112.

Haddad, S., Coatrieux, G., Moreau-Gaudry, A., & Cozic, M. (2020). Joint Watermarking-Encryption-JPEG-LS for Medical Image Reliability Control in Encrypted and Compressed Domains. *IEEE Transactions on Information Forensics and Security*, *15*, 2556–2569. doi:10.1109/TIFS.2020.2972159

Harahap, M., & Khairina, N. (2020). Dynamic steganography least significant bit with stretch on pixels neighborhood. *Journal of Information Systems Engineering and Business Intelligence*, *6*(2), 151. doi:10.20473/jisebi.6.2.151-158

Haridas, A. V., Marimuthu, R., & Sivakumar, V. G. (2018). A critical review and analysis on techniques of speech recognition: The road ahead. *International Journal of Knowledge-Based and Intelligent Engineering Systems*, *22*(1), 39–57. doi:10.3233/KES-180374

Harjito, B., & Suryani, E. (2017). Robust image watermarking using DWT and SVD for copyright protection. *AIP Conference Proceedings*, *1813*, 040003. doi:10.1063/1.4975968

Hassan, F. S., & Gutub, A. (2021). Efficient image reversible data hiding technique based on interpolation optimization. *Arabian Journal for Science and Engineering*, *46*(9), 8441–8456. doi:10.100713369-021-05529-3

Hassan, F., & Gutub, A. (2022). Improving data hiding within colour images using hue component of HSV colour space. *CAAI Transactions on Intelligence Technology*, *7*(1), 56–68. doi:10.1049/cit2.12053

Hassan, S., & Gutub, A. (2021). Efficient image reversible data hiding technique based on interpolation optimization Fatuma. *Journal for Science and Engineering*, *46*, 8441–8456.

Hastuty, A., Muh, B., & Amir, A. (2021). Sistem Pengenalan Ucapan Bahasa Daerah Menggunakan Metode Mel Frequency Cepstral Coefficient (MFCC) dan Adaptive Neuro-Fuzzy Inference System (ANFIS). *Jurnal Sintaks Logika*, *1*(2), 76–81.

Heindel, A., Wige, E., & Kaup, A. (2014, October). Sample-based weighted prediction for lossless enhancement layer coding in SHVC. In *IEEE International Conference on Image Processing (ICIP)* (pp. 3656-3660). 10.1109/ICIP.2014.7025742

Heindel, A., Wige, E., & Kaup, A. (2016). Low-complexity enhancement layer compression for scalable lossless video coding based on HEVC. *IEEE Transactions on Circuits and Systems for Video Technology*, *27*(8), 1749–1760. doi:10.1109/TCSVT.2016.2556338

He, L., Jin, G., & Tsai, S. B. (2021). Design and implementation of embedded real-time English speech recognition system based on big data analysis. *Mathematical Problems in Engineering*, *2021*, 1–12. doi:10.1155/2021/6561730

Hidayat, R., Bejo, A., Sumaryono, S., & Winursito, A. (2018, July). Denoising speech for MFCC feature extraction using wavelet transformation in speech recognition system. In *2018 10th international conference on information technology and electrical engineering (ICITEE)* (pp. 280-284). IEEE. 10.1109/ICITEED.2018.8534807

Hidayat, R., & Ikawijaya, W. (2015). Wavelet based feature extraction for the vowel sound. In *2015 International Conference on Information Technology Systems and Innovation (ICITSI)* (pp. 1-4). IEEE. 10.1109/ICITSI.2015.7437702

Hsieh, S., Chen, C., & Shen, W. (2014). Combining digital watermarking and fingerprinting techniques to identify copyrights for color images. *TheScientificWorldJournal*, *2014*, 1–14. doi:10.1155/2014/454867 PMID:25114966

Huang, H., Xu, H., Wang, X., & Silamu, W. (2015). Maximum F1-score discriminative training criterion for automatic mispronunciation detection. *IEEE/ACM Transactions on Audio, Speech, and Language Processing*, *23*(4), 787–797. doi:10.1109/TASLP.2015.2409733

Huffman, D. A. (1952). A method for the construction of minimum-redundancy codes. *Proceedings of the IRE*, *40*(9), 1098–1101. doi:10.1109/JRPROC.1952.273898

Hu, J., Shen, L., & Sun, G. (2018). Squeeze-and-excitation networks. In *Proceedings of IEEE Conference on Computer Vision and Pattern Recognition* (pp. 7132 - 7141). IEEE.

Hu, R., & Xiang, S. (2021). Cover-Lossless Robust Image Watermarking Against Geometric Deformations. *IEEE Transactions on Image Processing*, *30*, 318–331. doi:10.1109/TIP.2020.3036727 PMID:33186107

Hureib, E. S., & Gutub, A. A. (2020). Enhancing medical data security via combining elliptic curve cryptography and image steganography. *Int. J. Comput. Sci. Netw. Secur.*, *20*(8), 1–8.

Ian, T., Bouridane, A., Kurugollu, F., & Yan, W. (2008) Video watermarking using complex wavelets. In Multimedia Communication Security: Recent Advances (pp. 197-216). NOVA Publisher.

Ibrahim, Y. A., Odiketa, J. C., & Ibiyemi, T. S. (2017). Preprocessing technique in automatic speech recognition for human computer interaction: An overview. *Ann Comput Sci Ser*, *15*(1), 186–191.

Imen, N. (2018). *A novel blind and robust video watermarking technique in fast motion frames based on SVD and MR-SVD*. Hindawi Security and Communication Networks.

Iqbal, N., & Hanif, M. (2021). An efficient grayscale image encryption scheme based on variable length row-column swapping operations. *Multimed Tools Appl*, *80*, 36305–36339,

Isard, M. (1998). A mixed-state condensation tracker with automatic model-switching. *6th International Conference on Computer Vision (IEEE Cat. No.98CH36271)*. 10.1109/ICCV.1998.710707

Ismail, H., David, H., & Larry, S. (1998). A Real-Time System for Detecting and Tracking People in 2 1/2 D. *European Conference on Computer Vision (ECCV)*.

Iwana, B., & Uchida, S. (2021). An empirical survey of data augmentation for time series classification with neural networks. *PLoS One*, *16*(7), e0254841. doi:10.1371/journal.pone.0254841 PMID:34264999

Iwendi, C., Jalil, Z., Javed, A. R., Reddy G, T., Kaluri, R., Srivastava, G., & Jo, O. (2020). KeySplitWatermark: Zero Watermarking Algorithm for Software Protection Against Cyber-Attacks. *IEEE Access : Practical Innovations, Open Solutions*, *8*, 72650–72660. doi:10.1109/ACCESS.2020.2988160

Jamal, N. (2017). Automatic speech recognition (ASR) based approach for speech therapy of aphasic patients: A review. AIP Conference Proceedings, 1883(1). doi:10.1063/1.5002046

Jamali, M., Samavi, S., Karimi, N., Soroushmehr, S. M. R., Ward, K., & Najarian, K. (2016). Robust Watermarking in Non-ROI of Medical Images Based on DCT-DWT. *38th Annual International Conference of the IEEE Engineering in Medicine and Biology Society (EMBC)*. 10.1109/EMBC.2016.7590920

Jampour, M., & Sardar, A. K. (2021, April). Facial Expression Recognition using Multi-Feature Concatenation of Local Face Components and Hierarchical SVM. In *2021 5th International Conference on Pattern Recognition and Image Analysis (IPRIA)* (pp. 1-6). IEEE. 10.1109/IPRIA53572.2021.9483543

Jhawar, G., Nagraj, P., & Mahalakshmi, P. (2016). Speech disorder recognition using MFCC. In *2016 International Conference on Communication and Signal Processing (ICCSP)* (pp. 0246-0250). IEEE. 10.1109/ICCSP.2016.7754132

Jiao, M., He, J., & Zhang, B. (2018). Folding paper currency recognition and research based on convolution neural network. In *Proceedings of International Conference on Advances in Computing, Communications and Informatics* (pp. 18 - 23). 10.1109/ICACCI.2018.8554772

Jin, F., & Qiu, T. (2019). Adaptive time delay estimation based on the maximum correntropy criterion. *Digital Signal Processing, 88*, 23–32. doi:10.1016/j.dsp.2019.01.014

Jocher, G. (2020). *YOLOv5, Code repository, 2020.* https://github.com/ultralytics/yolov5

John, P., Mahesh, T. Y., & Sebastian, B. (2017). ECG signal de-noising, optimization and classification by wave atom transform. *International Conference on Intelligent Computing, Instrumentation and Control Technologies (ICICICT).* 10.1109/ICICICT1.2017.8342667

John, S. R. A., Mukhedkar, A. S., & Venkatesan, N. (2015). Performance Analysis of SOFM based Reduced Complexity Feature Extraction Methods with back Propagation Neural Network for Multilingual Digit Recognition Networks. *Indian Journal of Science and Technology, 8*(19), IPL098.

Junlin, Y., Kai, F., & Kaipeng, W. (2019, August). Intelligent recognition mobile platform based on STM32. In *2019 IEEE 3rd International Conference on Circuits, Systems and Devices (ICCSD)* (pp. 153-157). IEEE. 10.1109/ICCSD.2019.8842923

Kalpana, M., Suparshya, S., Susrutha, S., & Habibulla, K. (2013). FPGA implementation of moving object detection in frames by using background subtraction algorithm. *International Conference on Communication and Signal Processing.*

Kamal, S., Chawla, S. S., Goel, N., & Raman, B. (2015). Feature extraction and identification of Indian currency notes. In *Proceedings of National Conference on Computer Vision, Pattern Recognition, Image Processing and Graphics* (pp. 1 - 4), IEEE Press. 10.1109/NCVPRIPG.2015.7490005

Kavitha, N., & Ruba, K. (2017). Moving shadow detection based on stationary wavelet transform. *EURASIP Journal on Image and Video Processing, 49*, 1–19.

Kazemi, M. F., Pourmina, M. A., & Mazinan, A. H. (2020). Analysis of Watermarking Framework for Color Image through a Neural Network-based Approach. *Complex & Intelligent Systems, 6*(1), 213–220. doi:10.100740747-020-00129-4

Kerkeni, L., Serrestou, Y., Mbarki, M., Raoof, K., & Mahjoub, M. A. (2018). Speech Emotion Recognition: Methods and Cases Study. *ICAART*, (2), 20. doi:10.5220/0006611601750182

Khashan, O. A., & AlShaikh, M. (2020). Edge-based lightweight selective encryption scheme for digital medical images. *Multimed Tools Appl., 79*, 26369–26388.

Kheshaifaty, N., & Gutub, A. (2021). *Engineering graphical captcha and AES crypto Hash functions for secure online authentication. Journal of Engineering Research.*

Kim, B.-S., Choi, J.-G., Park, C.-H., Won, J.-U., Kwak, D.-M., Oh, S.-K., Koh, C.-R., & Park, K.-H. (2003). Robust digital image watermarking method against geometrical attacks. *Real-Time Imaging, 9*(2), 139–149. doi:10.1016/S1077-2014(03)00020-2

Kim, S. H., Kang, J. W., & Kuo, C. C. J. (2011). Improved H. 264/AVC lossless intra coding with two-layered residual coding (TRC). *IEEE Transactions on Circuits and Systems for Video Technology, 21*(7), 1005–1010. doi:10.1109/TCSVT.2011.2133170

Koppu & Viswanatham. (2020). An efficient image system-based grey wolf optimiser method for multimedia image security using reduced entropy-based 3D chaotic map. *International Journal of Computer Aided Engineering and Technology, 13*(3).

Koppu, S., & Viswanatham, V. M. (2018). Medical image security enhancement using two dimensional chaotic mapping optimized by self-adaptive grey wolf algorithm. *Evol. Intel., 11*, 53–71.

Krizhevsky, A., Sutskever, I., & Hinton, G. (2017). ImageNet classification with deep convolutional neural networks. *Communications of the ACM, 60*(6), 84–90. doi:10.1145/3065386

Küçüktopcu, O., Masazade, E., Ünsalan, C., & Varshney, P. K. (2019). A real-time bird sound recognition system using a low-cost microcontroller. *Applied Acoustics, 148*, 194–201. doi:10.1016/j.apacoust.2018.12.028

Kumar, R., Tripathi, R., Marchang, N., Srivastava, G., Gadekallu, T. R., & Xiong, N. N. (2021). A secured distributed detection system based on IPFS and blockchain for industrial image and video data security. *Journal of Parallel and Distributed Computing, 152*, 128–143. doi:10.1016/j.jpdc.2021.02.022

Kumar, V., Pathak, V., & Badal, N. (2022). *Complex entropy based encryption and decryption technique for securing medical images.* Multimed Tools Appl. doi:10.100711042-022-13546-z

Labied, M., & Belangour, A. (2021). Automatic Speech Recognition Features Extraction Techniques: A Multi-criteria Comparison. *International Journal of Advanced Computer Science and Applications, 12*(8). Advance online publication. doi:10.14569/IJACSA.2021.0120821

Lakshmanna & Khare. (2016). Constraint-Based Measures for DNA Sequence Mining using Group Search Optimization Algorithm. *International Journal of Intelligent Engineering and Systems, 9*(3).

Lakshmanna, K., Kaluri, R., & Thippa Reddy, G. (2016). An enhanced algorithm for frequent pattern mining from biological sequences. *Int J Pharm Technol, 8*, 12776–12784.

Langelaar, G. C., Setyawan, I., & Lagendijk, R. (2000). Watermarking digital image and video data. *IEEE Signal Processing Magazine, 17*(5), 20–46. doi:10.1109/79.879337

Lee, J., & Ahn, B. (2020). Real-time human action recognition with a low-cost RGB camera and mobile robot platform. *Sensors (Basel), 20*(10), 2886. doi:10.339020102886 PMID:32438776

Lee, Y., Im, D., & Shim, J. (2019). Data labeling research for deep learning based fire detection system. In *Proceedings of International Conference on Systems of Collaboration Big Data, Internet of Things & Security* (pp. 1 - 4). 10.1109/SysCoBIoTS48768.2019.9028029

Lei, B., Soon, Y., Zhou, F., Li, Z., & Lei, H. (2012). A robust audio watermarking scheme based on lifting wavelet transform and singular value decomposition. *Signal Processing, 92*(9), 1985–2001. doi:10.1016/j.sigpro.2011.12.021

Leylaz, Ma, & Sun. (2022). Identification of nonlinear dynamical systems with time delay. *International Journal of Dynamics and Control, 10*, 1–8. doi:10.1007/s40435-021-00783-7

Leylaz, G., Ma, S. F., & Sun, J. Q. (2021). An optimal model identiðcation algorithm of nonlinear dynamical systems with the algebraic method. *Journal of Vibration and Acoustics, 143*(2), 1–8. doi:10.1115/1.4048169

Li'skiewicz, M., Reischuk, R., & Wölfel, U. (2017). Security levels in steganography insecurity does not imply detectability. *Theoretical Computer Science*, 1–15.

Ligang, W. L., Hak-Keung, Z., Yuxin, S., & Zhan. (2015).Time-Delay Systems and Their Applications in Engineering. *Mathematical Problems in Engineering.*

Lin, Z., Feng, M., Santos, C., Yu, M., Xiang, B., Zhou, B., & Bengio, Y. (2017). A structured self-attentive sentence embedding. *Proceedings of ICLR.*

Liu, F., & Yan, W. (2014). *Visual cryptography for image processing and security: Theory, methods, and applications.* Springer. doi:10.1007/978-3-319-09644-5

Liu, T., Wang, Q. G., & Huang, H. P. (2013). A tutorial review on process identification from step or relay feedback test. *Journal of Process Control, 23*(10), 1597–1623. doi:10.1016/j.jprocont.2013.08.003

Liu, Y., Bi, J. W., & Fan, Z. P. (2017). A method for multi-class sentiment classification based on an improved one-vs-one (OVO) strategy and the support vector machine (SVM) algorithm. *Information Sciences, 394*, 38–52. doi:10.1016/j.ins.2017.02.016

Liu, Y., & Zheng, Y. F. (2005). One-against-all multi-class SVM classification using reliability measures. In *Proceedings 2005 IEEE International Joint Conference on Neural Network* (Vol. 2, pp. 849-854). IEEE. 10.1109/IJCNN.2005.1555963

Li, X., Yang, Y., Pang, Z., & Wu, X. (2015). A comparative study on selecting acoustic modeling units in deep neural networks based large vocabulary Chinese speech recognition. *Neurocomputing, 170*, 251–256. doi:10.1016/j.neucom.2014.07.087

Lubbad, M., Alhanjouri, M., & Alhalabi, H. (2019). Robust breast cancer classification using wave atom and back propagation neural networks. *Pertanika Journal of Science & Technology, 27*(3), 1247–1257.

Lucia, M., & Alfredo, P. (2012). The SOBS algorithm: What are the limits? *Computer Society Conference on Computer Vision and Pattern Recognition Workshops.*

Ma, X., & Yan, W. (2021). Banknote serial number recognition using deep learning. *Multimedia Tools and Applications*, *80*(12), 18445–18459. doi:10.100711042-020-10461-z

McLoughlin, Zhang, Xie, Song, & Xiao. (2015). Robust Sound Event Classification Using Deep Neural Networks. *IEEE/ACM Transactions on Audio, Speech, and Language Processing*, *23*, 540 - 552.

Mettripun, N. (2016). A Robust Medical Image Watermarking Based on DWT for Patient Identification. *13th International Conference on Electrical Engineering/Electronics, Computer, Telecommunications and Information Technology (ECTI-CON)*. 10.1109/ECTICon.2016.7561455

Mittal, S., & Mittal, S. (2018). Indian banknote recognition using convolutional neural network. In *Proceedings of International Conference on Internet of Things: Smart Innovation and Usages* (pp. 1 - 6). 10.1109/IoT-SIU.2018.8519888

Mnassri, A., Bennasr, M., & Adnane, C. (2019). A robust feature extraction method for real-time speech recognition system on a raspberry Pi 3 board. *Engineering, Technology & Applied Scientific Research*, *9*(2), 4066–4070.

Mohamed, B., & Aymen, M. (2022). Secure Images Transmission Using a Three-Dimensional S-Box-Based Encryption Algorithm. In *5th International Conference on Advanced Systems and Emergent Technologies (IC_ASET)* (pp. 17-22). IEEE

Mohamed, W., Souha, B., & Adnen, C. (2019). Speech recognition system based on discrete wave atoms transform partial noisy environment. *International Journal of Advanced Computer Science and Applications*, *10*(5).

Mohan, B. J. (2014). Speech recognition using MFCC and DTW. In 2014 international conference on advances in electrical engineering (ICAEE) (pp. 1-4). IEEE.

Mohd, W., Nasir, A., Muhammad, H., & Sahib, K. (2018) On combining MD5 for image authentication using LSB substitution in selected pixels. In *Proceedings of International Conference on Engineering and Emerging Technologies* (pp. 1-6). Academic Press.

Munir, N., Khan, M., & Al Karim Haj Ismail, A. (2022). Cryptanalysis and Improvement of Novel Image Encryption Technique Using Hybrid Method of Discrete Dynamical Chaotic Maps and Brownian Motion. *Multimed Tools Appl., 81*, 6571–6584.

Mun, K., & Son, C. (2019). Design of optimal blind watermarking technique based on MOEA/D. *IET Image Processing*. Advance online publication. doi:10.1049/iet-ipr.2019.1551

Mustafa, M. K., Allen, T., & Appiah, K. (2019). A comparative review of dynamic neural networks and hidden Markov model methods for mobile on-device speech recognition. *Neural Computing & Applications*, *31*(S2), 891–899. doi:10.100700521-017-3028-2

Muthumanickam, S., & Arun, C. (2018). Performance analysis of 2 levels DWT-SVD based non-blind and blind video watermarking using range conversion method. *Microsystem Technologies*, 1–9.

Na, J., Ren, X., & Xia, Y. (2014). Adaptive parameter identiðcation of linear SISO systems with unknown time-delay. *Systems & Control Letters, 66*, 43–50. doi:10.1016/j.sysconle.2014.01.005

Natarajan, M., & Govindarajan, Y. (2015). A study of DWT-SVD based multiple watermarking scheme for medical images. *International Journal of Network Security, 17*(5), 558–568.

Nazari, M., & Mehrabian, M. (2021). A novel chaotic IWT-LSB blind watermarking approach with flexible capacity for secure transmission of authenticated medical images. *Multimedia Tools and Applications, 80*(7), 10615–10655. doi:10.100711042-020-10032-2

Nguyen, S. C., Kha, H. H., & Nguyen, H. M. (2017). An Efficient Image Watermarking Scheme Using the Laplacian Pyramid based on Projection. *International Conference on Recent Advances in Signal Processing, Telecommunications & Computing (SigTelCom)*. 10.1109/SIGTELCOM.2017.7849804

Nurul, K., Muhammad, K., & Juanda, H. (2018). The authenticity of image using Hash MD5 and steganography least significant bit. *International Journal of Information System & Technology, 2*(1), 1–6.

Onyango, L. (2018). *Convolutional neural network to enhance stock taking*. University of Nairobi.

Oruh, J., Viriri, S., & Adegun, A. (2022). Long short-term Memory Recurrent neural network for Automatic speech recognition. *IEEE Access : Practical Innovations, Open Solutions, 10*, 30069–30079. doi:10.1109/ACCESS.2022.3159339

Ou, X., Yang, L., Zhang, G., Guo, L., Wu, J., & Tu, B. (2016). Improved Adaptive Transform for Residue in H. 264/AVC Lossless Video Coding. *Automatika: časopis za automatiku, mjerenje, elektroniku, računarstvo i komunikacije, 57*(4), 1045-1055.

Pallavi, M. (2018). Digital watermarking system for video authentication. *International Journal of Advanced Research in Computer and Communication Engineering*, 1–4.

Park, J., Woo, S., Lee, J., & Kweon, I. (2018). BAM: Bottleneck attention module. *Proceedings of BMVC*.

Parmar, N., Vaswani, A., Uszkoreit, J., Ukasz, K., Shazeer, N., & Ku, A. (2018). Image transformer. *Proceedings of International Conference on Machine Learning (ICML)*.

Patange, P. P., & Alex, J. S. R. (2017, March). Implementation of ANN based speech recognition system on an embedded board. In *2017 International Conference on Nextgen Electronic Technologies: Silicon to Software (ICNETS2)* (pp. 408-412). IEEE. 10.1109/ICNETS2.2017.8067968

Patel, S., John, S. R. A., & Venkatesan, N. (2015). Low-Power Multi-Layer Perceptron Neural Network Architecture for Speech Recognition Networks. *Indian Journal of Science and Technology, 8*(20). doi:10.17485/ijst/2015/v8i20/87516

Pisner, D. A., & Schnyer, D. M. (2020). Support vector machine. In *Machine learning* (pp. 101–121). Academic Press. doi:10.1016/B978-0-12-815739-8.00006-7

Po-Chyi, S., Chin-Song, W., Fan, C., Ching-Yu, W., & Ying-Chang, W. (2017). A practical design of digital watermarking for video streaming services. *Journal of Visual Communication and Image Representation, 42*, 161–172. doi:10.1016/j.jvcir.2016.11.018

Prabha & Sam. (2020). An Effective Robust and Imperceptible Blind Color Image Watermarking using WHT. *Journal of King Saud University - Computer and Information Sciences, 44*.

Pradhan, A., Sekhar, K., & Swain, G. (2018). Digital image steganography using LSB substitution, PVD, and EMD. *Mathematical Problems in Engineering, 2018*, 1–12. doi:10.1155/2018/1804953

Pramoun, T., & Amornraksa, T. (2012). Improved Image Watermarking Scheme based on DWT Coefficients Modification in LL Sub-band. Int. Proc. of IEEE on the 9th Electrical Engineering/Electronics, Computer, Telecommunications and Information Technology (ECTI-CON-2012), 1-4.

Preda, R. O., & Vizireanu, D. N. (2015). Watermarking-based image authentication robust to JPEG compression. *Electronics Letters, 51*(23), 1873–1875. doi:10.1049/el.2015.2522

Priya, S., & Santhi, B. (2019). A Novel Visual Medical Image Encryption for Secure Transmission of Authenticated Watermarked Medical Images. *Mobile Networks and Applications, 26*(6), 2501–2508. doi:10.100711036-019-01213-x

Prongnuch, S., & Sitjongsataporn, S. (2020). Thai voice-controlled analysis for car parking assistance in system-on-chip architecture. *Advances in Technology Innovation, 5*(4), 203. doi:10.46604/aiti.2020.5597

Qobbi, Y., Jarjar, A., Essaid, M., & Benazzi, A. (2022). Image encryption algorithm based on genetic operations and chaotic DNA encoding. *Soft Computing, 26*(12), 5823–5832. doi:10.100700500-021-06567-7

Rajput, D. S., Basha, S. M., & Xin, Q. (2021). *Providing diagnosis on diabetes using cloud computing environment to the people living in rural areas of India.* J Ambient Intell Human Comput. doi:10.100712652-021-03154-4

Ranftl, R., Bochkovskiy, A., & Koltun, V. (2021). Vision transformers for dense prediction. *Proceedings of ICCV.*

Rashid, H., Ahmed, I. U., Osman, S. B., Newaz, B., Rasheduzzaman, M., & Reza, S. T. (2017, January). Design and implementation of a voice controlled robot with human interaction ability. In *International Conference on Computer, Communication, Chemical, Materials and Electronic Engineering* (Vol. 65, pp. 148-151). Academic Press.

Ravi, D. J. (2021). Robust Perceptual Wavelet Packet Features for Recognition of Continuous Kannada Speech. *Wireless Personal Communications, 121*(3), 1781–1804. doi:10.100711277-021-08736-1

Redmon, J., Divvala, S., Girshick, R., & Farhadi, A. (2016). You Only Look Once: Unified, real-time object detection. In *Proceedings of IEEE Conference on Computer Vision and Pattern Recognition* (pp. 779 - 788). 10.1109/CVPR.2016.91

Redmon, J., & Farhadi, A. (2017). YOLO9000: Better, faster, stronger. In *Proceedings of IEEE Conference on Computer Vision and Pattern Recognition* (pp. 7263 - 7271). IEEE.

Ren, S., He, K., Girshick, R., & Sun, J. (2015). Faster R-CNN: Towards real-time object detection with region proposal networks. arXiv preprint arXiv:1506.01497. doi:10.4018/IJDCF.2018070105

Rey-Area, M., Guirado, E., Tabik, S., & Ruiz-Hidalgo, J. (2020). FuCiTNet: Improving the generalization of deep learning networks by the fusion of learned class-inherent transformations. *Information Fusion, 63*, 188–195. doi:10.1016/j.inffus.2020.06.015

Riaz, F., Hameed, S., Shafi, I., Kausar, R., & Ahmed, A. (2012). Enhanced Image Encryption Techniques Using Modified Advanced Encryption Standard. *Emerging Trends and Applications in Information Communication Technologies, 281*, 385–396.

Rolon-Heredia, J. A., Garrido-Arevalo, V. M., & Marulanda, J. (2019). Voice compression using discrete cosine transform and wavelet transform. *Journal of Physics: Conference Series, 1403*(1), 012001. doi:10.1088/1742-6596/1403/1/012001

Russakovsky, O., Deng, J., Su, H., Krause, J., Satheesh, S., Ma, S., Huang, Z., Karpathy, A., Khosla, A., Bernstein, M., Berg, A. C., & Fei-Fei, L. (2015). ImageNet large scale visual recognition challenge. *International Journal of Computer Vision, 115*(3), 211–252. doi:10.100711263-015-0816-y

Safta, M., Svasta, P., & Dima, M. O. (2017). Wavelet signal denoising applied on electromagnetic traces. In *2017 IEEE 23rd International Symposium for Design and Technology in Electronic Packaging (SIITME)* (pp. 399-402). IEEE. 10.1109/SIITME.2017.8259934

Sahib, K., Muneeza, W., Tawab, K., Nasir, A., & Muhammad, H. Z. (2018) Column level image authentication technique using hidden digital signatures. In *Proceedings of International Conference on Automation and Computing* (pp. 1-6). Academic Press.

Sahu, A., & Gutub, A. (2022). Improving grayscale steganography to protect personal information disclosure within hotel services. *Multimedia Tools and Applications, 81*(21), 30663–30683. doi:10.100711042-022-13015-7

Sanjaya, W. M., Anggraeni, D., & Santika, I. P. (2018, September). Speech recognition using linear predictive coding (LPC) and adaptive neuro-fuzzy (ANFIS) to control 5 DoF arm robot. *Journal of Physics: Conference Series, 1090*(1), 012046. doi:10.1088/1742-6596/1090/1/012046

Saqer, W., & Barhoom, T. (2016). Steganography and hiding data with indicators-based LSB using a secret key. Engineering, Technology &. *Applied Scientific Research, 6*(3), 1013–1017.

Sarić, R., Jokić, D., Beganović, N., Pokvić, L. G., & Badnjević, A. (2020). FPGA-based real-time epileptic seizure classification using Artificial Neural Network. *Biomedical Signal Processing and Control, 62*, 102106. doi:10.1016/j.bspc.2020.102106

Sasirekha, K., & Thangavel, K. (2014). A novel wavelet-based thresholding for denoising fingerprint image. *International Conference on Electronics, Communication and Computational Engineering (ICECCE).* 10.1109/ICECCE.2014.7086644

Saste, S. T., & Jagdale, S. M. (2017). Emotion recognition from speech using MFCC and DWT for security system. In 2017 international conference of electronics, communication and aerospace technology (ICECA) (Vol. 1, pp. 701-704). IEEE. doi:10.1109/ICECA.2017.8203631

Schlockermann. (2003). *Film grain coding in H.264/AVC.* JVTI034d2.doc.

Selvam, P., Balachandran, S., Iyer, S. P., & Jayabal, R. (2017). Hybrid transform based reversible watermarking technique for medical images in telemedicine applications. *Optik (Stuttgart), 145,* 655–671. doi:10.1016/j.ijleo.2017.07.060

Shaheen, A. M., Sheltami, T. R., Al-Kharoubi, T. M., & Shakshuki, E. (2019). Digital image encryption techniques for wireless sensor networks using image transformation methods: DCT and DWT. *Journal of Ambient Intelligence and Humanized Computing, 10*(12), 4733–4750. doi:10.100712652-018-0850-z

Sheng-Ke, W., Bo, Q., Zheng-Hua, F., & Zong-Shun, M. (2007). Fast shadow detection according to the moving region. *International Conference on Machine Learning and Cybernetics.*

Shen, T., Zhou, T., Long, G., Jiang, J., & Zhang, C. (2018). Bi-directional block self-attention for fast and memory-efficient sequence modeling. *Proceedings of ICLR.*

Shih, F. Y., & Zhong, X. (2016). High-capacity multiple regions of interest watermarking for medical images. *Information Sciences, 367–368,* 648–659. doi:10.1016/j.ins.2016.07.015

Shorten, C., & Khoshgoftaar, T. (2019). A survey on image data augmentation for deep learning. *Big Data, 6*(1), 60. doi:10.118640537-019-0197-0

Shymkovych, V., Telenyk, S., & Kravets, P. (2021). Hardware implementation of radial-basis neural networks with Gaussian activation functions on FPGA. *Neural Computing & Applications, 33*(15), 9467–9479. doi:10.100700521-021-05706-3

Simone, B., Gianluigi, C., & Raimondo, S. (2017). How Far Can You Get by Combining Change Detection Algorithms? *International Conference on Image Analysis and Processing.*

Simonyan, K., & Zisserman, A. (2015). Very deep convolutional networks for large-scale image recognition. *Proceedings of International Conference on Learning Representations.*

Singh, S., Tiwari, A., Shukla, S., & Pateriya, S. (2010). Currency recognition system using image processing. *International Journal of Engineering Applied Sciences and Technology.*

Singh, M. K., Kumar, S., Ali, M., & Saini, D. (2020). Application of a novel image moment computation in X-ray and MRI image watermarking. *IET Image Processing.* Advance online publication. doi:10.1049/ipr2.12052

Sneha, P. S., Sankar, S., & Kumar, A. S. (2020). A chaotic colour image encryption scheme combining Walsh–Hadamard transform and Arnold–Tent maps. *Journal of Ambient Intelligence and Humanized Computing, 11*(3), 1289–1308. doi:10.100712652-019-01385-0

Song, W., Fu, C., & Zheng, Y. (2022). Protection of image ROI using chaos-based encryption and DCNN-based object detection. *Neural Comput & Applic., 34*, 5743–5756.

Ssarma, M. K., Gajurel, A., Pokhrel, A., & Joshi, B. (2017). HMM based isolated word Nepali speech recognition. *2017 International Conference on Machine Learning and Cybernetics (ICMLC)*. 10.1109/ICMLC.2017.8107745

Suehring, K. (2015). *H. 264/AVC reference software*. http://iphome. hhi. de/suehring/tml/

Suehring, K., & Li, X. (2016). JVET common test conditions and software reference configurations. *Jurnal Veteriner*, B1010.

Sugumaran, S., & Prakash, V. R. (2015). PSoC based speech recognition system. *International Refereed Journal of Engineering and Science, 4*, 1-7.

Suryawanshi, U., & Ganorkar, S. R. (2014). Hardware Implementationof Speech Recognition Using MFCC and Euclidean Distance. *Int. J. Adv. Res. Electr. Electron. Instrum. Eng., 03*(08), 11248–11254.

Szegedy, C., Liu, W., Jia, Y., Sermanet, P., Reed, S., Anguelov, D., Erhan, D., Vanhoucke, V., & Rabinovich, A. (2015). Going deeper with convolutions. In *Proceedings of IEEE Conference on Computer Vision and Pattern Recognition* (pp. 1 - 9). IEEE.

Takore, Kumar, & Devi. (2016). A Modified Blind Image Watermarking Scheme Based on DWT, DCT and SVD domain Using GA to Optimize Robustness. *International Conference on Electrical, Electronics, and Optimization Techniques (ICEEOT)*.

Tang, Y., Pino, J., Wang, C., Ma, X., & Genzel, D. (2021). A general multi-task learning framework to leverage text data for speech to text tasks. In *ICASSP 2021-2021 IEEE International Conference on Acoustics, Speech and Signal Processing (ICASSP)* (pp. 6209-6213). IEEE. 10.1109/ICASSP39728.2021.9415058

Tasheva, A., Tasheva, Z., & Nakov, P. (2017) Image-based steganography using modified LSB insertion method with contrast stretching. *Proceedings of International Conference on Computer Systems and Technologies*.

Thanki, Borra, Dwivedi, & Borisagar. (2017). An efficient medical image watermarking scheme based on FDCuT–DCT. *Engineering Science and Technology, 20*(4), 1366-1379.

Thanki, R., & Kothari, A. (2021). A. Multi-level security of medical images based on encryption and watermarking for telemedicine applications. *Multimedia Tools and Applications, 80*(3), 4307–4325. doi:10.100711042-020-09941-z

Thompson, I., Bouridane, A., Kurugollu, F., & Yan, W. (2008). *Video watermarking using complex wavelets*. Nova Science Publishers.

Trinh, H., Vo, H., Pham, V., Nath, B., & Hoang, V. (2020). Currency recognition based on deep feature selection and classification. In *Proceedings of Asian Conference on Intelligent Information and Database Systems* (pp. 273 - 281), Springer. 10.1007/978-981-15-3380-8_24

Upadhyaya, A., Shokeen, V., & Srivastava, G. (2018). Analysis of counterfeit currency detection techniques for classification model. In *Proceedings of International Conference on Computing Communication and Automation* (pp. 1 - 6), IEEE Press. 10.1109/CCAA.2018.8777704

Vaswani, A., Shazeer, N., Parmar, N., Uszkoreit, J., Jones, L., Gomez, A. N., Kaiser, L., & Polosukhin, I. (2017). Attention is all you need. Proceedings of Advances in Neural Information Processing Systems.

Wahid, M., Ahmad, N., Zafar, M. H., & Khan, S. (2018) On combining MD5 for image authentication using LSB substitution in selected pixels. In *Proceedings of International Conference on Engineering and Emerging Technologies* (pp. 1-6). 10.1109/ICEET1.2018.8338621

Walid, M., Bousselmi, S., Dabbabi, K., & Cherif, A. (2019). Real-time implementation of isolated-word speech recognition system on raspberry Pi 3 using WAT-MFCC. *IJCSNS, 19*(3), 42.

Wang, X., Li, B., & Wang, Y. (2021). An efficient batch images encryption method based on DNA encoding and PWLCM. *Multimed Tools Appl, 80*, 943–971.

Wang, G., Wu, W., & Yan, W. (2017). The state-of-the-art technology of currency identification: A comparative study. *International Journal of Digital Crime and Forensics, 9*(3), 58–72. doi:10.4018/IJDCF.2017070106

Wang, J., Wan, W. B., Li, X. X., Sun, J. D., & Zhang, H. X. (2020). Color Image Watermarking Based on Orientation Diversity and Color Complexity. *Expert Systems with Applications, 140*, 112868. doi:10.1016/j.eswa.2019.112868

Wang, L. L., & Siu, W. C. (2011). Improved lossless coding algorithm in H. 264/AVC based on hierarchical intra prediction and coding-mode selection. *Journal of Electronic Imaging, 20*(4), 043001. doi:10.1117/1.3644573

Wang, Q., Wu, B., Zhu, P., Li, P., Zuo, W., & Hu, Q. (2020). ECA-Net: Efficient channel attention for deep convolutional neural networks. In *Proceedings of IEEE/CVF Conference on Computer Vision and Pattern Recognition* (pp. 11531 - 11539). 10.1109/CVPR42600.2020.01155

Wang, W., Xie, E., Li, X., Fan, D.-P., Song, K., Liang, D., Lu, T., Luo, P., & Shao, L. (2021). Pyramid vision transformer: A versatile backbone for dense prediction without convolutions. In *Proceedings of ICCV* (pp. 568-578). 10.1109/ICCV48922.2021.00061

Wang, Z. (2022). Audio Signal Acquisition and Processing System Based on Model DSP Rapid Design. *Security and Communication Networks*. doi:10.1155/2022/4593339

Weir, J., & Yan, W. (2011). A comprehensive study of visual cryptography. *Springer Transactions on DHMS, 6010*, 70–105.

Wei, S. T., Shen, S. R., Liu, B. D., & Yang, J. F. (2009, November). Lossless image and video coding based on H. 264/AVC intra predictions with simplified interpolations. In *16th IEEE International Conference on Image Processing (ICIP)* (pp. 633-636). IEEE.

Wei, S. T., Tien, C. W., Liu, B. D., & Yang, J. F. (2011). Adaptive truncation algorithm for Hadamard-transformed H. 264/AVC lossless video coding. *IEEE Transactions on Circuits and Systems for Video Technology*, *21*(5), 538–549. doi:10.1109/TCSVT.2011.2129030

Woo, S., Park, J., Lee, J. Y., & Kweon, I. (2018). CBAM: Convolutional block attention module. In *Proceedings of ECCV* (pp. 3 - 19). Academic Press.

Yağanoğlu, M. (2021). Real time wearable speech recognition system for deaf persons. *Computers & Electrical Engineering*, *91*, 107026. doi:10.1016/j.compeleceng.2021.107026

Yan, W., & Qi, D. (2001). Mapping-based watermarking of 2D engineering drawings. *International Conference on CAD/Graphics*, 464 – 469.

Yan, W. (2019). *Introduction to Intelligent Surveillance: Surveillance Data Capture, Transmission, and Analytics*. Springer London. doi:10.1007/978-3-030-10713-0

Yan, W. (2021). *Computational Methods for Deep Learning - Theoretic, Practice and Applications*. Springer. doi:10.1007/978-3-030-61081-4

Yan, W., & Chambers, J. (2013). An empirical approach for digital currency forensics. *IEEE International Symposium on Circuits and Systems (ISCAS)*, 2988-2991. 10.1109/ISCAS.2013.6572507

Yan, W., Chambers, J., & Garhwal, A. (2014). An empirical approach for currency identification. *Multimedia Tools and Applications*, *74*(7).

Yan, W., & Weir, J. (2010). *Fundamentals of Media Security*. Bookboon.

Yao, Y., & Cao, Y. (2020). A neural network enhanced hidden Markov model for tourism demand forecasting. *Applied Soft Computing*, *94*, 106465. doi:10.1016/j.asoc.2020.106465

Yin, R., Wang, D., Zhao, S., Lou, Z., & Shen, G. (2021). Wearable sensors-enabled human–machine interaction systems: From design to application. *Advanced Functional Materials*, *31*(11), 2008936. doi:10.1002/adfm.202008936

Yu, L., Qiu, T., & Song, A. M. (2017). A time delay estimation algorithm based on the weighted correntropy spectral density. *Circuits, Systems, and Signal Processing*, *36*(3), 1115–1128. doi:10.100700034-016-0347-y

Yuvaraj, S., Badholia, A., William, P., Vengatesan, K., & Bibave, R. (2022, May). Speech Recognition Based Robotic Arm Writing. In *Proceedings of International Conference on Communication and Artificial Intelligence: ICCAI 2021* (pp. 23-33). Springer Nature Singapore.

Zhang, Q., Dai, Y., & Kuo, C. C. J. (2009, May). Lossless video compression with residual image prediction and coding (RIPC). In *IEEE International Symposium on Circuits and Systems* (pp. 617-620). IEEE. 10.1109/ISCAS.2009.5117824

Zhang, Q., & Yan, W. (2018). Currency detection and recognition based on deep learning. In *Proceedings of IEEE International Conference on Advanced Video and Signal Based Surveillance* (pp. 1 - 6). 10.1109/AVSS.2018.8639124

Zhang, Q., Yan, W., & Kankanhalli, K. (2019). Overview of currency recognition using deep learning. *Journal of Banking and Financial Technology*, *3*(1), 59–69. doi:10.100742786-018-00007-1

Zhao, H., Jia, J., & Koltun, V. (2020). Exploring self-attention for image recognition. In *Proceedings of IEEE/CVF Conference on Computer Vision and Pattern Recognition* (pp. 10073-10082). IEEE.

Zheng, G., Barbot, J. P., & Boutat, D. (2015). Identiðcation of the delay parameter for nonlinear time-delay systems with unknown inputs. *Automatica*, *49*(6), 1755–1760. doi:10.1016/j.automatica.2013.02.020

Zhou, Z., Zhu, J., Su, Y., Wang, M., & Sun, X. (2021). Geometric correction code-based robust image watermarking. *IET Image Processing*, 1–10. doi:10.1049/ipr2.12143

Zivkovic, Z. (2004). Improved adaptive Gaussian mixture model for back-ground subtraction. *Proc. Int. Conf. Pattern Recognition.*

Zolotavkin & Juhola. (2014). A New QIM-Based Watermarking Method Robust to Gain Attack. *International Journal of Digital Multimedia Broadcasting.* doi:10.1155/2014/910808

Related References

To continue our tradition of advancing information science and technology research, we have compiled a list of recommended IGI Global readings. These references will provide additional information and guidance to further enrich your knowledge and assist you with your own research and future publications.

Abbas, R., Michael, K., & Michael, M. G. (2017). What Can People Do with Your Spatial Data?: Socio-Ethical Scenarios. In A. Marrington, D. Kerr, & J. Gammack (Eds.), *Managing Security Issues and the Hidden Dangers of Wearable Technologies* (pp. 206–237). Hershey, PA: IGI Global. doi:10.4018/978-1-5225-1016-1.ch009

Abulaish, M., & Haldar, N. A. (2018). Advances in Digital Forensics Frameworks and Tools: A Comparative Insight and Ranking. *International Journal of Digital Crime and Forensics*, *10*(2), 95–119. doi:10.4018/IJDCF.2018040106

Ahmad, F. A., Kumar, P., Shrivastava, G., & Bouhlel, M. S. (2018). Bitcoin: Digital Decentralized Cryptocurrency. In G. Shrivastava, P. Kumar, B. Gupta, S. Bala, & N. Dey (Eds.), *Handbook of Research on Network Forensics and Analysis Techniques* (pp. 395–415). Hershey, PA: IGI Global. doi:10.4018/978-1-5225-4100-4.ch021

Ahmed, A. A. (2017). Investigation Approach for Network Attack Intention Recognition. *International Journal of Digital Crime and Forensics*, *9*(1), 17–38. doi:10.4018/IJDCF.2017010102

Akhtar, Z. (2017). Biometric Spoofing and Anti-Spoofing. In M. Dawson, D. Kisku, P. Gupta, J. Sing, & W. Li (Eds.), Developing Next-Generation Countermeasures for Homeland Security Threat Prevention (pp. 121-139). Hershey, PA: IGI Global. doi:10.4018/978-1-5225-0703-1.ch007

Akowuah, F. E., Land, J., Yuan, X., Yang, L., Xu, J., & Wang, H. (2018). Standards and Guides for Implementing Security and Privacy for Health Information Technology. In Y. Maleh (Ed.), *Security and Privacy Management, Techniques, and Protocols* (pp. 214–236). Hershey, PA: IGI Global. doi:10.4018/978-1-5225-5583-4.ch008

Akremi, A., Sallay, H., & Rouached, M. (2018). Intrusion Detection Systems Alerts Reduction: New Approach for Forensics Readiness. In Y. Maleh (Ed.), *Security and Privacy Management, Techniques, and Protocols* (pp. 255–275). Hershey, PA: IGI Global. doi:10.4018/978-1-5225-5583-4.ch010

Aldwairi, M., Hasan, M., & Balbahaith, Z. (2017). Detection of Drive-by Download Attacks Using Machine Learning Approach. *International Journal of Information Security and Privacy*, *11*(4), 16–28. doi:10.4018/IJISP.2017100102

Alohali, B. (2017). Detection Protocol of Possible Crime Scenes Using Internet of Things (IoT). In M. Moore (Ed.), *Cybersecurity Breaches and Issues Surrounding Online Threat Protection* (pp. 175–196). Hershey, PA: IGI Global. doi:10.4018/978-1-5225-1941-6.ch008

AlShahrani, A. M., Al-Abadi, M. A., Al-Malki, A. S., Ashour, A. S., & Dey, N. (2017). Automated System for Crops Recognition and Classification. In N. Dey, A. Ashour, & S. Acharjee (Eds.), *Applied Video Processing in Surveillance and Monitoring Systems* (pp. 54–69). Hershey, PA: IGI Global. doi:10.4018/978-1-5225-1022-2.ch003

Anand, R., Shrivastava, G., Gupta, S., Peng, S., & Sindhwani, N. (2018). Audio Watermarking With Reduced Number of Random Samples. In G. Shrivastava, P. Kumar, B. Gupta, S. Bala, & N. Dey (Eds.), *Handbook of Research on Network Forensics and Analysis Techniques* (pp. 372–394). Hershey, PA: IGI Global. doi:10.4018/978-1-5225-4100-4.ch020

Anand, R., Sinha, A., Bhardwaj, A., & Sreeraj, A. (2018). Flawed Security of Social Network of Things. In G. Shrivastava, P. Kumar, B. Gupta, S. Bala, & N. Dey (Eds.), *Handbook of Research on Network Forensics and Analysis Techniques* (pp. 65–86). Hershey, PA: IGI Global. doi:10.4018/978-1-5225-4100-4.ch005

Aneja, M. J., Bhatia, T., Sharma, G., & Shrivastava, G. (2018). Artificial Intelligence Based Intrusion Detection System to Detect Flooding Attack in VANETs. In G. Shrivastava, P. Kumar, B. Gupta, S. Bala, & N. Dey (Eds.), *Handbook of Research on Network Forensics and Analysis Techniques* (pp. 87–100). Hershey, PA: IGI Global. doi:10.4018/978-1-5225-4100-4.ch006

Antunes, F., Freire, M., & Costa, J. P. (2018). From Motivation and Self-Structure to a Decision-Support Framework for Online Social Networks. In V. Ahuja & S. Rathore (Eds.), *Multidisciplinary Perspectives on Human Capital and Information Technology Professionals* (pp. 116–136). Hershey, PA: IGI Global. doi:10.4018/978-1-5225-5297-0.ch007

Atli, D. (2017). Cybercrimes via Virtual Currencies in International Business. In M. Moore (Ed.), *Cybersecurity Breaches and Issues Surrounding Online Threat Protection* (pp. 121–143). Hershey, PA: IGI Global. doi:10.4018/978-1-5225-1941-6.ch006

Baazeem, R. M. (2018). The Role of Religiosity in Technology Acceptance: The Case of Privacy in Saudi Arabia. In J. McAlaney, L. Frumkin, & V. Benson (Eds.), *Psychological and Behavioral Examinations in Cyber Security* (pp. 172–193). Hershey, PA: IGI Global. doi:10.4018/978-1-5225-4053-3.ch010

Bailey, W. J. (2017). Protection of Critical Homeland Assets: Using a Proactive, Adaptive Security Management Driven Process. In M. Dawson, D. Kisku, P. Gupta, J. Sing, & W. Li (Eds.), Developing Next-Generation Countermeasures for Homeland Security Threat Prevention (pp. 17-50). Hershey, PA: IGI Global. https://doi.org/doi:10.4018/978-1-5225-0703-1.ch002

Bajaj, S. (2018). Current Drift in Energy Efficiency Cloud Computing: New Provocations, Workload Prediction, Consolidation, and Resource Over Commitment. In S. Aljawarneh & M. Malhotra (Eds.), *Critical Research on Scalability and Security Issues in Virtual Cloud Environments* (pp. 283–303). Hershey, PA: IGI Global. doi:10.4018/978-1-5225-3029-9.ch014

Balasubramanian, K. (2018). Hash Functions and Their Applications. In K. Balasubramanian & M. Rajakani (Eds.), *Algorithmic Strategies for Solving Complex Problems in Cryptography* (pp. 66–77). Hershey, PA: IGI Global. doi:10.4018/978-1-5225-2915-6.ch005

Balasubramanian, K. (2018). Recent Developments in Cryptography: A Survey. In K. Balasubramanian & M. Rajakani (Eds.), *Algorithmic Strategies for Solving Complex Problems in Cryptography* (pp. 1–22). Hershey, PA: IGI Global. doi:10.4018/978-1-5225-2915-6.ch001

Balasubramanian, K. (2018). Secure Two Party Computation. In K. Balasubramanian & M. Rajakani (Eds.), *Algorithmic Strategies for Solving Complex Problems in Cryptography* (pp. 145–153). Hershey, PA: IGI Global. doi:10.4018/978-1-5225-2915-6.ch012

Balasubramanian, K. (2018). Securing Public Key Encryption Against Adaptive Chosen Ciphertext Attacks. In K. Balasubramanian & M. Rajakani (Eds.), *Algorithmic Strategies for Solving Complex Problems in Cryptography* (pp. 134–144). Hershey, PA: IGI Global. doi:10.4018/978-1-5225-2915-6.ch011

Balasubramanian, K. (2018). Variants of the Diffie-Hellman Problem. In K. Balasubramanian & M. Rajakani (Eds.), *Algorithmic Strategies for Solving Complex Problems in Cryptography* (pp. 40–54). Hershey, PA: IGI Global. doi:10.4018/978-1-5225-2915-6.ch003

Balasubramanian, K., & K., M. (2018). Secure Group Key Agreement Protocols. In K. Balasubramanian, & M. Rajakani (Eds.), *Algorithmic Strategies for Solving Complex Problems in Cryptography* (pp. 55-65). Hershey, PA: IGI Global. https://doi.org/ doi:10.4018/978-1-5225-2915-6.ch004

Balasubramanian, K., & M., R. (2018). Problems in Cryptography and Cryptanalysis. In K. Balasubramanian, & M. Rajakani (Eds.), *Algorithmic Strategies for Solving Complex Problems in Cryptography* (pp. 23-39). Hershey, PA: IGI Global. https://doi.org/ doi:10.4018/978-1-5225-2915-6.ch002

Balasubramanian, K., & Abbas, A. M. (2018). Integer Factoring Algorithms. In K. Balasubramanian & M. Rajakani (Eds.), *Algorithmic Strategies for Solving Complex Problems in Cryptography* (pp. 228–240). Hershey, PA: IGI Global. doi:10.4018/978-1-5225-2915-6.ch017

Balasubramanian, K., & Abbas, A. M. (2018). Secure Bootstrapping Using the Trusted Platform Module. In K. Balasubramanian & M. Rajakani (Eds.), *Algorithmic Strategies for Solving Complex Problems in Cryptography* (pp. 167–185). Hershey, PA: IGI Global. doi:10.4018/978-1-5225-2915-6.ch014

Balasubramanian, K., & Mathanan, J. (2018). Cryptographic Voting Protocols. In K. Balasubramanian & M. Rajakani (Eds.), *Algorithmic Strategies for Solving Complex Problems in Cryptography* (pp. 124–133). Hershey, PA: IGI Global. doi:10.4018/978-1-5225-2915-6.ch010

Balasubramanian, K., & Rajakani, M. (2018). Secure Multiparty Computation. In K. Balasubramanian & M. Rajakani (Eds.), *Algorithmic Strategies for Solving Complex Problems in Cryptography* (pp. 154–166). Hershey, PA: IGI Global. doi:10.4018/978-1-5225-2915-6.ch013

Balasubramanian, K., & Rajakani, M. (2018). The Quadratic Sieve Algorithm for Integer Factoring. In K. Balasubramanian & M. Rajakani (Eds.), *Algorithmic Strategies for Solving Complex Problems in Cryptography* (pp. 241–252). Hershey, PA: IGI Global. doi:10.4018/978-1-5225-2915-6.ch018

Barone, P. A. (2017). Defining and Understanding the Development of Juvenile Delinquency from an Environmental, Sociological, and Theoretical Perspective. In S. Egharevba (Ed.), *Police Brutality, Racial Profiling, and Discrimination in the Criminal Justice System* (pp. 215–238). Hershey, PA: IGI Global. doi:10.4018/978-1-5225-1088-8.ch010

Beauchere, J. F. (2018). Encouraging Digital Civility: What Companies and Others Can Do. In R. Luppicini (Ed.), *The Changing Scope of Technoethics in Contemporary Society* (pp. 262–274). Hershey, PA: IGI Global. doi:10.4018/978-1-5225-5094-5.ch014

Behera, C. K., & Bhaskari, D. L. (2017). Malware Methodologies and Its Future: A Survey. *International Journal of Information Security and Privacy, 11*(4), 47–64. doi:10.4018/IJISP.2017100104

Benson, V., McAlaney, J., & Frumkin, L. A. (2018). Emerging Threats for the Human Element and Countermeasures in Current Cyber Security Landscape. In J. McAlaney, L. Frumkin, & V. Benson (Eds.), *Psychological and Behavioral Examinations in Cyber Security* (pp. 266–271). Hershey, PA: IGI Global. doi:10.4018/978-1-5225-4053-3.ch016

Berbecaru, D. (2018). On Creating Digital Evidence in IP Networks With NetTrack. In G. Shrivastava, P. Kumar, B. Gupta, S. Bala, & N. Dey (Eds.), *Handbook of Research on Network Forensics and Analysis Techniques* (pp. 225–245). Hershey, PA: IGI Global. doi:10.4018/978-1-5225-4100-4.ch012

Berki, E., Valtanen, J., Chaudhary, S., & Li, L. (2018). The Need for Multi-Disciplinary Approaches and Multi-Level Knowledge for Cybersecurity Professionals. In V. Ahuja & S. Rathore (Eds.), *Multidisciplinary Perspectives on Human Capital and Information Technology Professionals* (pp. 72–94). Hershey, PA: IGI Global. doi:10.4018/978-1-5225-5297-0.ch005

Bhardwaj, A. (2017). Ransomware: A Rising Threat of new age Digital Extortion. In S. Aljawarneh (Ed.), *Online Banking Security Measures and Data Protection* (pp. 189–221). Hershey, PA: IGI Global. doi:10.4018/978-1-5225-0864-9.ch012

Bhattacharjee, J., Sengupta, A., Barik, M. S., & Mazumdar, C. (2018). An Analytical Study of Methodologies and Tools for Enterprise Information Security Risk Management. In M. Gupta, R. Sharman, J. Walp, & P. Mulgund (Eds.), *Information Technology Risk Management and Compliance in Modern Organizations* (pp. 1–20). Hershey, PA: IGI Global. doi:10.4018/978-1-5225-2604-9.ch001

Bruno, G. (2018). Handling the Dataflow in Business Process Models. In V. Ahuja & S. Rathore (Eds.), *Multidisciplinary Perspectives on Human Capital and Information Technology Professionals* (pp. 137–151). Hershey, PA: IGI Global. doi:10.4018/978-1-5225-5297-0.ch008

Bush, C. L. (2021). Policing Strategies and Approaches to Improving Community Relations: Black Citizens' Perceptions of Law Enforcement Efforts to Intentionally Strengthen Relationships. In M. Pittaro (Ed.), *Global Perspectives on Reforming the Criminal Justice System* (pp. 56–75). IGI Global. https://doi.org/10.4018/978-1-7998-6884-2.ch004

Carneiro, A. D. (2017). Defending Information Networks in Cyberspace: Some Notes on Security Needs. In M. Dawson, D. Kisku, P. Gupta, J. Sing, & W. Li (Eds.), Developing Next-Generation Countermeasures for Homeland Security Threat Prevention (pp. 354-375). Hershey, PA: IGI Global. https://doi.org/ doi:10.4018/978-1-5225-0703-1.ch016

Chakraborty, S., Patra, P. K., Maji, P., Ashour, A. S., & Dey, N. (2017). Image Registration Techniques and Frameworks: A Review. In N. Dey, A. Ashour, & S. Acharjee (Eds.), *Applied Video Processing in Surveillance and Monitoring Systems* (pp. 102–114). Hershey, PA: IGI Global. doi:10.4018/978-1-5225-1022-2.ch005

Chaudhari, G., & Mulgund, P. (2018). Strengthening IT Governance With COBIT 5. In M. Gupta, R. Sharman, J. Walp, & P. Mulgund (Eds.), *Information Technology Risk Management and Compliance in Modern Organizations* (pp. 48–69). Hershey, PA: IGI Global. doi:10.4018/978-1-5225-2604-9.ch003

Cheikh, M., Hacini, S., & Boufaida, Z. (2018). Visualization Technique for Intrusion Detection. In Y. Maleh (Ed.), *Security and Privacy Management, Techniques, and Protocols* (pp. 276–290). Hershey, PA: IGI Global. doi:10.4018/978-1-5225-5583-4.ch011

Chen, G., Ding, L., Du, J., Zhou, G., Qin, P., Chen, G., & Liu, Q. (2018). Trust Evaluation Strategy for Single Sign-on Solution in Cloud. *International Journal of Digital Crime and Forensics*, *10*(1), 1–11. doi:10.4018/IJDCF.2018010101

Chen, J., & Peng, F. (2018). A Perceptual Encryption Scheme for HEVC Video with Lossless Compression. *International Journal of Digital Crime and Forensics*, *10*(1), 67–78. doi:10.4018/IJDCF.2018010106

Chen, K., & Xu, D. (2018). An Efficient Reversible Data Hiding Scheme for Encrypted Images. *International Journal of Digital Crime and Forensics*, *10*(2), 1–22. doi:10.4018/IJDCF.2018040101

Chen, Z., Lu, J., Yang, P., & Luo, X. (2017). Recognizing Substitution Steganography of Spatial Domain Based on the Characteristics of Pixels Correlation. *International Journal of Digital Crime and Forensics, 9*(4), 48–61. doi:10.4018/IJDCF.2017100105

Cherkaoui, R., Zbakh, M., Braeken, A., & Touhafi, A. (2018). Anomaly Detection in Cloud Computing and Internet of Things Environments: Latest Technologies. In K. Munir (Ed.), *Cloud Computing Technologies for Green Enterprises* (pp. 251–265). Hershey, PA: IGI Global. doi:10.4018/978-1-5225-3038-1.ch010

Chowdhury, A., Karmakar, G., & Kamruzzaman, J. (2017). Survey of Recent Cyber Security Attacks on Robotic Systems and Their Mitigation Approaches. In R. Kumar, P. Pattnaik, & P. Pandey (Eds.), *Detecting and Mitigating Robotic Cyber Security Risks* (pp. 284–299). Hershey, PA: IGI Global. doi:10.4018/978-1-5225-2154-9.ch019

Cortese, F. A. (2018). The Techoethical Ethos of Technic Self-Determination: Technological Determinism as the Ontic Fundament of Freewill. In R. Luppicini (Ed.), *The Changing Scope of Technoethics in Contemporary Society* (pp. 74–104). Hershey, PA: IGI Global. doi:10.4018/978-1-5225-5094-5.ch005

Crosston, M. D. (2017). The Fight for Cyber Thoreau: Distinguishing Virtual Disobedience from Digital Destruction. In M. Korstanje (Ed.), *Threat Mitigation and Detection of Cyber Warfare and Terrorism Activities* (pp. 198–219). Hershey, PA: IGI Global. doi:10.4018/978-1-5225-1938-6.ch009

da Costa, F., & de Sá-Soares, F. (2017). Authenticity Challenges of Wearable Technologies. In A. Marrington, D. Kerr, & J. Gammack (Eds.), *Managing Security Issues and the Hidden Dangers of Wearable Technologies* (pp. 98–130). Hershey, PA: IGI Global. doi:10.4018/978-1-5225-1016-1.ch005

Dafflon, B., Guériau, M., & Gechter, F. (2017). Using Physics Inspired Wave Agents in a Virtual Environment: Longitudinal Distance Control in Robots Platoon. *International Journal of Monitoring and Surveillance Technologies Research, 5*(2), 15–28. doi:10.4018/IJMSTR.2017040102

Dash, S. R., Sheeraz, A. S., & Samantaray, A. (2018). Filtration and Classification of ECG Signals. In C. Pradhan, H. Das, B. Naik, & N. Dey (Eds.), *Handbook of Research on Information Security in Biomedical Signal Processing* (pp. 72–94). Hershey, PA: IGI Global. doi:10.4018/978-1-5225-5152-2.ch005

Dhavale, S. V. (2018). Insider Attack Analysis in Building Effective Cyber Security for an Organization. In J. McAlaney, L. Frumkin, & V. Benson (Eds.), *Psychological and Behavioral Examinations in Cyber Security* (pp. 222–238). Hershey, PA: IGI Global. doi:10.4018/978-1-5225-4053-3.ch013

Dixit, P. (2018). Security Issues in Web Services. In G. Shrivastava, P. Kumar, B. Gupta, S. Bala, & N. Dey (Eds.), *Handbook of Research on Network Forensics and Analysis Techniques* (pp. 57–64). Hershey, PA: IGI Global. doi:10.4018/978-1-5225-4100-4.ch004

Doraikannan, S. (2018). Efficient Implementation of Digital Signature Algorithms. In K. Balasubramanian & M. Rajakani (Eds.), *Algorithmic Strategies for Solving Complex Problems in Cryptography* (pp. 78–86). Hershey, PA: IGI Global. doi:10.4018/978-1-5225-2915-6.ch006

E., J. V., Mohan, J., & K., A. (2018). Automatic Detection of Tumor and Bleed in Magnetic Resonance Brain Images. In C. Pradhan, H. Das, B. Naik, & N. Dey (Eds.), *Handbook of Research on Information Security in Biomedical Signal Processing* (pp. 291-303). Hershey, PA: IGI Global. https://doi.org/ doi:10.4018/978-1-5225-5152-2.ch015

Escamilla, I., Ruíz, M. T., Ibarra, M. M., Soto, V. L., Quintero, R., & Guzmán, G. (2018). Geocoding Tweets Based on Semantic Web and Ontologies. In M. Lytras, N. Aljohani, E. Damiani, & K. Chui (Eds.), *Innovations, Developments, and Applications of Semantic Web and Information Systems* (pp. 372–392). Hershey, PA: IGI Global. doi:10.4018/978-1-5225-5042-6.ch014

Essefi, E. (2022). Advances in Forensic Geophysics: Magnetic Susceptibility as a Tool for Environmental Forensic Geophysics. In C. Chen, W. Yang, & L. Chen (Eds.), *Technologies to Advance Automation in Forensic Science and Criminal Investigation* (pp. 15-36). IGI Global. https://doi.org/10.4018/978-1-7998-8386-9.ch002

Farhadi, M., Haddad, H. M., & Shahriar, H. (2018). Compliance of Electronic Health Record Applications With HIPAA Security and Privacy Requirements. In Y. Maleh (Ed.), *Security and Privacy Management, Techniques, and Protocols* (pp. 199–213). Hershey, PA: IGI Global. doi:10.4018/978-1-5225-5583-4.ch007

Fatma, S. (2018). Use and Misuse of Technology in Marketing: Cases from India. *International Journal of Technoethics*, 9(1), 27–36. doi:10.4018/IJT.2018010103

Fazlali, M., & Khodamoradi, P. (2018). Metamorphic Malware Detection Using Minimal Opcode Statistical Patterns. In Y. Maleh (Ed.), *Security and Privacy Management, Techniques, and Protocols* (pp. 337–359). Hershey, PA: IGI Global. doi:10.4018/978-1-5225-5583-4.ch014

Filiol, É., & Gallais, C. (2017). Optimization of Operational Large-Scale (Cyber) Attacks by a Combinational Approach. *International Journal of Cyber Warfare & Terrorism*, 7(3), 29–43. doi:10.4018/IJCWT.2017070103

Forge, J. (2018). The Case Against Weapons Research. In R. Luppicini (Ed.), *The Changing Scope of Technoethics in Contemporary Society* (pp. 124–134). Hershey, PA: IGI Global. doi:10.4018/978-1-5225-5094-5.ch007

G., S., & Durai, M. S. (2018). Big Data Analytics: An Expedition Through Rapidly Budding Data Exhaustive Era. In D. Lopez, & M. Durai (Eds.), *HCI Challenges and Privacy Preservation in Big Data Security* (pp. 124-138). Hershey, PA: IGI Global. https://doi.org/ doi:10.4018/978-1-5225-2863-0.ch006

Gammack, J., & Marrington, A. (2017). The Promise and Perils of Wearable Technologies. In A. Marrington, D. Kerr, & J. Gammack (Eds.), *Managing Security Issues and the Hidden Dangers of Wearable Technologies* (pp. 1–17). Hershey, PA: IGI Global. doi:10.4018/978-1-5225-1016-1.ch001

Gamoura, S. C. (2018). A Cloud-Based Approach for Cross-Management of Disaster Plans: Managing Risk in Networked Enterprises. In S. Aljawarneh & M. Malhotra (Eds.), *Critical Research on Scalability and Security Issues in Virtual Cloud Environments* (pp. 240–268). Hershey, PA: IGI Global. doi:10.4018/978-1-5225-3029-9.ch012

Gao, L., Gao, T., Zhao, J., & Liu, Y. (2018). Reversible Watermarking in Digital Image Using PVO and RDWT. *International Journal of Digital Crime and Forensics*, *10*(2), 40–55. doi:10.4018/IJDCF.2018040103

Ghany, K. K., & Zawbaa, H. M. (2017). Hybrid Biometrics and Watermarking Authentication. In S. Zoughbi (Ed.), *Securing Government Information and Data in Developing Countries* (pp. 37–61). Hershey, PA: IGI Global. doi:10.4018/978-1-5225-1703-0.ch003

Ghosh, P., Sarkar, D., Sharma, J., & Phadikar, S. (2021). An Intrusion Detection System Using Modified-Firefly Algorithm in Cloud Environment. *International Journal of Digital Crime and Forensics*, *13*(2), 77–93. https://doi.org/10.4018/IJDCF.2021030105

Grant, B. S. (2022). All the World's a Stage: Achieving Deliberate Practice and Performance Improvement Through Story-Based Learning. In *Research Anthology on Advancements in Cybersecurity Education* (pp. 394-413). IGI Global. https://doi.org/10.4018/978-1-6684-3554-0.ch019

Hacini, S., Guessoum, Z., & Cheikh, M. (2018). False Alarm Reduction: A Profiling Mechanism and New Research Directions. In Y. Maleh (Ed.), *Security and Privacy Management, Techniques, and Protocols* (pp. 291–320). Hershey, PA: IGI Global. doi:10.4018/978-1-5225-5583-4.ch012

Hadlington, L. (2018). The "Human Factor" in Cybersecurity: Exploring the Accidental Insider. In J. McAlaney, L. Frumkin, & V. Benson (Eds.), *Psychological and Behavioral Examinations in Cyber Security* (pp. 46-63). Hershey, PA: IGI Global. https://doi.org/ doi:10.4018/978-1-5225-4053-3.ch003

Haldorai, A., & Ramu, A. (2018). The Impact of Big Data Analytics and Challenges to Cyber Security. In G. Shrivastava, P. Kumar, B. Gupta, S. Bala, & N. Dey (Eds.), *Handbook of Research on Network Forensics and Analysis Techniques* (pp. 300–314). Hershey, PA: IGI Global. doi:10.4018/978-1-5225-4100-4.ch016

Hariharan, S., Prasanth, V. S., & Saravanan, P. (2018). Role of Bibliographical Databases in Measuring Information: A Conceptual View. In J. Jeyasekar & P. Saravanan (Eds.), *Innovations in Measuring and Evaluating Scientific Information* (pp. 61–71). Hershey, PA: IGI Global. doi:10.4018/978-1-5225-3457-0.ch005

Hore, S., Chatterjee, S., Chakraborty, S., & Shaw, R. K. (2017). Analysis of Different Feature Description Algorithm in object Recognition. In N. Dey, A. Ashour, & P. Patra (Eds.), *Feature Detectors and Motion Detection in Video Processing* (pp. 66–99). Hershey, PA: IGI Global. doi:10.4018/978-1-5225-1025-3.ch004

Hurley, J. S. (2017). Cyberspace: The New Battlefield - An Approach via the Analytics Hierarchy Process. *International Journal of Cyber Warfare & Terrorism*, *7*(3), 1–15. doi:10.4018/IJCWT.2017070101

Hussain, M., & Kaliya, N. (2018). An Improvised Framework for Privacy Preservation in IoT. *International Journal of Information Security and Privacy*, *12*(2), 46–63. doi:10.4018/IJISP.2018040104

Ilahi-Amri, M., Cheniti-Belcadhi, L., & Braham, R. (2018). Competence E-Assessment Based on Semantic Web: From Modeling to Validation. In V. Ahuja & S. Rathore (Eds.), *Multidisciplinary Perspectives on Human Capital and Information Technology Professionals* (pp. 246–267). Hershey, PA: IGI Global. doi:10.4018/978-1-5225-5297-0.ch013

Jambhekar, N., & Dhawale, C. A. (2018). Cryptography in Big Data Security. In D. Lopez & M. Durai (Eds.), *HCI Challenges and Privacy Preservation in Big Data Security* (pp. 71–94). Hershey, PA: IGI Global. doi:10.4018/978-1-5225-2863-0.ch004

Jansen van Vuuren, J., Leenen, L., Plint, G., Zaaiman, J., & Phahlamohlaka, J. (2017). Formulating the Building Blocks for National Cyberpower. *International Journal of Cyber Warfare & Terrorism*, *7*(3), 16–28. doi:10.4018/IJCWT.2017070102

Jaswal, S., & Malhotra, M. (2018). Identification of Various Privacy and Trust Issues in Cloud Computing Environment. In S. Aljawarneh & M. Malhotra (Eds.), *Critical Research on Scalability and Security Issues in Virtual Cloud Environments* (pp. 95–121). Hershey, PA: IGI Global. doi:10.4018/978-1-5225-3029-9.ch005

Jaswal, S., & Singh, G. (2018). A Comprehensive Survey on Trust Issue and Its Deployed Models in Computing Environment. In S. Aljawarneh & M. Malhotra (Eds.), *Critical Research on Scalability and Security Issues in Virtual Cloud Environments* (pp. 150–166). Hershey, PA: IGI Global. doi:10.4018/978-1-5225-3029-9.ch007

Javid, T. (2018). Secure Access to Biomedical Images. In C. Pradhan, H. Das, B. Naik, & N. Dey (Eds.), *Handbook of Research on Information Security in Biomedical Signal Processing* (pp. 38–53). Hershey, PA: IGI Global. doi:10.4018/978-1-5225-5152-2.ch003

Jeyakumar, B., Durai, M. S., & Lopez, D. (2018). Case Studies in Amalgamation of Deep Learning and Big Data. In D. Lopez & M. Durai (Eds.), *HCI Challenges and Privacy Preservation in Big Data Security* (pp. 159–174). Hershey, PA: IGI Global. doi:10.4018/978-1-5225-2863-0.ch008

Jeyaprakash, H. M. K., K., & S., G. (2018). A Comparative Review of Various Machine Learning Approaches for Improving the Performance of Stego Anomaly Detection. In G. Shrivastava, P. Kumar, B. Gupta, S. Bala, & N. Dey (Eds.), Handbook of Research on Network Forensics and Analysis Techniques (pp. 351-371). Hershey, PA: IGI Global. https://doi.org/ doi:10.4018/978-1-5225-4100-4.ch019

Jeyasekar, J. J. (2018). Dynamics of Indian Forensic Science Research. In J. Jeyasekar & P. Saravanan (Eds.), *Innovations in Measuring and Evaluating Scientific Information* (pp. 125–147). Hershey, PA: IGI Global. doi:10.4018/978-1-5225-3457-0.ch009

Jones, H. S., & Moncur, W. (2018). The Role of Psychology in Understanding Online Trust. In J. McAlaney, L. Frumkin, & V. Benson (Eds.), *Psychological and Behavioral Examinations in Cyber Security* (pp. 109–132). Hershey, PA: IGI Global. doi:10.4018/978-1-5225-4053-3.ch007

Jones, H. S., & Towse, J. (2018). Examinations of Email Fraud Susceptibility: Perspectives From Academic Research and Industry Practice. In J. McAlaney, L. Frumkin, & V. Benson (Eds.), *Psychological and Behavioral Examinations in Cyber Security* (pp. 80–97). Hershey, PA: IGI Global. doi:10.4018/978-1-5225-4053-3.ch005

Joseph, A., & Singh, K. J. (2018). Digital Forensics in Distributed Environment. In G. Shrivastava, P. Kumar, B. Gupta, S. Bala, & N. Dey (Eds.), *Handbook of Research on Network Forensics and Analysis Techniques* (pp. 246–265). Hershey, PA: IGI Global. doi:10.4018/978-1-5225-4100-4.ch013

K., I., & A, V. (2018). Monitoring and Auditing in the Cloud. In K. Munir (Ed.), *Cloud Computing Technologies for Green Enterprises* (pp. 318-350). Hershey, PA: IGI Global. https://doi.org/ doi:10.4018/978-1-5225-3038-1.ch013

Kashyap, R., & Piersson, A. D. (2018). Impact of Big Data on Security. In G. Shrivastava, P. Kumar, B. Gupta, S. Bala, & N. Dey (Eds.), *Handbook of Research on Network Forensics and Analysis Techniques* (pp. 283–299). Hershey, PA: IGI Global. doi:10.4018/978-1-5225-4100-4.ch015

Kastrati, Z., Imran, A. S., & Yayilgan, S. Y. (2018). A Hybrid Concept Learning Approach to Ontology Enrichment. In M. Lytras, N. Aljohani, E. Damiani, & K. Chui (Eds.), *Innovations, Developments, and Applications of Semantic Web and Information Systems* (pp. 85–119). Hershey, PA: IGI Global. doi:10.4018/978-1-5225-5042-6.ch004

Kaur, H., & Saxena, S. (2018). UWDBCSN Analysis During Node Replication Attack in WSN. In C. Pradhan, H. Das, B. Naik, & N. Dey (Eds.), *Handbook of Research on Information Security in Biomedical Signal Processing* (pp. 210–227). Hershey, PA: IGI Global. doi:10.4018/978-1-5225-5152-2.ch011

Kaushal, P. K., & Sobti, R. (2018). Breaching Security of Full Round Tiny Encryption Algorithm. *International Journal of Information Security and Privacy*, *12*(1), 89–98. doi:10.4018/IJISP.2018010108

Kavati, I., Prasad, M. V., & Bhagvati, C. (2017). Search Space Reduction in Biometric Databases: A Review. In M. Dawson, D. Kisku, P. Gupta, J. Sing, & W. Li (Eds.), Developing Next-Generation Countermeasures for Homeland Security Threat Prevention (pp. 236-262). Hershey, PA: IGI Global. doi:10.4018/978-1-5225-0703-1.ch011

Kaye, L. K. (2018). Online Research Methods. In J. McAlaney, L. Frumkin, & V. Benson (Eds.), *Psychological and Behavioral Examinations in Cyber Security* (pp. 253–265). Hershey, PA: IGI Global. doi:10.4018/978-1-5225-4053-3.ch015

Kenekar, T. V., & Dani, A. R. (2017). Privacy Preserving Data Mining on Unstructured Data. In S. Tamane, V. Solanki, & N. Dey (Eds.), *Privacy and Security Policies in Big Data* (pp. 167–190). Hershey, PA: IGI Global. doi:10.4018/978-1-5225-2486-1.ch008

Kenny, P., & Leonard, L. J. (2021). Restorative Justice as an "Informal" Alternative to "Formal" Court Processes. In L. Leonard (Ed.), *Global Perspectives on People, Process, and Practice in Criminal Justice* (pp. 226–244). IGI Global. https://doi.org/10.4018/978-1-7998-6646-6.ch014

Khaire, P. A., & Kotkondawar, R. R. (2017). Measures of Image and Video Segmentation. In N. Dey, A. Ashour, & S. Acharjee (Eds.), *Applied Video Processing in Surveillance and Monitoring Systems* (pp. 28–53). Hershey, PA: IGI Global. doi:10.4018/978-1-5225-1022-2.ch002

Knibbs, C., Goss, S., & Anthony, K. (2017). Counsellors' Phenomenological Experiences of Working with Children or Young People who have been Cyberbullied: Using Thematic Analysis of Semi Structured Interviews. *International Journal of Technoethics*, 8(1), 68–86. doi:10.4018/IJT.2017010106

Ko, A., & Gillani, S. (2018). Ontology Maintenance Through Semantic Text Mining: An Application for IT Governance Domain. In M. Lytras, N. Aljohani, E. Damiani, & K. Chui (Eds.), *Innovations, Developments, and Applications of Semantic Web and Information Systems* (pp. 350–371). Hershey, PA: IGI Global. doi:10.4018/978-1-5225-5042-6.ch013

Kohler, J., Lorenz, C. R., Gumbel, M., Specht, T., & Simov, K. (2017). A Security-By-Distribution Approach to Manage Big Data in a Federation of Untrustworthy Clouds. In S. Tamane, V. Solanki, & N. Dey (Eds.), *Privacy and Security Policies in Big Data* (pp. 92–123). Hershey, PA: IGI Global. doi:10.4018/978-1-5225-2486-1.ch005

Korstanje, M. E. (2017). English Speaking Countries and the Culture of Fear: Understanding Technology and Terrorism. In M. Korstanje (Ed.), *Threat Mitigation and Detection of Cyber Warfare and Terrorism Activities* (pp. 92–110). Hershey, PA: IGI Global. doi:10.4018/978-1-5225-1938-6.ch005

Korstanje, M. E. (2018). How Can World Leaders Understand the Perverse Core of Terrorism?: Terror in the Global Village. In C. Akrivopoulou (Ed.), *Global Perspectives on Human Migration, Asylum, and Security* (pp. 48–67). Hershey, PA: IGI Global. doi:10.4018/978-1-5225-2817-3.ch003

Krishnamachariar, P. K., & Gupta, M. (2018). Swimming Upstream in Turbulent Waters: Auditing Agile Development. In M. Gupta, R. Sharman, J. Walp, & P. Mulgund (Eds.), *Information Technology Risk Management and Compliance in Modern Organizations* (pp. 268–300). Hershey, PA: IGI Global. doi:10.4018/978-1-5225-2604-9.ch010

Ksiazak, P., Farrelly, W., & Curran, K. (2018). A Lightweight Authentication and Encryption Protocol for Secure Communications Between Resource-Limited Devices Without Hardware Modification: Resource-Limited Device Authentication. In Y. Maleh (Ed.), *Security and Privacy Management, Techniques, and Protocols* (pp. 1–46). Hershey, PA: IGI Global. doi:10.4018/978-1-5225-5583-4.ch001

Kukkuvada, A., & Basavaraju, P. (2018). Mutual Correlation-Based Anonymization for Privacy Preserving Medical Data Publishing. In C. Pradhan, H. Das, B. Naik, & N. Dey (Eds.), *Handbook of Research on Information Security in Biomedical Signal Processing* (pp. 304–319). Hershey, PA: IGI Global. doi:10.4018/978-1-5225-5152-2.ch016

Kumar, G., & Saini, H. (2018). Secure and Robust Telemedicine using ECC on Radix-8 with Formal Verification. *International Journal of Information Security and Privacy*, *12*(1), 13–28. doi:10.4018/IJISP.2018010102

Kumar, M., & Bhandari, A. (2017). Performance Evaluation of Web Server's Request Queue against AL-DDoS Attacks in NS-2. *International Journal of Information Security and Privacy*, *11*(4), 29–46. doi:10.4018/IJISP.2017100103

Kumar, M., & Vardhan, M. (2018). Privacy Preserving and Efficient Outsourcing Algorithm to Public Cloud: A Case of Statistical Analysis. *International Journal of Information Security and Privacy*, *12*(2), 1–25. doi:10.4018/IJISP.2018040101

Kumar, R. (2018). A Robust Biometrics System Using Finger Knuckle Print. In G. Shrivastava, P. Kumar, B. Gupta, S. Bala, & N. Dey (Eds.), *Handbook of Research on Network Forensics and Analysis Techniques* (pp. 416–446). Hershey, PA: IGI Global. doi:10.4018/978-1-5225-4100-4.ch022

Kumar, R. (2018). DOS Attacks on Cloud Platform: Their Solutions and Implications. In S. Aljawarneh & M. Malhotra (Eds.), *Critical Research on Scalability and Security Issues in Virtual Cloud Environments* (pp. 167–184). Hershey, PA: IGI Global. doi:10.4018/978-1-5225-3029-9.ch008

Kumari, R., & Sharma, K. (2018). Cross-Layer Based Intrusion Detection and Prevention for Network. In G. Shrivastava, P. Kumar, B. Gupta, S. Bala, & N. Dey (Eds.), *Handbook of Research on Network Forensics and Analysis Techniques* (pp. 38–56). Hershey, PA: IGI Global. doi:10.4018/978-1-5225-4100-4.ch003

Lapke, M. (2018). A Semiotic Examination of the Security Policy Lifecycle. In Y. Maleh (Ed.), *Security and Privacy Management, Techniques, and Protocols* (pp. 237–253). Hershey, PA: IGI Global. doi:10.4018/978-1-5225-5583-4.ch009

Liang, Z., Feng, B., Xu, X., Wu, X., & Yang, T. (2018). Geometrically Invariant Image Watermarking Using Histogram Adjustment. *International Journal of Digital Crime and Forensics*, *10*(1), 54–66. doi:10.4018/IJDCF.2018010105

Liu, Z. J. (2017). A Cyber Crime Investigation Model Based on Case Characteristics. *International Journal of Digital Crime and Forensics*, *9*(4), 40–47. doi:10.4018/IJDCF.2017100104

Loganathan, S. (2018). A Step-by-Step Procedural Methodology for Improving an Organization's IT Risk Management System. In M. Gupta, R. Sharman, J. Walp, & P. Mulgund (Eds.), *Information Technology Risk Management and Compliance in Modern Organizations* (pp. 21–47). Hershey, PA: IGI Global. doi:10.4018/978-1-5225-2604-9.ch002

Long, M., Peng, F., & Gong, X. (2018). A Format-Compliant Encryption for Secure HEVC Video Sharing in Multimedia Social Network. *International Journal of Digital Crime and Forensics*, *10*(2), 23–39. doi:10.4018/IJDCF.2018040102

M., S., & M., J. (2018). Biosignal Denoising Techniques. In C. Pradhan, H. Das, B. Naik, & N. Dey (Eds.), *Handbook of Research on Information Security in Biomedical Signal Processing* (pp. 26-37). Hershey, PA: IGI Global. https://doi.org/ doi:10.4018/978-1-5225-5152-2.ch002

Mahapatra, C. (2017). Pragmatic Solutions to Cyber Security Threat in Indian Context. In R. Kumar, P. Pattnaik, & P. Pandey (Eds.), *Detecting and Mitigating Robotic Cyber Security Risks* (pp. 172–176). Hershey, PA: IGI Global. doi:10.4018/978-1-5225-2154-9.ch012

Majumder, A., Nath, S., & Das, A. (2018). Data Integrity in Mobile Cloud Computing. In K. Munir (Ed.), *Cloud Computing Technologies for Green Enterprises* (pp. 166–199). Hershey, PA: IGI Global. doi:10.4018/978-1-5225-3038-1.ch007

Maleh, Y., Zaydi, M., Sahid, A., & Ezzati, A. (2018). Building a Maturity Framework for Information Security Governance Through an Empirical Study in Organizations. In Y. Maleh (Ed.), *Security and Privacy Management, Techniques, and Protocols* (pp. 96–127). Hershey, PA: IGI Global. doi:10.4018/978-1-5225-5583-4.ch004

Malhotra, M., & Singh, A. (2018). Role of Agents to Enhance the Security and Scalability in Cloud Environment. In S. Aljawarneh & M. Malhotra (Eds.), *Critical Research on Scalability and Security Issues in Virtual Cloud Environments* (pp. 19–47). Hershey, PA: IGI Global. doi:10.4018/978-1-5225-3029-9.ch002

Mali, A. D. (2017). Recent Advances in Minimally-Obtrusive Monitoring of People's Health. *International Journal of Monitoring and Surveillance Technologies Research*, *5*(2), 44–56. doi:10.4018/IJMSTR.2017040104

Mali, A. D., & Yang, N. (2017). On Automated Generation of Keyboard Layout to Reduce Finger-Travel Distance. *International Journal of Monitoring and Surveillance Technologies Research*, *5*(2), 29–43. doi:10.4018/IJMSTR.2017040103

Mali, P. (2018). Defining Cyber Weapon in Context of Technology and Law. *International Journal of Cyber Warfare & Terrorism*, *8*(1), 43–55. doi:10.4018/IJCWT.2018010104

Malik, A., & Pandey, B. (2018). CIAS: A Comprehensive Identity Authentication Scheme for Providing Security in VANET. *International Journal of Information Security and Privacy*, *12*(1), 29–41. doi:10.4018/IJISP.2018010103

Manikandakumar, M., & Ramanujam, E. (2018). Security and Privacy Challenges in Big Data Environment. In G. Shrivastava, P. Kumar, B. Gupta, S. Bala, & N. Dey (Eds.), *Handbook of Research on Network Forensics and Analysis Techniques* (pp. 315–325). Hershey, PA: IGI Global. doi:10.4018/978-1-5225-4100-4.ch017

Manogaran, G., Thota, C., & Lopez, D. (2018). Human-Computer Interaction With Big Data Analytics. In D. Lopez & M. Durai (Eds.), *HCI Challenges and Privacy Preservation in Big Data Security* (pp. 1–22). Hershey, PA: IGI Global. doi:10.4018/978-1-5225-2863-0.ch001

Mbale, J. (2018). Computer Centres Resource Cloud Elasticity-Scalability (CRECES): Copperbelt University Case Study. In S. Aljawarneh & M. Malhotra (Eds.), *Critical Research on Scalability and Security Issues in Virtual Cloud Environments* (pp. 48–70). Hershey, PA: IGI Global. doi:10.4018/978-1-5225-3029-9.ch003

McAvoy, D. (2017). Institutional Entrepreneurship in Defence Acquisition: What Don't We Understand? In K. Burgess & P. Antill (Eds.), *Emerging Strategies in Defense Acquisitions and Military Procurement* (pp. 222–241). Hershey, PA: IGI Global. doi:10.4018/978-1-5225-0599-0.ch013

McKeague, J., & Curran, K. (2018). Detecting the Use of Anonymous Proxies. *International Journal of Digital Crime and Forensics*, *10*(2), 74–94. doi:10.4018/IJDCF.2018040105

Meitei, T. G., Singh, S. A., & Majumder, S. (2018). PCG-Based Biometrics. In C. Pradhan, H. Das, B. Naik, & N. Dey (Eds.), *Handbook of Research on Information Security in Biomedical Signal Processing* (pp. 1–25). Hershey, PA: IGI Global. doi:10.4018/978-1-5225-5152-2.ch001

Menemencioğlu, O., & Orak, İ. M. (2017). A Simple Solution to Prevent Parameter Tampering in Web Applications. In M. Korstanje (Ed.), *Threat Mitigation and Detection of Cyber Warfare and Terrorism Activities* (pp. 1–20). Hershey, PA: IGI Global. doi:10.4018/978-1-5225-1938-6.ch001

Minto-Coy, I. D., & Henlin, M. G. (2017). The Development of Cybersecurity Policy and Legislative Landscape in Latin America and Caribbean States. In M. Moore (Ed.), *Cybersecurity Breaches and Issues Surrounding Online Threat Protection* (pp. 24–53). Hershey, PA: IGI Global. doi:10.4018/978-1-5225-1941-6.ch002

Mohamed, J. H. (2018). Scientograph-Based Visualization of Computer Forensics Research Literature. In J. Jeyasekar & P. Saravanan (Eds.), *Innovations in Measuring and Evaluating Scientific Information* (pp. 148–162). Hershey, PA: IGI Global. doi:10.4018/978-1-5225-3457-0.ch010

Mohan Murthy, M. K., & Sanjay, H. A. (2018). Scalability for Cloud. In S. Aljawarneh & M. Malhotra (Eds.), *Critical Research on Scalability and Security Issues in Virtual Cloud Environments* (pp. 1–18). Hershey, PA: IGI Global. doi:10.4018/978-1-5225-3029-9.ch001

Moorthy, U., & Gandhi, U. D. (2018). A Survey of Big Data Analytics Using Machine Learning Algorithms. In D. Lopez & M. Durai (Eds.), *HCI Challenges and Privacy Preservation in Big Data Security* (pp. 95–123). Hershey, PA: IGI Global. doi:10.4018/978-1-5225-2863-0.ch005

Mountantonakis, M., Minadakis, N., Marketakis, Y., Fafalios, P., & Tzitzikas, Y. (2018). Connectivity, Value, and Evolution of a Semantic Warehouse. In M. Lytras, N. Aljohani, E. Damiani, & K. Chui (Eds.), *Innovations, Developments, and Applications of Semantic Web and Information Systems* (pp. 1–31). Hershey, PA: IGI Global. doi:10.4018/978-1-5225-5042-6.ch001

Moussa, M., & Demurjian, S. A. (2017). Differential Privacy Approach for Big Data Privacy in Healthcare. In S. Tamane, V. Solanki, & N. Dey (Eds.), *Privacy and Security Policies in Big Data* (pp. 191–213). Hershey, PA: IGI Global. doi:10.4018/978-1-5225-2486-1.ch009

Mugisha, E., Zhang, G., El Abidine, M. Z., & Eugene, M. (2017). A TPM-based Secure Multi-Cloud Storage Architecture grounded on Erasure Codes. *International Journal of Information Security and Privacy*, *11*(1), 52–64. doi:10.4018/IJISP.2017010104

Nachtigall, L. G., Araujo, R. M., & Nachtigall, G. R. (2017). Use of Images of Leaves and Fruits of Apple Trees for Automatic Identification of Symptoms of Diseases and Nutritional Disorders. *International Journal of Monitoring and Surveillance Technologies Research*, *5*(2), 1–14. doi:10.4018/IJMSTR.2017040101

Nagesh, K., Sumathy, R., Devakumar, P., & Sathiyamurthy, K. (2017). A Survey on Denial of Service Attacks and Preclusions. *International Journal of Information Security and Privacy, 11*(4), 1–15. doi:10.4018/IJISP.2017100101

Nanda, A., Popat, P., & Vimalkumar, D. (2018). Navigating Through Choppy Waters of PCI DSS Compliance. In M. Gupta, R. Sharman, J. Walp, & P. Mulgund (Eds.), *Information Technology Risk Management and Compliance in Modern Organizations* (pp. 99–140). Hershey, PA: IGI Global. doi:10.4018/978-1-5225-2604-9.ch005

Newton, S. (2017). The Determinants of Stock Market Development in Emerging Economies: Examining the Impact of Corporate Governance and Regulatory Reforms (I). In M. Ojo & J. Van Akkeren (Eds.), *Value Relevance of Accounting Information in Capital Markets* (pp. 114–125). Hershey, PA: IGI Global. doi:10.4018/978-1-5225-1900-3.ch008

Nidhyananthan, S. S. A., J. V., & R., S. S. (2018). Wireless Enhanced Security Based on Speech Recognition. In C. Pradhan, H. Das, B. Naik, & N. Dey (Eds.), Handbook of Research on Information Security in Biomedical Signal Processing (pp. 228-253). Hershey, PA: IGI Global. https://doi.org/ doi:10.4018/978-1-5225-5152-2.ch012

Norri-Sederholm, T., Huhtinen, A., & Paakkonen, H. (2018). Ensuring Public Safety Organisations' Information Flow and Situation Picture in Hybrid Environments. *International Journal of Cyber Warfare & Terrorism, 8*(1), 12–24. doi:10.4018/IJCWT.2018010102

Nunez, S., & Castaño, R. (2017). Building Brands in Emerging Economies: A Consumer-Oriented Approach. In Rajagopal, & R. Behl (Eds.), Business Analytics and Cyber Security Management in Organizations (pp. 183-194). Hershey, PA: IGI Global. doi:10.4018/978-1-5225-0902-8.ch013

Odella, F. (2018). Privacy Awareness and the Networking Generation. *International Journal of Technoethics, 9*(1), 51–70. doi:10.4018/IJT.2018010105

Ojo, M., & DiGabriele, J. A. (2017). Fundamental or Enhancing Roles?: The Dual Roles of External Auditors and Forensic Accountants. In M. Ojo & J. Van Akkeren (Eds.), *Value Relevance of Accounting Information in Capital Markets* (pp. 59–78). Hershey, PA: IGI Global. doi:10.4018/978-1-5225-1900-3.ch004

Olomojobi, Y., & Omotola, O. T. (2021). Social Media: A Protagonist for Terrorism. *International Journal of Cyber Warfare & Terrorism, 11*(1), 31–44. https://doi.org/10.4018/IJCWT.2021010103

Pandey, S. (2018). An Empirical Study of the Indian IT Sector on Typologies of Workaholism as Predictors of HR Crisis. In V. Ahuja & S. Rathore (Eds.), *Multidisciplinary Perspectives on Human Capital and Information Technology Professionals* (pp. 202–224). Hershey, PA: IGI Global. doi:10.4018/978-1-5225-5297-0.ch011

Pattabiraman, A., Srinivasan, S., Swaminathan, K., & Gupta, M. (2018). Fortifying Corporate Human Wall: A Literature Review of Security Awareness and Training. In M. Gupta, R. Sharman, J. Walp, & P. Mulgund (Eds.), *Information Technology Risk Management and Compliance in Modern Organizations* (pp. 142–175). Hershey, PA: IGI Global. doi:10.4018/978-1-5225-2604-9.ch006

Prachi. (2018). Detection of Botnet Based Attacks on Network: Using Machine Learning Techniques. In G. Shrivastava, P. Kumar, B. Gupta, S. Bala, & N. Dey (Eds.), *Handbook of Research on Network Forensics and Analysis Techniques* (pp. 101-116). Hershey, PA: IGI Global. https://doi.org/ doi:10.4018/978-1-5225-4100-4.ch007

Pradhan, P. L. (2017). Proposed Round Robin CIA Pattern on RTS for Risk Assessment. *International Journal of Digital Crime and Forensics*, 9(1), 71–85. doi:10.4018/IJDCF.2017010105

Prentice, S., & Taylor, P. J. (2018). Psychological and Behavioral Examinations of Online Terrorism. In J. McAlaney, L. Frumkin, & V. Benson (Eds.), *Psychological and Behavioral Examinations in Cyber Security* (pp. 151–171). Hershey, PA: IGI Global. doi:10.4018/978-1-5225-4053-3.ch009

Priyadarshini, I. (2017). Cyber Security Risks in Robotics. In R. Kumar, P. Pattnaik, & P. Pandey (Eds.), *Detecting and Mitigating Robotic Cyber Security Risks* (pp. 333–348). Hershey, PA: IGI Global. doi:10.4018/978-1-5225-2154-9.ch022

R., A., & D., E. (2018). Cyber Crime Toolkit Development. In G. Shrivastava, P. Kumar, B. Gupta, S. Bala, & N. Dey (Eds.), *Handbook of Research on Network Forensics and Analysis Techniques* (pp. 184-224). Hershey, PA: IGI Global. https:// doi.org/ doi:10.4018/978-1-5225-4100-4.ch011

Raghunath, R. (2018). Research Trends in Forensic Sciences: A Scientometric Approach. In J. Jeyasekar & P. Saravanan (Eds.), *Innovations in Measuring and Evaluating Scientific Information* (pp. 108–124). Hershey, PA: IGI Global. doi:10.4018/978-1-5225-3457-0.ch008

Ramadhas, G., Sankar, A. S., & Sugathan, N. (2018). The Scientific Communication Process in Homoeopathic Toxicology: An Evaluative Study. In J. Jeyasekar & P. Saravanan (Eds.), *Innovations in Measuring and Evaluating Scientific Information* (pp. 163–179). Hershey, PA: IGI Global. doi:10.4018/978-1-5225-3457-0.ch011

Ramani, K. (2018). Impact of Big Data on Security: Big Data Security Issues and Defense Schemes. In G. Shrivastava, P. Kumar, B. Gupta, S. Bala, & N. Dey (Eds.), *Handbook of Research on Network Forensics and Analysis Techniques* (pp. 326–350). Hershey, PA: IGI Global. doi:10.4018/978-1-5225-4100-4.ch018

Ramos, P., Funderburk, P., & Gebelein, J. (2018). Social Media and Online Gaming: A Masquerading Funding Source. *International Journal of Cyber Warfare & Terrorism*, *8*(1), 25–42. doi:10.4018/IJCWT.2018010103

Rao, N., & Srivastava, S., & K.S., S. (2017). PKI Deployment Challenges and Recommendations for ICS Networks. *International Journal of Information Security and Privacy*, *11*(2), 38–48. doi:10.4018/IJISP.2017040104

Rath, M., Swain, J., Pati, B., & Pattanayak, B. K. (2018). Network Security: Attacks and Control in MANET. In G. Shrivastava, P. Kumar, B. Gupta, S. Bala, & N. Dey (Eds.), *Handbook of Research on Network Forensics and Analysis Techniques* (pp. 19–37). Hershey, PA: IGI Global. doi:10.4018/978-1-5225-4100-4.ch002

Ricci, J., Baggili, I., & Breitinger, F. (2017). Watch What You Wear: Smartwatches and Sluggish Security. In A. Marrington, D. Kerr, & J. Gammack (Eds.), *Managing Security Issues and the Hidden Dangers of Wearable Technologies* (pp. 47–73). Hershey, PA: IGI Global. doi:10.4018/978-1-5225-1016-1.ch003

Rossi, J. A. (2017). Revisiting the Value Relevance of Accounting Information in the Italian and UK Stock Markets. In M. Ojo & J. Van Akkeren (Eds.), *Value Relevance of Accounting Information in Capital Markets* (pp. 102–113). Hershey, PA: IGI Global. doi:10.4018/978-1-5225-1900-3.ch007

Sabillon, R., Serra-Ruiz, J., Cavaller, V., & Cano, J. J. (2017). Digital Forensic Analysis of Cybercrimes: Best Practices and Methodologies. *International Journal of Information Security and Privacy*, *11*(2), 25–37. doi:10.4018/IJISP.2017040103

Sadasivam, U. M., & Ganesan, N. (2021). Detecting Fake News Using Deep Learning and NLP. In S. Misra, C. Arumugam, S. Jaganathan, & S. S. (Ed.), *Confluence of AI, Machine, and Deep Learning in Cyber Forensics* (pp. 117-133). IGI Global. https://doi.org/10.4018/978-1-7998-4900-1.ch007

Sample, C., Cowley, J., & Bakdash, J. Z. (2018). Cyber + Culture: Exploring the Relationship. In J. McAlaney, L. Frumkin, & V. Benson (Eds.), *Psychological and Behavioral Examinations in Cyber Security* (pp. 64–79). Hershey, PA: IGI Global. doi:10.4018/978-1-5225-4053-3.ch004

Sarıgöllü, S. C., Aksakal, E., Koca, M. G., Akten, E., & Aslanbay, Y. (2018). Volunteered Surveillance. In J. McAlaney, L. Frumkin, & V. Benson (Eds.), *Psychological and Behavioral Examinations in Cyber Security* (pp. 133–150). Hershey, PA: IGI Global. doi:10.4018/978-1-5225-4053-3.ch008

Shahriar, H., Clincy, V., & Bond, W. (2018). Classification of Web-Service-Based Attacks and Mitigation Techniques. In Y. Maleh (Ed.), *Security and Privacy Management, Techniques, and Protocols* (pp. 360–378). Hershey, PA: IGI Global. doi:10.4018/978-1-5225-5583-4.ch015

Shet, S., Aswath, A. R., Hanumantharaju, M. C., & Gao, X. (2017). Design of Reconfigurable Architectures for Steganography System. In N. Dey, A. Ashour, & S. Acharjee (Eds.), *Applied Video Processing in Surveillance and Monitoring Systems* (pp. 145–168). Hershey, PA: IGI Global. doi:10.4018/978-1-5225-1022-2.ch007

Shrivastava, G., Sharma, K., Khari, M., & Zohora, S. E. (2018). Role of Cyber Security and Cyber Forensics in India. In G. Shrivastava, P. Kumar, B. Gupta, S. Bala, & N. Dey (Eds.), *Handbook of Research on Network Forensics and Analysis Techniques* (pp. 143–161). Hershey, PA: IGI Global. doi:10.4018/978-1-5225-4100-4.ch009

Singh, N., Mittal, T., & Gupta, M. (2018). A Tale of Policies and Breaches: Analytical Approach to Construct Social Media Policy. In M. Gupta, R. Sharman, J. Walp, & P. Mulgund (Eds.), *Information Technology Risk Management and Compliance in Modern Organizations* (pp. 176–212). Hershey, PA: IGI Global. doi:10.4018/978-1-5225-2604-9.ch007

Singh, R., & Jalota, H. (2018). A Study of Good-Enough Security in the Context of Rural Business Process Outsourcing. In J. McAlaney, L. Frumkin, & V. Benson (Eds.), *Psychological and Behavioral Examinations in Cyber Security* (pp. 239–252). Hershey, PA: IGI Global. doi:10.4018/978-1-5225-4053-3.ch014

Sivasubramanian, K. E. (2018). Authorship Pattern and Collaborative Research Productivity of Asian Journal of Dairy and Food Research During the Year 2011 to 2015. In J. Jeyasekar & P. Saravanan (Eds.), *Innovations in Measuring and Evaluating Scientific Information* (pp. 213–222). Hershey, PA: IGI Global. doi:10.4018/978-1-5225-3457-0.ch014

Somasundaram, R., & Thirugnanam, M. (2017). IoT in Healthcare: Breaching Security Issues. In N. Jeyanthi & R. Thandeeswaran (Eds.), *Security Breaches and Threat Prevention in the Internet of Things* (pp. 174–188). Hershey, PA: IGI Global. doi:10.4018/978-1-5225-2296-6.ch008

Sonam, & Khari, M. (2018). Wireless Sensor Networks: A Technical Survey. In G. Shrivastava, P. Kumar, B. Gupta, S. Bala, & N. Dey (Eds.), *Handbook of Research on Network Forensics and Analysis Techniques* (pp. 1-18). Hershey, PA: IGI Global. https://doi.org/ doi:10.4018/978-1-5225-4100-4.ch001

Soni, P. (2018). Implications of HIPAA and Subsequent Regulations on Information Technology. In M. Gupta, R. Sharman, J. Walp, & P. Mulgund (Eds.), *Information Technology Risk Management and Compliance in Modern Organizations* (pp. 71–98). Hershey, PA: IGI Global. doi:10.4018/978-1-5225-2604-9.ch004

Sönmez, F. Ö., & Günel, B. (2018). Security Visualization Extended Review Issues, Classifications, Validation Methods, Trends, Extensions. In Y. Maleh (Ed.), *Security and Privacy Management, Techniques, and Protocols* (pp. 152–197). Hershey, PA: IGI Global. doi:10.4018/978-1-5225-5583-4.ch006

Srivastava, S. R., & Dube, S. (2018). Cyberattacks, Cybercrime and Cyberterrorism. In G. Shrivastava, P. Kumar, B. Gupta, S. Bala, & N. Dey (Eds.), *Handbook of Research on Network Forensics and Analysis Techniques* (pp. 162–183). Hershey, PA: IGI Global. doi:10.4018/978-1-5225-4100-4.ch010

Stacey, E. (2017). Contemporary Terror on the Net. In *Combating Internet-Enabled Terrorism: Emerging Research and Opportunities* (pp. 16–44). Hershey, PA: IGI Global. doi:10.4018/978-1-5225-2190-7.ch002

Sumana, M., Hareesha, K. S., & Kumar, S. (2018). Semantically Secure Classifiers for Privacy Preserving Data Mining. In Y. Maleh (Ed.), *Security and Privacy Management, Techniques, and Protocols* (pp. 66–95). Hershey, PA: IGI Global. doi:10.4018/978-1-5225-5583-4.ch003

Suresh, N., & Gupta, M. (2018). Impact of Technology Innovation: A Study on Cloud Risk Mitigation. In M. Gupta, R. Sharman, J. Walp, & P. Mulgund (Eds.), *Information Technology Risk Management and Compliance in Modern Organizations* (pp. 229–267). Hershey, PA: IGI Global. doi:10.4018/978-1-5225-2604-9.ch009

Tank, D. M. (2017). Security and Privacy Issues, Solutions, and Tools for MCC. In K. Munir (Ed.), *Security Management in Mobile Cloud Computing* (pp. 121–147). Hershey, PA: IGI Global. doi:10.4018/978-1-5225-0602-7.ch006

Thackray, H., & McAlaney, J. (2018). Groups Online: Hacktivism and Social Protest. In J. McAlaney, L. Frumkin, & V. Benson (Eds.), *Psychological and Behavioral Examinations in Cyber Security* (pp. 194–209). Hershey, PA: IGI Global. doi:10.4018/978-1-5225-4053-3.ch011

Thandeeswaran, R., Pawar, R., & Rai, M. (2017). Security Threats in Autonomous Vehicles. In N. Jeyanthi & R. Thandeeswaran (Eds.), *Security Breaches and Threat Prevention in the Internet of Things* (pp. 117–141). Hershey, PA: IGI Global. doi:10.4018/978-1-5225-2296-6.ch006

Thota, C., Manogaran, G., Lopez, D., & Vijayakumar, V. (2017). Big Data Security Framework for Distributed Cloud Data Centers. In M. Moore (Ed.), *Cybersecurity Breaches and Issues Surrounding Online Threat Protection* (pp. 288–310). Hershey, PA: IGI Global. doi:10.4018/978-1-5225-1941-6.ch012

Thukral, S., & Rodriguez, T. D. (2018). Child Sexual Abuse: Intra- and Extra-Familial Risk Factors, Reactions, and Interventions. In R. Gopalan (Ed.), *Social, Psychological, and Forensic Perspectives on Sexual Abuse* (pp. 229–258). Hershey, PA: IGI Global. doi:10.4018/978-1-5225-3958-2.ch017

Tidke, S. (2017). MonogDB: Data Management in NoSQL. In S. Tamane, V. Solanki, & N. Dey (Eds.), *Privacy and Security Policies in Big Data* (pp. 64–91). Hershey, PA: IGI Global. doi:10.4018/978-1-5225-2486-1.ch004

Tierney, M. (2018). #TerroristFinancing: An Examination of Terrorism Financing via the Internet. *International Journal of Cyber Warfare & Terrorism*, 8(1), 1–11. doi:10.4018/IJCWT.2018010101

Topal, R. (2018). A Cyber-Psychological and Behavioral Approach to Online Radicalization. In J. McAlaney, L. Frumkin, & V. Benson (Eds.), *Psychological and Behavioral Examinations in Cyber Security* (pp. 210–221). Hershey, PA: IGI Global. doi:10.4018/978-1-5225-4053-3.ch012

Tripathy, B. K., & Baktha, K. (2018). Clustering Approaches. In *Security, Privacy, and Anonymization in Social Networks: Emerging Research and Opportunities* (pp. 51–85). Hershey, PA: IGI Global. doi:10.4018/978-1-5225-5158-4.ch004

Tripathy, B. K., & Baktha, K. (2018). De-Anonymization Techniques. In *Security, Privacy, and Anonymization in Social Networks: Emerging Research and Opportunities* (pp. 137–147). Hershey, PA: IGI Global. doi:10.4018/978-1-5225-5158-4.ch007

Tripathy, B. K., & Baktha, K. (2018). Fundamentals of Social Networks. In *Security, Privacy, and Anonymization in Social Networks: Emerging Research and Opportunities* (pp. 1–22). Hershey, PA: IGI Global. doi:10.4018/978-1-5225-5158-4.ch001

Tripathy, B. K., & Baktha, K. (2018). Graph Modification Approaches. In *Security, Privacy, and Anonymization in Social Networks: Emerging Research and Opportunities* (pp. 86–115). Hershey, PA: IGI Global. doi:10.4018/978-1-5225-5158-4.ch005

Tripathy, B. K., & Baktha, K. (2018). Social Network Anonymization Techniques. In *Security, Privacy, and Anonymization in Social Networks: Emerging Research and Opportunities* (pp. 36–50). Hershey, PA: IGI Global. doi:10.4018/978-1-5225-5158-4.ch003

Tsimperidis, I., Rostami, S., & Katos, V. (2017). Age Detection Through Keystroke Dynamics from User Authentication Failures. *International Journal of Digital Crime and Forensics*, *9*(1), 1–16. doi:10.4018/IJDCF.2017010101

Wadkar, H. S., Mishra, A., & Dixit, A. M. (2017). Framework to Secure Browser Using Configuration Analysis. *International Journal of Information Security and Privacy*, *11*(2), 49–63. doi:10.4018/IJISP.2017040105

Wahlgren, G., & Kowalski, S. J. (2018). IT Security Risk Management Model for Handling IT-Related Security Incidents: The Need for a New Escalation Approach. In Y. Maleh (Ed.), *Security and Privacy Management, Techniques, and Protocols* (pp. 129–151). Hershey, PA: IGI Global. doi:10.4018/978-1-5225-5583-4.ch005

Wall, H. J., & Kaye, L. K. (2018). Online Decision Making: Online Influence and Implications for Cyber Security. In J. McAlaney, L. Frumkin, & V. Benson (Eds.), *Psychological and Behavioral Examinations in Cyber Security* (pp. 1–25). Hershey, PA: IGI Global. doi:10.4018/978-1-5225-4053-3.ch001

Wu, J. B., Zhang, Y., Luo, C. W., Yuan, L. F., & Shen, X. K. (2021). A Modification-Free Steganography Algorithm Based on Image Classification and CNN. *International Journal of Digital Crime and Forensics*, *13*(3), 47–58. https://doi.org/10.4018/IJDCF.20210501.oa4

Xylogiannopoulos, K. F., Karampelas, P., & Alhajj, R. (2017). Advanced Network Data Analytics for Large-Scale DDoS Attack Detection. *International Journal of Cyber Warfare & Terrorism*, *7*(3), 44–54. doi:10.4018/IJCWT.2017070104

Yan, W. Q., Wu, X., & Liu, F. (2018). Progressive Scrambling for Social Media. *International Journal of Digital Crime and Forensics*, *10*(2), 56–73. doi:10.4018/IJDCF.2018040104

Yassein, M. B., Mardini, W., & Al-Abdi, A. (2018). Security Issues in the Internet of Things: A Review. In S. Aljawarneh & M. Malhotra (Eds.), *Critical Research on Scalability and Security Issues in Virtual Cloud Environments* (pp. 186–200). Hershey, PA: IGI Global. doi:10.4018/978-1-5225-3029-9.ch009

Yassein, M. B., Shatnawi, M., & l-Qasem, N. (2018). A Survey of Probabilistic Broadcast Schemes in Mobile Ad Hoc Networks. In S. Aljawarneh, & M. Malhotra (Eds.), *Critical Research on Scalability and Security Issues in Virtual Cloud Environments* (pp. 269-282). Hershey, PA: IGI Global. https://doi.org/doi:10.4018/978-1-5225-3029-9.ch013

Yue, C., Tianliang, L., Manchun, C., & Jingying, L. (2018). Evaluation of the Attack Effect Based on Improved Grey Clustering Model. *International Journal of Digital Crime and Forensics*, *10*(1), 92–100. doi:10.4018/IJDCF.2018010108

Zhang, P., He, Y., & Chow, K. (2018). Fraud Track on Secure Electronic Check System. *International Journal of Digital Crime and Forensics*, *10*(2), 137–144. doi:10.4018/IJDCF.2018040108

Zhou, L., Yan, W. Q., Shu, Y., & Yu, J. (2018). CVSS: A Cloud-Based Visual Surveillance System. *International Journal of Digital Crime and Forensics*, *10*(1), 79–91. doi:10.4018/IJDCF.2018010107

Zhu, J., Guan, Q., Zhao, X., Cao, Y., & Chen, G. (2017). A Steganalytic Scheme Based on Classifier Selection Using Joint Image Characteristics. *International Journal of Digital Crime and Forensics*, *9*(4), 1–14. doi:10.4018/IJDCF.2017100101

Zoughbi, S. (2017). Major Technology Trends Affecting Government Data in Developing Countries. In S. Zoughbi (Ed.), *Securing Government Information and Data in Developing Countries* (pp. 127–135). Hershey, PA: IGI Global. doi:10.4018/978-1-5225-1703-0.ch008

Zubairu, B. (2018). Security Risks of Biomedical Data Processing in Cloud Computing Environment. In C. Pradhan, H. Das, B. Naik, & N. Dey (Eds.), *Handbook of Research on Information Security in Biomedical Signal Processing* (pp. 177–197). Hershey, PA: IGI Global. doi:10.4018/978-1-5225-5152-2.ch009

About the Contributors

Boussif Mohamed was born in Zaghouan, Tunisia in 1989. He received a Master's thesis and a Ph.D. degree in Electronics from the Faculty of Sciences of Tunis, University of El Manar Tunis, in 2013 and 2018, respectively. In 2019, he was an assistant at the Preparatory Institute for Engineering Nabeul, Carthage University. From 2020, he is an assistant at the Higher School of Science and Technology of Hammam Sousse, University of Sousse. His research interests include multimedia data processing, security, and embedded systems. He has authored more than 10 papers on encryption and watermarking of images and co-authored more than four papers. He is a reviewer for many well-known journals.

* * *

Donia Ammous obtained her bachelor's degree at FSS (Faculty of Sciences of Sfax), Tunisia, in 2008. She received her MS degree in Electrical Engineers from the National School of Engineering (ENIS), Sfax, Tunisia, in 2012. She is currently a PhD student in the Laboratory of Electronics and Information Technology (LETI) ENIS, University of Sfax. Her main research activities include image\video processing on H.264/AVC and artificial intelligence system.

Mnassri Aymen received his PhD degree in Electronic from Tunis Elmanar University in 2020. Currently, Mnassri Aymen is an assistant professor of Computer Science at Private Graduate School of Engineering and Technology ESPRIT. He is conducting research activities in the areas of human computer interaction, speech recognition and embedded system at Analysis and Processing of Signals and Electrical and Energy Systems Laboratory.

Oussama Boufares is an assistant professor at the private engineering school of Gafsa since 2019.

Milan Gupta received his Master of Philosophy (MPhil) degree from Auckland University of Technology in 2021. His research interests include digital watermarking and information security.

Fahmi Kammoun received the DEA degree in automatic and signal processing from the University of Pierre et Marie Curie (Paris VI)-France in 1987, the Ph.D. degree in signal processing from the University of Orsay (Paris XI)-France in 1991. His doctoral work focused on the luminance uniformity, the contrast enhancement, the edges detection and gray-level video analysis. He received the HDR degree in electrical engineering from Sfax National School of Engineering (ENIS)-Tunisia in 2007. He is currently a professor in the department of physics at the Faculty of Sciences of Sfax (FSS)-University of Sfax. He is a member of the Laboratory of Electronics and Information Technology (LETI) -Tunisia. His current research interests include video quality metrics, video compression, video encryption, and image processing

Amina Kessentini was born in Sfax, Tunisia, in 1983. She received her degree in Electrical Engineering and her Masters in Electronic Engineering from Sfax National School of Engineering (ENIS), Tunisia, in 2007 and 2008, respectively. She received the Ph.D degrees in Electronics Engineering from Sfax National School of Engineering in 2013. In 2015, she joined the Higher Institute of Computing and Multimedia of Gabes, Tunisia, as an assistant professor. She is a member of Sfax Laboratory of Electronics and Information Technology. Her current research interests include video coding and development of video compression algorithms.

Naziha Khlif received her diploma in Electrical Engineering in 2006, the master degree in Electronics in 2011 and the PhD in Electrical Engineering in 2016 from the National Engineering School of Sfax University of Sfax. She is currently a postdoctoral research fellow at Sfax University. Her research interests include image processing, video coding, cryptography and data security.

Nouri Masmoudi received his electrical engineering degree from the Faculty of Sciences and Techniques, Sfax, Tunisia, in 1982, the DEA degree from the National Institute of Applied Sciences, Lyon and University Claude Bernard, Lyon, France in 1984. From 1986 to 1990, he achieved his Ph.D. degree at the National School Engineering of Tunis (ENIT), Tunisia and obtained in 1990. He is currently a professor at the electrical engineering department, ENIS. Since 2000, he has been a director of 'Circuits and Systems' in the Laboratory of Electronics and Information

Technology. Since 2003, he has been responsible for the Electronic Master Program at ENIS. His research activities have been devoted to several topics: Design, Telecommunication, Embedded Systems, Information Technology, Video Coding and Image Processing.

Duo Tong received her Master's degree from the Auckland University of Technology, New Zealand in 2021, her research interests are currency watermark and computer vision as well as deep learning.

Wei Qi Yan is the Director of Centre for Robotics & Vision (CeRV), Auckland University of Technology (AUT), his expertise is in deep learning, intelligent surveillance, computer vision, multimedia, etc. Dr. Yan has published over 250 research papers, his research distinctions include the published Springer monographs: Computational Methods for Deep Learning (2021), Introduction to Intelligent Surveillance (2019), etc. Dr. Yan is the Chair of the ACM Multimedia Chapter of New Zealand, a Member of the ACM, a Senior Member of the IEEE, TC members of the IEEE. Dr. Yan was a visiting professor with the National University of Singapore, Singapore.

Index